Introduction to Multimedia Systems

Introduction to Multimedia Systems

Editors
Gaurav Bhatnagar
Shikha Mehta
Sugata Mitra

Centre for Research in Cognitive Systems (CRCS)
NIIT Ltd.
New Delhi, India

ACADEMIC PRESS
A Harcourt Science and Technology Company

San Diego San Francisco New York Boston London Sydney Tokyo

This book is printed on acid-free paper. ∞

Academic Press
A division of Harcourt, Inc.
525 B Street, Suite 1900, San Diego, California 92101-4495, USA
http://www.academicpress.com

Academic Press
Harcourt Place, 32 Jamestown Road, London NW1 7BY, UK
http://www.academicpress.com

Library of Congress Catalog Card Number: 2001092781

International Standard Book Number: 0-12-500452-4
International Standard Book Number: 0-12-500453-2 (International edition)

PRINTED IN THE UNITED STATES OF AMERICA
01 02 03 04 05 06 MB 9 8 7 6 5 4 3 2 1

Contents

Preface

Learning to make digital multimedia on a computer is a bit like learning a language. Not a computer language like Visual Basic or C++ but languages like English or German. This is because multimedia is more about communication between human beings than about technology.

Digital multimedia is defined as any combination of graphics (2-D and/or 3-D), audio, text, animation and real-life video delivered through the computer. In addition, the notion of interactivity differentiates digital multimedia from the traditional forms of media and is an integral part of multimedia.

Since we are dealing with digital multimedia, all of the above-mentioned elements have to be stored in a digital or discrete format, as opposed to the largely analog formats used by traditional mass media. Thus the multimedia expert will have to be able to do the following, for each media:

Convert analog media into a suitable discrete format.

For example, a photograph may have to be scanned and stored on the hard drive of the computer. Or a video may have to be "grabbed" or digitized.

Since data in digital format is discrete, a decision needs to be made about how to sample the analog data. For example, theoretically, the straight line that you draw on paper has an infinite number of points. But when drawn on the monitor, only a finite number of points can be drawn. How close should the points be so that our eyes cannot tell the difference? Similarly, when using a printer to print a line, how many dots of ink per inch should the printer throw on the paper, for our eyes to perceive it as a straight line? Obviously, the more data that you keep to describe the analog media, the better quality you will get. However, a large amount of data may be impossible to store given the restrictions of your hard disk. Thus the multimedia programmer should be able to:

Decide the "resolution" to be used when storing the data, based on the application, the quality of the desired output, and the restrictions of the storage medium.

Obviously, if possible, we would like to have the highest quality possible. Using appropriate compression technologies, it is possible to compress digital data and reduce the file size but still keep adequate quality. For example, on the Internet, currently two graphics file formats are very popular and supported widely. These are the GIF and JPEG formats. While GIFs give good quality for cartoons and animated characters, JPEG is used for putting photographs on the Internet. A graphics expert in a Web-development team is able to use the right format, and adjusts the file size using these compression technologies. In general, the multimedia programmer should be able to:

Use appropriate compression technologies and file formats for storing the media elements.

Once the file is stored in a particular file format, you may require a special player or an editor to view and/or edit the files. For example, MP3 is a popular format for CD quality music files on the Internet. When such a song is downloaded on your PC, you will need a special MP3 player to play the song. As another example, consider Paint Shop Pro, a popular graphics software. Using this package you can edit various graphics files and save them in JPEG or GIF formats as required. You may also be able to give "special effects" to previously made or scanned graphics. You can make screen grabs. And you can do all this, regardless of whether you took any art classes in school! In general, for any media element, a multimedia expert should be able to:

Edit a given media element using an appropriate editor.

Finally, the multimedia expert should be able to:

Integrate all the media elements into one multimedia system using a programming language or an authoring package.

In this book we cover these topics for each media element.

We believe that people learn much more by experimenting with software packages and talking to friends, rather than by reading any large tomes or by messing with the complicated manuals written for practicing professionals. Our book gives exercises to encourage these constructionist learning mechanisms. A Web page containing links to many of these free software packages **www.academicpress.com/multimedia**. There are also links to sample images, sounds, etc., that the students can use for educational purposes.

Each chapter tries to highlight the main features of software packages, without referring to any commercial (and expensive) software. The philosophy is that multimedia experts should not be software dependent, since a specific software package may not be available at a given time. We enable our readers to become self-educated when where it comes to learning software packages, by showing them the principles behind their central features. All the software packages that are referred to in this book are freeware or have evaluation versions freely available on the Internet.

As far as the Internet is concerned, we discuss the concerns of the Web developer in terms of file formats and bandwidth restrictions. Since this is a very fast growing area, the emphasis is on fundamentals and how developers can keep in touch with the changing trends and technologies in this area.

We prepared this book using a process analogous to multimedia production. Experts in the R&D Centre of NIIT Ltd. wrote the various sections. Later, the various elements of this book were stitched together by its editors. Their role was similar to the role played by the designers and programmers in a multimedia production. A preliminary version of this book was used in one of NIIT's centers, for a 10-week course on multimedia.

This book should be suitable for young adults in high school or college who have some programming background and have worked on the Windows platform, and who are keen to learn how to make multimedia systems. If students already know some programming language like Visual Basic or Java, they will be able to make their own stand-alone or Web-based multimedia systems. If not, they can still use MS-PowerPoint and make interesting interactive presentations.

Gaurav Bhatnagar, Shikha Mehta, and Sugata Mitra
New Delhi, December 6, 1999

Note to Students

This book is on the topic of Digital Interactive Multimedia. The word multimedia is derived from the words multiple media, and involves sound, 2-D and 3-D graphics, animation, video, and text. All of these elements are stitched together by the programmer, based on the conceptualization of the designer. Nevertheless, it turns out there are a few principles common to all the different parts of digital multimedia. These principles are largely due to the word Digital—and that, of course, is something extremely familiar to you.

There are a few things you—the student—must do to become a multimedia expert. First, play and experiment with the various software mentioned in this book—or any other multimedia software you can acquire. Remember, playing for 1 hr with a software package is worth reading 10,000 words from the manual.

Second, it is important to share notes with your friends. Talk and discuss the kinds of things you were able to do with this software, and what could possibly be the concepts that are involved in making and using these products. Learning by talking to friends is much, much easier than listening to lectures!

And finally, the most important thing that can do is to remember that Multimedia is first and foremost a medium of communication, just like a movie, a television program, or a radio show. Constantly observe these other multiple media, think about the way they convey messages, and discuss them with your friends and family. Seeing movies and watching TV can be productive, provided you think about what you have observed!

As you nead this book, try your best to discover the principles of Multimedia. All the best!

Prelude to Multimedia

You can read a newspaper to learn what is going on in the world. Or you could watch a news broadcast on TV. Both times, chances are that you will get the same information.

But is there a difference between news as it is presented in a newspaper and shown on TV?

I am sure you will realize that there is a difference. Understanding this difference is very important to your understanding of multimedia.

Watch a news broadcast in the evening. Notice how each news item is communicated. Read about the same news in the following morning's newspaper. How different was the experience?

To help you identify the differences, use the form below. Discuss the differences in the classroom and with other students. Did everybody find the same differences?

Table 1 lists the main things to notice about media.

Table 1 Newspaper versus Television

Things to notice	Newspaper	Television
What role does color play?		
Which is more "real"?		
Where do you have to imagine more?		
Are you free to make a choice about what you want to see or read?		
Where is the editor's role more important?		
For the same news item, which takes less time?		
How is a political speech represented?		
What about dance?		
Which do you remember more, text or pictures?		

CHAPTER 1

Overview of Multimedia Systems

INTRODUCTION TO MULTIMEDIA

We perceive the universe through our senses. These senses—sight and hearing among them—are brought into play as soon as we interact with our surroundings. Our sensory organs send signals to the brain, which constructs an interpretation of this interaction. The process of communication, of sending messages from one person to another, is dependent on our understanding of the senses. In general, the more information that is perceived by the receiver, the more likely it is that an effective communication will take place.

For example, suppose you are talking to a friend on the telephone. What is missing from this conversation, as opposed to a regular face-to-face conversation? For one thing, you cannot see the other person's face. The expressions, and the gestures that accompany what we say, have a lot to do with communication. Now consider a letter you have written describing a fun trip you took. Here your friend only gets to read the text that you have written and cannot hear your voice saying the things you have written. Besides, the communication is just one way. You have to wait a while before finding out what your friend wishes to reply to you. Now suppose you send a picture of yourself to your friend, along with the letter. Now you are sending some more visual information and your friend can visualize the fun you are having. However, the impact would have been tremendous if you had sent a video shot during the trip.

As you can see, the more information you send, the greater the impact of the communication.

The medium of communication—for example, a letter or a telephone call—restricts the usage of the various elements. Indeed, the development of communication devices is aimed at increasing the amount of information that can be transmitted. From the early letters involving just text, to the telephone where we could speak, we now are seeing the development of video telephony.

The development of computers is also moving in this direction. Earlier, the computer was capable of giving only simple text as output, now we can get sound, pictures, and more. At present, the multimedia computer—a personal computer that has the capability to play sounds, accurately reproduce pictures, and play videos—is easily available and widely in use.

We define digital multimedia as any combination of text, graphics (still and animated), sound, and motion video delivered to you by a computer. The computer is an intrinsic part of multimedia. All these elements—text, graphics, sound, and video—are either computer generated, or transmitted through a computer.

The development of powerful multimedia computers and the evolution of the Internet have led to an explosion of applications of multimedia worldwide. These days multimedia systems are used for education, in presentations, as information kiosks, and in the gaming industry. In fact, multimedia has applications everywhere: in businesses, at schools and universities, at home, and even in public places.

The word multimedia is a combination derived from multiple and media. The word medium (the singular of media) means a transmission channel. For example, sound is transmitted through the medium of air, or electricity is transmitted through the medium of wires. Similarly, poetry could be considered a medium for transmitting our thoughts. Or for that matter, a painting is a medium for conveying what we observe. Similarly, a Hollywood director uses the medium of movies to tell a story. Multimedia is also a medium. To use it effectively, we have to understand not only how to create specific elements of multimedia, but also to design our multimedia system so that the messages we wish to convey are conveyed effectively. To be able to create effective multimedia, it is important for us to be sensitive to other multiple-media—such as TV and films. Nevertheless, it is also necessary to keep in mind that the two are different in many ways. We will understand the differences and similarities between the two as we go along.

The most important difference between traditional multiple media such as radio and television and digital multimedia is the notion of interactivity. The power of computers allows users to interact with the programs. Since interactivity is such a powerful concept, many experts in the field of multimedia consider interactivity to be an integral part of multimedia. We will also follow this convention. Thus, whenever we say the word multimedia, you should understand that we are referring to digital, interactive multimedia.

ELEMENTS OF MULTIMEDIA

We have seen that a multimedia system consists of several elements such as sound, graphics, text, and video. We now describe what each one contains.

The first element of multimedia we consider is audio. The word audio is slightly different from sound. Audio consists of the sounds we can hear. This may seem contradictory, but it is well known that humans do not hear all possible sounds. For example, the sound emitted by the dog-whistle is recognized by dogs but not by humans. Audio is one of the most appealing elements of any successful multimedia presentation. The impact of sound sets the mood and establishes the ambience of a presentation. It can be used in a number of ways in a multimedia application, for example, to reinforce a message or theme, to set the mood, or to catch the interest and alert the audience. As part of audio content in a multimedia system, we may use music, sound effects, or speech to accomplish the goals of our presentation. The audio that appears in a multimedia presentation is of two types. It is either computer generated, or recorded and converted into a digital format.

Perhaps the most important element of multimedia is the graphic element. Multimedia presentations are predominantly graphics based. Information communicated through pictures is easier to understand and retain. Graphic elements in a multimedia system could be still pictures (like photographs) converted to digital format with the help of scanners, or generated on the computer. They may be flat (or two-dimensional), such as photographs and paintings, or they may appear solid (or three-dimensional), like sculptures and objects around us. They may be either static graphic elements or animated. Further, animations may be two-dimensional, as in old cartoon films, or three-dimensional.

Computer-generated text is another element of multimedia. A few words appearing in a predominantly graphic multimedia system can have a powerful effect. On the Internet, text is used much more than on stand-alone multimedia products, so it takes on an added importance. Also, text and art can be mixed together in interesting ways to reinforce the message being transmitted. Text can also be animated in interesting ways.

Figure 1 shows the main screen of a multimedia product, with some of its graphics and text elements.

Finally, we mention that video is another element of multimedia. Obviously, video and audio are closely related, and together they are the most effective means of communication that can be a part of the multimedia system.

MASS MEDIA VERSUS MULTIMEDIA—DIGITAL AND ANALOG DATA

Recall that the computer is an intrinsic part of multimedia. Thus all the elements of multimedia have to be in digital format. In contrast, other multiple media such as TV programs and films are analog in nature. It is important to understand the difference between the two formats.

First there is the difference between discrete and continuous. Consider a line segment connecting two points. There are an infinite number of points on any line segment. However, when we wish to write a program to draw a line segment on the screen connecting two points, we will not be able to draw an infinite number of points. This is because the number of pixels

FIGURE 1
The main screen of a multimedia product.

on the screen is finite, and only a finite number of pixels have to be colored black (on a white screen) to draw a line segment. In other words, we can say that the line segment (as defined in geometry books) is continuous and the line made on the computer screen is discrete. However, since the pixels on the screen are very close to each other, our eyes cannot tell the difference, and we perceive a continuous line.

To return to the difference between analog and digital data, we can say that analog is continuous data, and digital is discrete. The plants and trees that we see around us are continuous, but their digital pictures are forced to be discrete. Nevertheless, we have seen that if we include enough data in our digital representation, our eyes cannot tell the difference. One advantage of working with digitally stored media is the comparative ease of editing media files. This is the primary reason why even analog media studios employ computers in their work. For example, the 2-D and 3-D animations that you see these days on television and in movies are almost all done by using computers.

One consequence of requiring all multimedia elements to be in a digital format is that we need special hardware and software to convert from analog to digital format. For example, we may shoot a video to incorporate in our multimedia project, but we need some special software and hardware to convert it into a digital format, aside from the software to edit it. Moreover, multimedia files usually take up a lot of space on the disk, so we usually use different techniques to reduce the file size of (or compress) the data. We may also need to find special programs to view or play the files.

For example, to compress music files using a technique called MP3 compression, we use an MP3 encoder. To play the music files, we need (aside from the usual multimedia computer) software that can play the music in this format—an MP3 Player. In addition, we need special software to edit the sound files. Thus, creating a multimedia system involves working with many kinds of software for each element of multimedia, aside from the usual programming language to stitch all the elements together.

INTERACTIVITY

In a multimedia system, if the user has the ability to control what elements are delivered and when, the system is called an interactive system. Traditional mass media include television, film, radio, and newspapers. These are called mass media, since the communication processes are one way, originating from a source and being delivered to a mass audience. These technologies also combine audio, video, graphics, and text, but in a way that is inflexible. For example, a film has a predefined beginning, middle, and end, irrespective of the audience watching it. With the power of the computer, the same media could be manipulated by the audience. In this manner, the audience does not need to remain passive, but becomes the user of the system. Thus, the key difference between mass media and multimedia is the shift from audience to users, and one-way communication to two-way communication. This is accomplished through interactivity.

To communicate with the system, the user can use a variety of devices such as the keyboard, mouse, tracking ball, touch screen, and pen-based mouse. Thus while designing a multimedia application, we have to decide the level of interactivity we wish to provide to the user of the system. For example, in a direct-sales application, you can give different choices for a single product with different schemes. The buyers can select the products they wish to buy.

One important thing to notice is that well-designed products always give feedback to the user once the user interacts with the computer. In our example, once the user selects the products to buy, the program can provide feedback to the user, such as, "you will get your requested product within 36 hours from now."

MULTIMEDIA PRODUCTION

Multimedia production is a complicated process, usually involving many people. Typically, one or more of the following people may be involved in making a multimedia product: producer, multimedia designer/creative designer, subject matter expert, programmer, instructional designer, scriptwriter, computer graphic artist, audio/video specialist, and webmaster. A brief description of each of these roles follows.

- PRODUCER—The role of the producer is to define, coordinate, and facilitate the production of the project. Other tasks performed by the producer include negotiating with the client; securing financial resources, equipment, and facilities, and coordinating the development team. The person should be aware of the capabilities and limitations of the technology, which helps in discussions with the client.
- MULTIMEDIA DESIGNER—A multimedia designer visualizes the system and determines its structure. The designer defines the look, feel, format, and style of the entire multimedia system.
- SUBJECT MATTER EXPERT—The subject matter expert provides the program content for the multimedia architect.
- PROGRAMMER/AUTHOR—The programmer integrates all the multimedia elements like graphics, text, audio, music, photos, and animation, and codes the functionality of the product.
- INSTRUCTIONAL DESIGNER—The team may include a specialist who can take the information provided by the content specialists and decide how to present it using suitable strategies and practices. The instructional designer makes sure that the information is presented in such a manner that the audience easily understands it.
- SCRIPTWRITER—A script is a description of events that happen in a production. The scriptwriter makes the flowchart of the entire system and decides the level of interactivity of the system.
- COMPUTER GRAPHIC ARTIST—The computer graphic artist creates the graphic elements of the program such as backgrounds, photos, 3-D objects, logos, animation, and so on.
- AUDIO AND VIDEO SPECIALISTS—Audio and video specialists are needed when intensive use of narration and digitized video are integrated into a multimedia presentation. The audio specialist is responsible for recording and editing narration and for selecting, recording, or editing sound effects. The video specialist is responsible for video capturing, editing, and digitizing.
- WEBMASTER—This individual has the responsibility of creating and maintaining a Web page. The person should be capable of converting a multimedia application into a Web page or creating a Web page with multimedia elements.

STAGES IN MULTIMEDIA PRODUCTION

Multimedia production is a complex process that can be categorized broadly into the following different stages:

- RESEARCH AND ANALYSIS—At this stage, we should find out as much as possible about the audience: their education, technology skill level, needs, and so on. We also gather information on the content to be presented and the system on which the multimedia product will be used.

- SCRIPTING/FLOWCHARTING—Scripting (or flowcharting) involves deciding the overall structure of the multimedia project. This is done by placing the various segments of the project in order, using arrows to reflect flow and interactive decision making. A flowchart has information about the major headings/options given to the user, what comes in the main menu of the program, and the subsequent branching when the user takes an action. For example, if we were designing our home pages with information about our education, our interests, and our favorite sites as subpages, we would draw a flowchart, starting with our main screen and indicate the other screens and how they are linked up together.
- STORYBOARDING—The storyboard is a detailed design plan that the designer creates, indicating what each screen looks like, which media elements are used in the screen, and all the specifications of the media elements. For example, a storyboard of a screen will contain information about the buttons being used on the screen, what they look like (a rough sketch), and what happens when the user clicks on a button. The storyboarding stage is where the detailed visualization of the multimedia system takes place.
- CONSTRUCTION/COLLECTION OF MEDIA ELEMENTS—Usually after the storyboard, a prototype is made and tested, and the design is reviewed. After this stage, the graphic designer is given detailed specifications of the project and begins creating graphics and other media elements.
- PROGRAMMING—When the development team has created and collected the various interface and content elements, they are assembled into a final product using a programming language like Visual Basic. One trend has been the development of easy-to-use authoring programs such as the Macromedia Director, Hypercard, and Authorware.
- TESTING—The final production stage is the testing phase. It determines that everything works on the system it is supposed to work on and also whether typical users will find the design intuitive enough.

EXERCISES

1. Which of the following are interactive?
   a. A radio broadcast
   b. A talk show on TV
   c. A newspaper
   d. A computer game

State whether the following statements are true or false.

2. The instructional designer is responsible for the information to be presented in a multimedia system.
3. The storyboard contains a description of the navigation buttons to be used in a system.
4. The audience analysis is done before the scripting stage of multimedia production.
5. The webmaster is not involved in every multimedia production team.

Projects

1. Multimedia programs primarily appeal to only two of our senses—sight and hearing. Many computer-based applications may become possible once multimedia computers can also deliver the "smells" of the world. For example, the smell of a pizza may entice more users to order pizza from a Web site. Make a list of all the applications that may

become possible once this sense is also available over the digital medium. Discuss these with your friends.

2. Carefully watch an advertisement (several times) for a popular product on television. Can you figure out the intended audience? Can you figure out the main message the advertisement is trying to project to its audience? By looking at the advertisement several times, try to go back and recreate brief notes on what must have been the findings at the Research and Analysis stage. What was contained in the script and storyboard? Recreate these documents by looking at the ad.

Solutions

1. d (A computer game)
2. False
3. True
4. True
5. True

Prelude to Audio

Voice is the predominant method by which human beings communicate. We are so accustomed to speaking and listening that we take sound for granted. But sound exists in many different forms and each form has its own purpose and characteristics. Here are some things you can do:

- Listen to a song on a radio. Try and tune to a clear station on an AM frequency.
- Watch a music video. (Imagine, today you can "watch" a song!)
- Listen to a song from a CD player or a good quality audiotape.
- Speak to a friend on the phone.

How do the sounds from the above exercises differ from each other?

Table 1 will help you identify the differences:

Table 1 Identify the Differences in Sound in Various Media

Things to notice	Telephone	Radio	Television	CD/Hi-fi tape
Which sounds most like a "real" voice?				
Do voices sound distorted?				
Is it noisy?				
How is music different from speech?				

CHAPTER 2

The Nature of Sound

SOUND

What Is Sound?

Sound is a key component in communication. Imagine what you would experience if the television program you are watching becomes very noisy. Or, if the sound system stops working in the middle of a gripping film!

The presence of sound greatly enhances the effect of a mostly graphic presentation, especially in a video or with animation. In a multimedia project, you can use sound in many different ways, some of which will be discussed shortly.

Sound is the brain's interpretation of electrical impulses being sent by the inner ear through the nervous system. There are some sounds the human ear cannot perceive—those which have a very high or low frequency. Your dog can help you with those because dogs can hear these very high or low frequency sounds and their ears are very susceptible to sound variations.

How Do We Hear?

If a tree falls in the forest, and there is no one to hear it, will there be a sound?

This is a very old philosophical dilemma, which relies on using the word sound for two different purposes. One use is as a description of a particular type of physical disturbance—sound is an organized movement of molecules caused by a vibrating body in some medium—water, air, rock, etc.

The other use is as a description of a sensation—sound is the auditory sensation produced through the ear by the alteration in pressure, particle displacement, or particle velocity which is propagated in an elastic medium. Both these definitions are correct. They differ only in the first being a cause and the second being an effect.

When an object moves back and forth (vibrates), it pushes the air immediately next to it a bit to one side and, when coming back, creates a slight vacuum. This process of oscillation creates a wave similar to the ripples that are created when you throw a stone in still waters.

The air particles that move in waves make the eardrum oscillate. This movement is registered [illegible] and the stirrup—that transmit these vibr[illegible]n, send impulses to the brain, which pe[illegible]

For exa[illegible]itar string. The plucked string vibrates, [illegible] decompressions—in the air surroundi[illegible] move through the air. When these sou[illegible] vibrate, which in turn results in signals [illegible]

Heari[illegible]

The wa[illegible]ou hear your voice the way you do. Ev[illegible] you will find that your voice sounds [illegible]f. This is because sound waves inside [illegible]es between your voice box and your in[illegible]travel through the air and reach your e[illegible]

Use of Audio in Multimedia

You can use sound in a multimedia project in two ways. In fact, all sounds fall into two broad categories:

- Content sound
- Ambient sound

Content sound provides information to audiences, for example, dialogs in movies or theater. Some examples of content sound used in multimedia are:

- Narration: Narration provides information about an animation that is playing on the screen.
- Testimonials: These could be auditory or video sound tracks used in presentations or movies.
- Voice-overs: These are used for short instructions, for example, to navigate the multimedia application.
- Music: Music may be used to communicate (as in a song).

Ambient sound consists of an array of background and sound effects. These include:

- Message reinforcement: The background sounds you hear in real life, such as the crowds at a ball game, can be used to reinforce the message that you wish to communicate.
- Background music: Set the mood for the audience to receive and process information by starting and ending a presentation with music.
- Sound effects: Sound effects are used in presentations to liven up the mood and add effects to your presentations, such as sound attached to bulleted lists.

SOME PHYSICS BACKGROUND

Properties of Sound

Many of the terms that we learned in our high school physics class are used by audio experts. In this section we review some of these terms.

As we have seen, sound waves are disturbances in the air (or other mediums of transmission). The wave consists of compressions and rarefactions of air and is a longitudinal wave. However, all waves can be represented by a standard waveform depicting the compressions and rarefactions. The compressions can map to the troughs and the rarefactions to crests in Figure 1, which depicts a typical waveform. A waveform gives a measurement of the speed of the air particles and the distance that they travel for a given sound in a given medium. The amplitude measures the relative loudness of the sound, which is the distance between a valley and a crest as shown in Figure 1. The amplitude determines the volume of the sound.

The unit of measurement of volume is a decibel. Have you ever stood on the tarmac when an airplane takes off? The sound produced is of such a high decibel value that you want to shut your ears because they hurt.

Frequency

The difference in time between the formation of two crests is termed as the period. It is measured in seconds (see Figure 1). A number of crests (peaks) may occur within a second. The number of peaks that occur in one second is the frequency. Another term associated with frequency is pitch. If an object oscillates rapidly, it creates a "high-pitched" sound. A low-frequency sound on the other hand is produced by an object that vibrates slowly, such as the thicker strings of a piano or guitar. Frequency is measured by the number of cycles (vibrations) per second and the unit of frequency is hertz (Hz). Frequency may also be defined as the number of waves passing a point in one second.

The human ear can perceive a range of frequencies from 20–20,000 Hz (or 20 kHz). However, it is most sensitive to sounds in the range of 2–4 kHz.

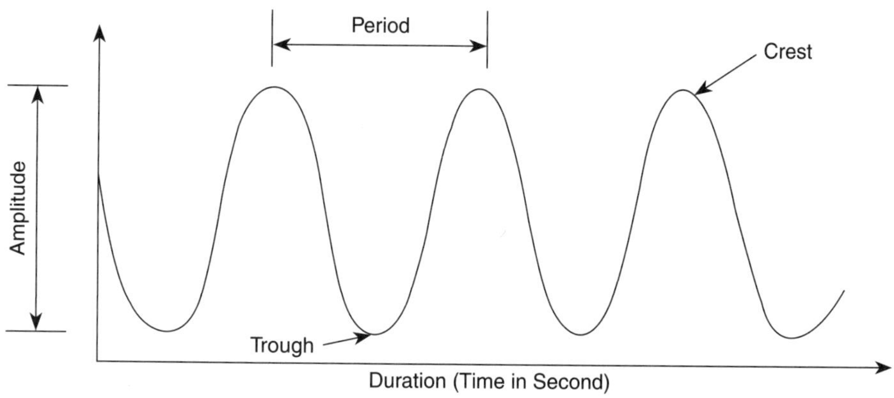

FIGURE 1
Sound in a waveform.

Wavelength

Wavelength is the distance from the midpoint of one crest to the midpoint of the next crest. It is represented by the symbol λ (refer Figure 2).

Doppler Effect

Sound waves, as we said earlier, are compressions and rarefactions of air. When the object making the sound is moving toward you, the frequency goes up due to the waves getting pushed more tightly together. The opposite happens when the object moves away from you and the pitch goes down. This is called the Doppler effect.

Why does the horn of an approaching car sound high-pitched when it is coming close to you, yet suddenly becomes low when it moves away? As a car and its horn move toward you, the pushes of sound—the sound waves—get crammed together, which makes them higher pitched.

On the other hand, when the car and the horn move away from you, the sound waves are spread out further apart. That makes a lower pitched sound. This is depicted in Figure 3.

Bandwidth

Bandwidth is defined as the difference between the highest and the lowest frequency

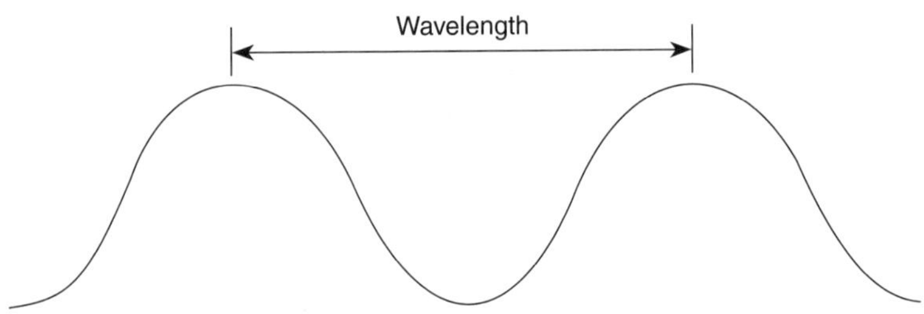

FIGURE 2
Wavelength.

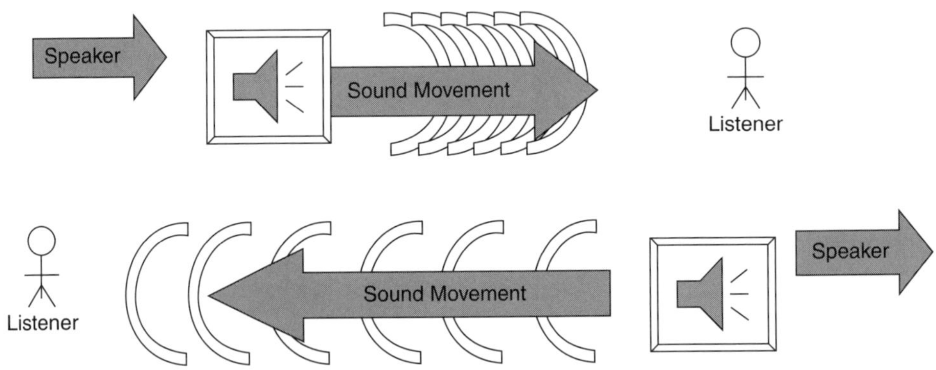

FIGURE 3
Doppler effect.

contained in a signal. A signal which spans the range of 200–3200 Hz has a bandwidth (BW) of:

$$BW = 3200 - 200 = 3000 \text{ Hz}.$$

Harmonics

Few objects produce sound of a single frequency. Most musical instruments, for example, generate multiple frequencies for each note. That is really the way one can tell the difference between musical instruments, for example, a violin and a flute, even though both produce notes of precisely the same pitch. The combinations of frequencies generated by an instrument are known as the timbre. A timbre consists of a fundamental or main frequency and other minor frequencies known as overtones or harmonics (see Figure 4).

Consider a string of length L stretched between two fixed supports. When a wave is set up in the string, the wave will travel in both directions and will be reflected at each end (see Figure 5). For a stationary wave to exist in the string, each end, $x = 0$ and $x = L$, must be a node. From the conditions stated at $x = L$, $L = N\,\lambda/2$ (λ is the wavelength), and the string must be an integral number of half wavelengths. Now this string may vibrate with the lowest frequency f, called the fundamental frequency, and any integral multiple of the lowest frequency. These possible modes of vibration whose frequencies are all multiples of the lowest frequency are called harmonic frequencies, or simply harmonics. The fundamental is the first harmonic, and each of the higher frequencies is named by the integer used to express its frequency in terms of the fundamental, for example (d) in Figure 5 is the fourth harmonic.

The sounds that we hear from vibrating objects are complex in the sense that they contain many different frequencies. This is due to the complex way the objects vibrate.

A "note" (say, Middle C) played on a piano sounds different from the same "note" played on a saxophone. In both cases, different frequencies above the common fundamental note sounded are present. These different frequencies along with the difference in timbre enable you to distinguish between different instruments.

The harmonic series is a series of frequencies that are whole number multiples of a fundamental frequency. For example, taking the tone Middle C, whose fundamental frequency is approximately 261 Hz, the harmonic series (HS) on this frequency is:

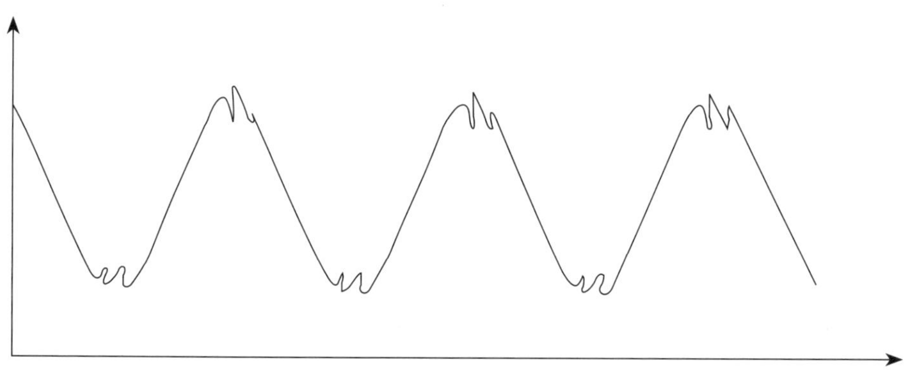

FIGURE 4
A complex sound wave.

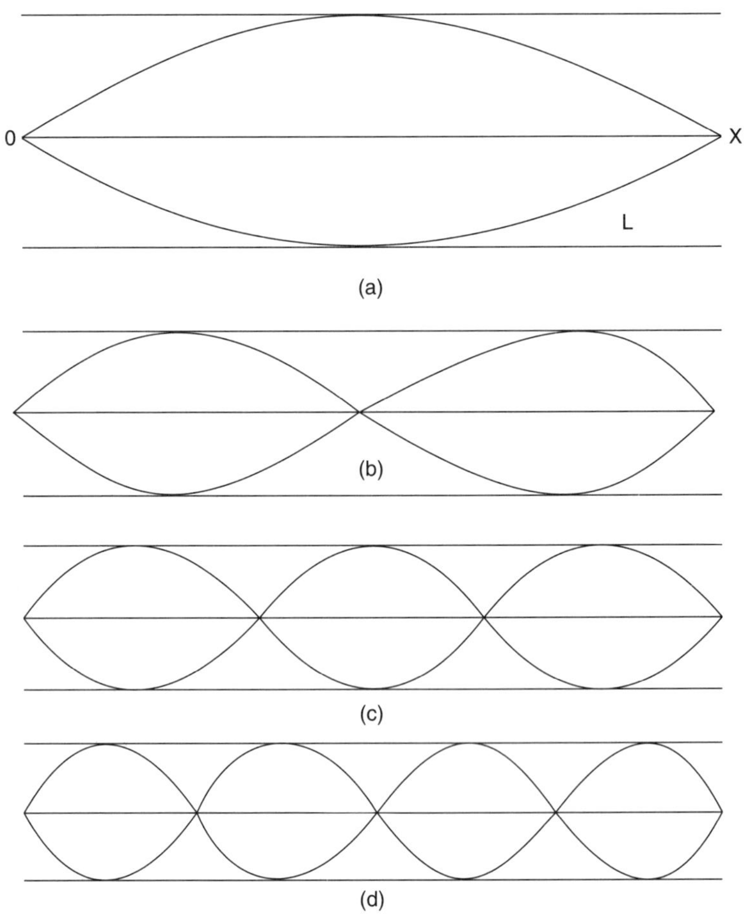

FIGURE 5
Vibrations in a stretched string.

$$\text{HS} = f,\ 2f,\ 3f,\ 4f,\ \ldots,\ nf, \text{ where } f = 261 \text{ Hz.}$$

Or,

$$\text{HS} = 261,\ 522,\ 783,\ 1044 \text{ Hz},\ \ldots,\ n \times 261 \text{ Hz.}$$

A tone with only the first harmonic is a "pure" tone. A tone with many harmonics is a "rich" tone. The proportion of harmonics produced by a piano are different from those produced by an organ.

Velocity of Sound

The velocity of sound may be found directly by measuring the time required for the waves to travel a measured distance. The velocity varies greatly with the medium through which it travels. The velocity of sound increases as the temperature rises and decreases as the temperature falls. Table 1 provides the values for the speed of sound at 0°C in various media.

Table 1 The Speed of Sound in Various Media

Medium	Meters/second
Air	331.5
Hydrogen	1270
Carbon dioxide	258
Water	1450
Iron	5100
Glass	5500

If you watch the firing of a gun at a considerable distance, you will see the smoke of the discharge before you hear the sound. This delay represents the time required for the sound to travel from the gun to you (since the light reaches you almost instantaneously).

EXERCISES

1. Sound effects can be used:
   a. To impress the audience.
   b. To liven up the mood of the audience.
   c. To distract the audience.
2. Sound is the result of:
   a. A vibration.
   b. Strumming a guitar.
   c. Talking.
3. I hear my voice differently from others because:
   a. I talk differently to others.
   b. They hear me differently.
   c. They hear me through air as the medium whereas I hear myself through my body.
   d. They hear me through my body as the medium whereas I hear myself through air.
4. Can you think of a situation where the sound produced is close to the threshold of pain?
5. You can see two people talking in the distance, but you do not hear them speak because:
   a. The decibel value of the sound is below 1 decibel.
   b. The decibel value of the sound is above 115 decibels.
   c. The decibel value of the sound is above 120 decibels.
6. Close your eyes and imagine it is night and a train whistles past you. Think about what happens when the train moves past you, and write one paragraph describing the experience. If you haven't heard a train whistle past you, find a movie which has such a scenario, and describe the audio effects used.
7. The bandwidth of a signal which spans the range of 2–4 kHz is:
   a. 2000 Hz
   b. 2000 kHz
   c. 4 kHz
8. You are underwater and there is an explosion at a distance of 2900 meters from where

you are scuba diving. Approximately how long will the sound take to reach you?

a. 5 seconds
b. 2 minutes
c. < 2 seconds
d. 2 seconds

Project

1. Watch an action movie of your choice. Choose 5 minutes of action-packed footage, and list all the sounds that you hear in this clip. Classify them into content or ambient sounds, and further describe in one line what message the audio is conveying, or what effect it is having on you. Discuss your answers with friends.

Solutions

1. b
2. a
3. c
5. a
7. a
8. d

CHAPTER 3

Introduction to Digital Audio

DIGITAL AUDIO

The sound heard by the ear (also called audio) is analog in nature and is a continuous waveform. Acoustic instruments produce analog sounds. A computer needs to transfer the analog sound wave into its digital representation, consisting of discrete numbers.

In this section, we will try to understand the basic principles of digital audio that are critical in understanding the storage, transmission, and applications of audio data. With the Internet providing an unrestricted medium for audio transmission, a large amount of research is focused on compression techniques, speed of transmission, and audio quality.

A microphone converts the sound waves into electrical signals. This signal is then amplified, filtered, and sent to an analog-to-digital converter. This information can then be retrieved and edited using a computer. If you want to output this data as sound, the stream of data is sent to the speakers via a digital-to-analog converter, a reconstruction filter, and the audio is amplified. This produces the analog sound wave that we hear.

SAMPLING

The audio input from a source is sampled several thousand times per second. Each sample is a snapshot of the original signal at a particular time. For example, Figure 1 shows samples taken at intervals of 0.125 seconds.

Let us make an analogy. Consider the making of a motion picture. A dynamic scene is captured on film or videotape 24–30 times a second. The eye perceives a rapid succession of individual photographic frames as movement on the screen. Due to the speed of display of the frames, the eye perceives it as a continuum. Similarly, sound sampling transfers a continuous sound wave into discrete numbers.

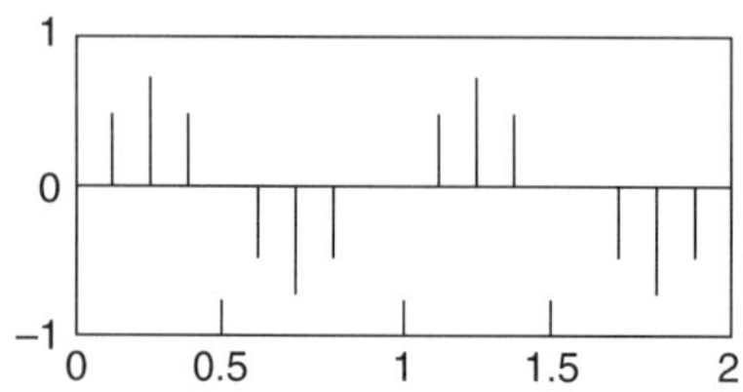

FIGURE 1
Sampled and digitized signal.

SAMPLING RATE

When sampling a sound, the computer processes snapshots of the waveform. The frequency of these snapshots is called the *sampling rate*. The rate can vary typically from 5000–90,000 samples per second.

Sampling rate is an important (though not the only) factor in determining how accurately the digitized sound represents the original analog sound. Let us take an example. Your mother is scolding you for breaking her precious vase kept in the living room. Your sister hears only bits and pieces of the conversation because she is not interested in the matter. Later you ask your sister if the scolding was justified and your sister replies that she did not listen to the whole conversation. This is because she sampled the voices at a very wide range.

DIGITIZATION

Digitization is the process of assigning a discrete value to each of the sampled values. It is performed by an Integrated Chip (IC) called an A to D Converter. In the case of 8-bit digitization, this value is between 0 and 255 (or –128 and 127). In 16-bit digitization, this value is between 0 and 65,535 (or –32,768 and 32,767). An essential thing to remember is that a digitized signal can take only certain (discrete) values. The process of digitization introduces noise in a signal. This is related to the number of bits per sample. A higher number of bits used to store the sampled value leads to a more accurate sample, with less noise.

This process can be compared to measuring the liquid level using a measuring cylinder (as in Figure 2). While the liquid level can have any value between 0 and 100 ml, the reading accuracy is restricted by the number of graduations on the scale. On a scale with higher resolution, one might know that it was actually 43 ml.

FIDELITY

Fidelity is defined as the closeness of the recorded version to the original sound. In the case of digital speech, it depends upon the number of bits per sample and the sampling rate. A really high-fidelity (hi-fi) recording takes up a lot of memory space (176.4 Kb for every second of audio of stereo quality sampled at 16 bits, 44.1 kHz per channel). Fortunately for most computer multimedia applications, it is not necessary to have very high fidelity sound.

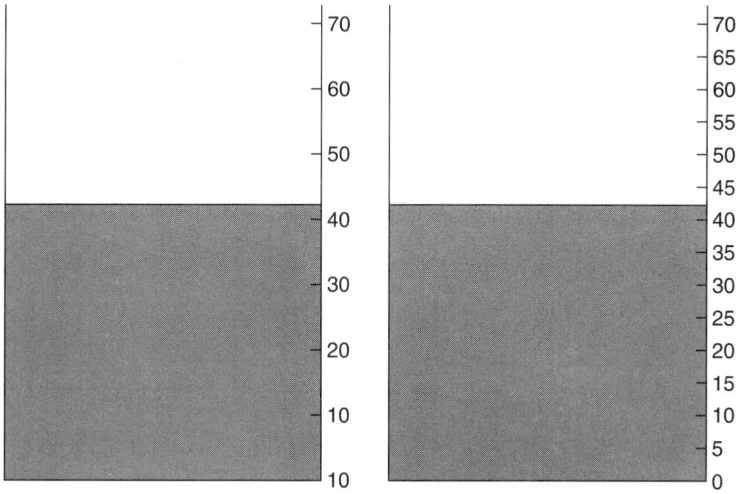

FIGURE 2
A smaller measure means more accurate reading.

NYQUIST THEOREM

The sampling frequency determines the limit of audio frequencies that can be reproduced digitally. According to Nyquist theorem, a minimum of two samples (per cycle) is necessary to represent a given sound wave. Thus, to represent a sound with a frequency of 440 Hz, it is necessary to sample that sound at a minimum rate of 880 samples per second. Therefore, Sampling rate = 2 × Highest frequency.

If it is not sampled above this rate, a distortion known as "aliasing" occurs and it cannot be removed by postprocessing the digitized audio signal. So frequencies that are above half the sampling rate are filtered out prior to sampling to remove any aliasing effects.

SOUND FORMATS AND SETTINGS

As discussed, the sampling rate determines the frequency makeup of the recording. Recording at high sampling rates produces a more accurate capture of the high-frequency content of the sound. Another aspect to consider is the "bit-resolution." Along with sampling rate, the resolution determines the accuracy with which a sound is digitized. The increase in the number of bits in a recording makes the sound playback increasingly realistic.

Stereo recordings are made by recording on two channels, and are lifelike and realistic. Mono sounds are less realistic, flat, and not as dramatic, but they have a smaller file size. Stereo sounds require twice the space as compared to mono recordings. To calculate the storage space required, the following formula are used:

Mono Recording:
File size = Sampling rate × duration of recording in seconds × (bits per sample/8) × 1

Stereo Recording:
File size = Sampling rate × duration of recording in seconds × (bits per sample/8) × 2

Sound formats are standard in most audio editing software. Sampling rates of 8, 11, 22, and 44 kHz are used more often.

Table 1 shows a comparative analysis of sound files with reference to file resolution and sampling rates.

Unlike magnetic duplication techniques (taping) which lose a portion of the quality with every transfer, there is no loss of quality when reproducing digital audio. This is its chief advantage over other audio reproduction techniques.

Table 1 The Sound Quality of Digitized Sound

Sampling rate (kHz)	Bit-resolution (bits)	Stereo/Mono	Bytes needed for one minute (MB)	Comments
44	16	Stereo	10.5	CD-quality sound.
44	16	Mono	5.25	Good quality for voice-overs.
44	8	Stereo	5.25	Good quality for playback.
44	8	Mono	2.6	Good quality for recording a mono audio source.
22	16	Stereo	5.25	Good quality reproduction but not CD quality.
22	16	Mono	2.6	OK for narration.
22	8	Stereo	2.6	Good for stereo recording when playback equipment quality is low.
22	8	Mono	1.3	Sounds like good AM radio quality.
11	16	Stereo	2.64	No advantage in using stereo.
11	16	Mono	1.32	Sounds muffled. The lowest standard you should use, unless you are using for telephony applications.

QUALITY OF SOUND

Quality of Sound in a Telephone

The telephone until very recently was considered an independent office or home appliance. The advent of voice mail systems was the first step in changing the role of the telephone. Voice mail servers convert the analog voice and store it in digital form. With the standards for voice mail file formats and digital storage of sound for computer systems coming closer together, use of a computer system to manage the phone system is a natural extension of the user's desktop. The bandwidth of telephone conversation is 3300 Hz. The frequency ranges from 200–3500 Hz. The signal of course is inherently analog.

Quality of Sound in a CD

CD-ROMs have become the media choice for the music industry in a very short period of time. The reasons are as follows:

- Ease of use and durability of the media

- Random access capability as compared to audiotapes
- Very high quality sound
- Large storage volumes

CD-ROMs are becoming important media for multimedia applications. The sampling rate is typically 44 kHz for each channel (left and right).

For example, take an audiocassette and listen to a song by your favorite singer. Then listen to the same song on a CD. Do you hear the difference? This difference in audio quality is because of the difference in recording the song on the two different media.

Criteria for Selecting a Particular Quality Audio

As you already know, audio objects generate large volumes of data. This requires a large volume of on-line disk space to store the data; and second, it takes longer to transmit this larger volume of data over a network. To solve these problems, the data are compressed. The compression and decompression techniques are discussed below.

The choice of sampling rate and compression for a particular piece of audio depends upon the use for that clip of sound. If you are going to use it for embedding sound in your HTML pages and these pages will be downloaded over the Internet it makes sense to use a low or medium sampling rate with compression. If you are going to record a song which will be pressed on a CD, then go for the highest sampling rate of 44.1 kHz. Remember, higher quality audio will always be associated with higher storage and access time so the quality is purely application dependent.

COMPRESSION

Introduction

An important aspect of communication is transfer of data from the creator to the recipient. Transfer of data in the Internet age is very time-dependent. Take for instance speech, which is nothing but changes in the intensity of sound over a fixed period. This speech is transferred across networks in the form of sound files. If the size of the sound files is too large, the time taken to transfer the files increases. This increase in the transfer time deteriorates the quality of the sound at the receiver's end. The time taken to transfer a file can be decreased using compression.

Compression in computer terms means reducing the physical size of data such that it occupies less storage space and memory. Compressed files are, therefore, easier to transfer because there is a sizable amount of reduction in the size of data to be transferred. This results in a reduction in the time needed for file transfer as well as a reduction in the bandwidth utilization thus providing good sound quality even over a slow network.

The following examples of digital media show the amount of storage space required for one second of playback of an audio file:

- An uncompressed audio signal of telephone quality (8-bit sampled at 8 kHz) leads to a bandwidth requirement of 64 Kbps and storage requirement of 8 KB to store one second of playback.
- An uncompressed stereo audio signal of CD quality (16-bit sampled at 44.1 kHz) leads to a bandwidth requirement of 44.1 kHz $\times$ 16 bits = 705.6 Kbps and storage requirement of 88.2 KB for one second of playback.

Compression Requirements

In the case of audio, processing data in a multimedia system leads to storage requirements in the range of several megabytes. Compressions in multimedia systems are subjected to certain constraints. These constraints are:

- The quality of the reproduced data should be adequate for applications.
- The complexity of the technique used should be minimal, to make a cost-effective compression technique.
- The processing of the algorithm should not take too long.
- Various audio data rates should be supported. Thus, depending on specific system conditions the data rates can be adjusted.
- It should be possible to generate data on one multimedia system and reproduce data on another system. The compression technique should be compatible with various reproduction systems.

As many applications exchange multimedia data using communication networks, the compatibility of compression is required. Standards like CCITT (International Consultative Committee for Telephone and Telegraph), ISO (International Standard Organization), and MPEG (Moving Picture Experts Group) are used to achieve this compatibility.

Common Compression Methods

An array of compression techniques have been set by the CCITT Group—an international organization that develops communication standards known as "Recommendations" for all digitally controlled forms of communication.

There are two types of compression:

- Lossless Compression
- Lossy Compression

Lossless Compression

In lossless compression, data are not altered or lost in the process of compression or decompression. Decompression produces a replica of the compressed object. This compression technique is used for text documents, databases, and text-related objects. The following are some of the commonly used lossless standards:

- Packbits encoding (run-length encoding)
- CCITT Group 3 1-D (compression standard based on run-length encoding scheme)
- CCITT Group 3 2-D (compression standard based on run-length encoding scheme modified by two-dimensional encoding)
- CCITT Group 4 (compression standards based on two-dimensional compression)
- Lempel-Ziv and Welch algorithm LZW (Techniques used by ARJ/PKZIP)

Lossy Compression

There is loss of some information when lossy compression is used. The loss of this data is such that the object looks more or less like the original. This method is used where absolute data accuracy is not essential. Lossy compression is the most commonly used compression type. This compression technique is used for image documents, audio, and video objects. The following are some of the commonly used lossy standards:

- Joint Photographic Experts Group (JPEG)
- Motion Picture Experts Group (MPEG)
- Adaptive Differential Pulse Code Modulation (ADPCM)
- CCITT H.261 (Px64) Video Coding Algorithm
- Intel DVI (Digital Video Interactive)

Schemes of Audio Compression

The most commonly used compression schemes for audio are:

- ADPCM (Adaptive Differential Pulse Code Modulation)
- MPEG (Motion Picture Experts Group)

ADPCM

ADPCM stands for Adaptive Differential Pulse Code Modulation. It is a family of speech compression and decompression algorithms. Using this technique one can achieve about 40–80% compression.

Audio signals are waves, which are smooth in nature. Complex sounds, such as music, consist of a series of overlaid waves at different frequencies. These wave patterns have amplitudes of the signal that change with time. Digital encoding of the signal is achieved by sampling the audio signal at different frequencies. The primary source of encoding algorithms is CCITT. Recommendations defined by CCITT include the following:

- G.711:1988—Coding of analog signals by 64-Kbps Pulse Code Modulation (PCM)
- G.721:1988—32 Kbps ADPCM
- G.723:1988—Extensions of Rec. G.721 ADPCM to 24 and 40 Kbps

ADPCM performs compression by encoding and storing only the differences between the values of successive samples in the data stream. For example, normal speech consists of 75% silence, which can be compressed.

MPEG

MPEG stands for Motion Picture Experts Group. In 1987, a very powerful algorithm was developed that was standardized as ISO-MPEG Audio Layer-3. Using MPEG audio coding you can compress the original audio on a CD by a factor of 12 without losing the sound quality. Factors of 24 or even more are also possible, but these are achieved only by getting a sound output of reduced sampling rate and reduced resolution of the samples.

The family of audio coding schemes that achieve compression without losing the CD sound quality, along with their compression ratio are:

- MPEG Layer 1 (corresponds with 384 Kbps of data transferred to the player in case of a stereo signal)—compression ratio is 1:4.
- MPEG Layer 2 (corresponds with 256–192 Kbps of data transferred to the player in case of a stereo signal)—compression ratio is 1:6–1:8.

- MPEG Layer 3 (corresponds with 128–112 Kbps of data transferred to the player in case of a stereo signal)—compression ratio is 1:10–1:12.

AUDIO FILE FORMATS

Common Audio File Formats

Until the early 1990s, PC applications were only visual, without any audio output capability. Occasionally, an application would use the internal speaker of the PC to produce sound such as an alert in case of error. Game applications on the other hand made use of the PC speaker to produce sounds of varying frequencies to create good sound effects. Numerous audio file formats have been introduced over the years. Each has made its own mark in the field of multimedia across various platforms. Audio is one of the most important components of any multimedia system. Can you imagine watching a movie without sound—it would be so lifeless. Some commonly used audio file formats with their brief description are listed in Table 2.

Table 2 File Formats

Name of the audio file	File extension	Description	Platforms
m-law	.au .snd	Most frequently used file format on the Internet. It is not the highest quality audio available, but the size is small and it has a player on almost all platforms. It is sampled at 8 kHz.	Sun and NeXT
Audio Interchange File Format (AIFF)	.aif .aiff .aifc	This format allows for storage of multi-channel sampled sound at a variety of sample rates. Its an interchange format, which can be easily converted to other formats. It is often used in high-end audio recording applications where storage space is not a problem. For example, one minute of 16-bit stereo audio sampled at 44 kHz occupies about 10MB.	Macintosh and Silicon Graphics
Resource Interleave File Format (RIFF) Wave	.wav	This format is very similar to the AIFF format and supports multichannel samples and variety of sampling rates. They follow the RIFF (Resource Interchange File Format) specification and is commonly found on Windows based PCs. WAV files require approx. 10 MB/min for a 16-bit sampling rate of 44 kHz.	Microsoft and IBM
Motion Picture Experts Group (MPEG)	.mpg .mp2 .mp3	The most popular of the standards today, defined by ISO's MPEG. Supports three layers, and compression techniques use the psycho-acoustic models. Layer I takes the	Almost all platforms

(Continues)

Table 2 File Formats *(Continued)*

Name of the audio file	File extension	Description	Platforms
		least amount of time to compress while Layer III takes more time.	
Creative Voice	.voc	Sound recorded by Creative Lab's Sound Blaster and Sound Blaster Pro audio cards. Supports only 8 bit mono audio files sampled at 44 kHz and stereo files at 22 kHz.	Almost all platforms
Musical Instrument Digital Interface (MIDI)	.mid midi	Unlike, the above format, the MIDI is not a specification for sampled audio data. This is a serial communications protocol designed to allow transmission of control data between electronic musical instruments. It is a PostScript language for music. The MIDI Manufacturer Association (MMA), a group of electronic musical instrument manufacturers, is responsible for the evolution of the MIDI protocol since its birth in 1983.	Almost all platforms
Modules (MOD)	.mod	Originally designed for Amiga. This format is a cross between MIDI files and Digitized audio files. This format also has simple digital signal processing (DSP) capabilities for adding effects.	Almost all platforms
AD Lib	.smp	Used by the AD lib Gold Card. Its sampled instruments, available in 8 or 16 bit, stereo or mono with 4-bit Yamaha ADPCM compression. Generally used by game engines.	DOS and Windows platforms
Dialogic	.vox	This is a 4-bit mono ADPCM format, which expands to 16 bit on execution. Works on specialized speech-data sound boards. Usually used for games.	DOS and Windows platforms

EXERCISES

1. Suppose a song is played from a CD, sampled at 44 kHz as usual. The maximum frequency you can hear is:
   a. 44 kHz
   b. 20 kHz
   c. 22 kHz
   d. 2 kHz
2. How many bytes will a one-minute recording of CD-quality music at a 44.1 kHz sampling rate and 16-bit resolution generate? Now if you record the same music in stereo, then what will be the amount of uncompressed data generated?

3. You are listening to a song which when recorded was sampled at 22,000 samples per second. Will this sound better or worse than the same song recorded at 44,000 samples per second?
4. If the highest frequency of a signal is 5.5 kHz, what should be the minimum sampling rate?
5. What are the benefits of using compression in multimedia applications?
   a. Audio becomes clear
   b. Unwanted frequencies are removed
   c. Saves disk space and memory
6. What happens when one uses the lossy compression technique to compress audio?
   a. Some data is lost but the clarity of the audio file remains almost the same.
   b. No data is lost but the clarity of the audio file is lost.
7. Which of the following file formats use lossless compression techniques?
   a. MPEG.
   b. ZIP or any archive file.
   c. ADPCM Wave.
8. MPEG stands for
   a. Moving Pictures Engineers Group.
   b. Motion Picture Experts Group.
   c. Movie Pictures Expert Group.
   d. Movie Picture Engineers Group.

Project

Find all the sound files on your computer: WAV files (.wav), MIDI (.mid or .rmi), and any others (like .mp3 files) that you are able to download from the Web. Listen to several files of each format carefully, check their properties (right-click→ properties→ advanced), and compare their quality with the properties like the size of file, time of the clip, compression used if any, sampling rate, etc. Make a table and record your results in the table. Mention whether these sounds are used (or can be used) as content audio or ambient audio, and explain in one sentence the message they give (if any).

Solutions

1. b. Can you tell why it is b and not c?
3. The song recorded at 44,000 samples per second will definitely sound better.
4. 11 kHz
5. c
6. a
7. b
8. b

CHAPTER 4

Audio Editing

AUDIO EDITING

Introduction

One can record or manipulate audio files using various audio editors. You must have a sound card installed on your PC to edit stored or recorded audio data. Recording sound for multimedia applications is only the first step in the process of sound processing. After the audio has been recorded and stored, it has to be modified to improve the level of quality. Unwanted sound or silences have to be removed. Mistakes in recording can be erased or modified. Sounds can be mixed to get a better effect. Also adding effects to the audio file gives that extra touch to the listener who will hear the audio. Some common audio editing software packages for Windows are:

- Cool Edit
- Sound Forge XP
- Wave Flow

Using these wave editors, one can perform functions like copy and paste, just as one would use any text editor. You can also concatenate, append, or mix two or more audio files. We assume that the audio files are saved in the WAV format. So the files would have a .wav extension. This is a popular format for use on the windows platform. However, many editors will allow editing in other formats as well. We have also used the Wave Flow Editor (that is packaged with the sound blaster card) to illustrate some common editing options. You can also experiment with these effects using other editors.

Special Effects

Sound and music effects are a part of our daily lives. Every environment, whether it be a highway, an office, or a home, has its own set of sounds to characterize it. These include a car being driven, office equipment in operation, or household appliances. Sounds not only provide a realistic sense of the scene but can also provide important input for sensing a scene change.

Sound effects can be incorporated in audio files using audio editors. Sound effects are generated by simply manipulating the amplitude or wavelength of the audio waveform. There is a variety of special effects built into audio editors. The most commonly used effects are echo, reverb, fade-in, fade-out, and amplify.

Reverb Special Effect

A person could receive sound directly from the sound source as well as reflected from other objects around him. Consider the room shown in the Figure 1. LS is the sound source and A is the listener who receives both the direct sound from the source as well as the reflected sound. The sound persists even after the sound source has stopped producing sound waves. The sound gradually fades away after some time. This gradual fading is called reverberation.

Reverberation is different from echo. In the case of an echo, there is a time gap between the finish of the original sound and the arrival of the echo. Echo sometimes causes irritation and undesirable effects, while reverberation is pleasing to hear and should be incorporated in the design of any room.

The steps to add the Reverb effect to an audio file in Wave Flow are as follows:

1. Activate the wave editor, Wave Flow.
2. Open a .wav file. The .wav file is displayed (see Figure 2).
3. Click on the Edit option from the main menu toolbar, and select the Select All option.
4. The entire waveform will be selected.
5. Click on the Tools option from the main menu toolbar and select the Reverb option. The Reverb screen is displayed (see Figure 3).
6. Select the Big Empty Room preset reverb setting from the Reverb list box.
7. Play the changed .wav file and notice the difference.

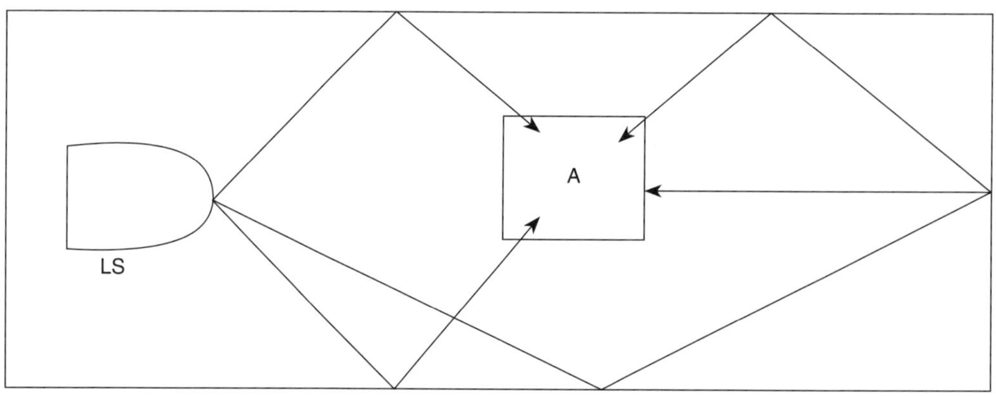

FIGURE 1
Reverberation.

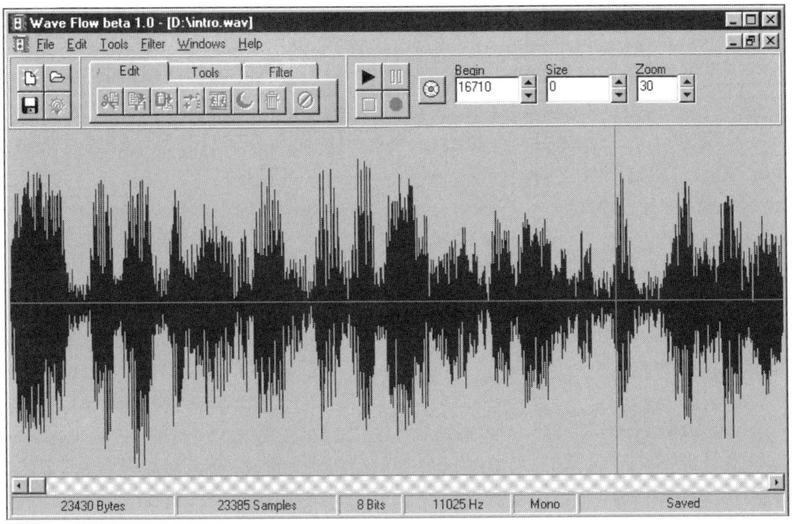

FIGURE 2
A .wav file.

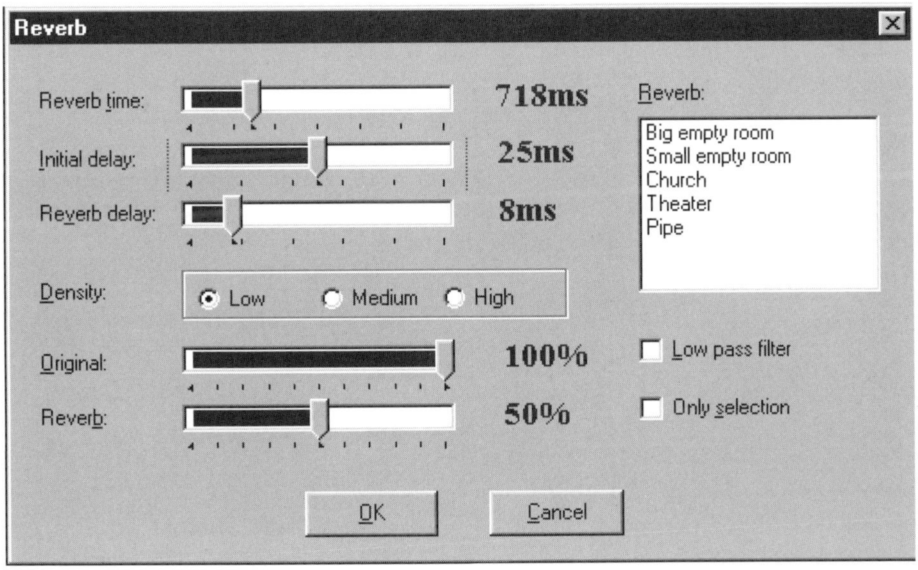

FIGURE 3
Reverb dialog box.

The Fade-In Effect

Imagine that you are about to give a multimedia presentation before an audience. The projector is on and the speakers are set to a high volume to give realistic sound effects. As soon as you start your multimedia application, the first screen of the presentation is projected. The audio starts with a bang, which may cause some damage to the speakers and the audience is left stunned. This is because of the abrupt beginning of the audio which is sometimes not desirable.

To avoid these audio problems we make use of the fade-in effect, which performs a progressive increase of the volume of the waveform making the initial volume lower than the final volume. This effect is also used in CD or tape audio. Even if the volume of the speakers is set to the maximum value, the audio file will gradually increase in volume until it reaches its peak value. Listen to a music cassette or a CD and notice that the beginning of each song has a fade-in effect.

The gradual increase in the sound of an approaching train is another example of the fade-in effect.

The steps to add the fade-in effect in Wave Flow are as follows:

1. Activate the wave editor, Wave Flow.
2. Open a .wav file.
3. Select the first 25% of the waveform by holding the left mouse button down and dragging the mouse until the selection is made.
4. Click on the Tools option from the main menu toolbar and select the Fade-In option. The fade-in dialog box is displayed (Figure 4).
5. Set the Initial Percent to 0% and select the Progression type as Linear. Click on the OK button.
6. Click on the waveform to remove the selection and play the changed wave file to the audience.
7. Note the steady increase in volume of the wave file over a period of time.

Note the change in amplitude of the selected waveform to the audience. Amplitude is linked to the volume of the sound.

The Fade-Out Effect

The fade-out effect is the exact opposite of the fade-in effect. When audio ends, you may

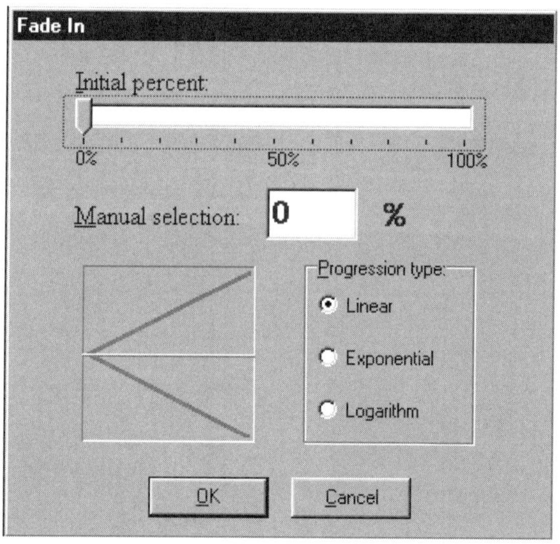

FIGURE 4
Fade-In effect dialog box.

want the audio to just fade out and die, instead of stopping abruptly. This effect can also be used to fade out of one type of audio to another type of audio. Any audio that ends abruptly is not very pleasing to the ear. Therefore, it is preferable to let it fade out and die. This is known as the fade-out effect. You may have heard some medley music on a cassette player or a CD player which has many songs joined together to form one single song.

The train that has arrived at the station platform in the fade-in example is now ready to leave the station. The sound of the train is now at its peak and gradually keeps decreasing as it leaves the station. This effect is the fade-out effect.

The steps to add the Fade-Out effect in Wave Flow are as follows:

1. Activate the wave editor, Wave Flow.
2. Open a .wav file.
3. Select the last 25% of the waveform by holding the left mouse button down and dragging the mouse until the selection is made.
4. Click on the Tools option from the main menu toolbar and select the Fade-Out option. The Fade-Out dialog box is displayed (see Figure 5).
5. Set the Initial percent to 0% and select the Progression type as Linear. Click on the OK button.
6. Note the change in amplitude of the selected waveform to the audience.
7. Click on the waveform to remove the selection and play the changed wave file to the audience.
8. Note the steady decrease in output of the wave file over a period of time. If time permits, try out the other fade-out options on the wave file.

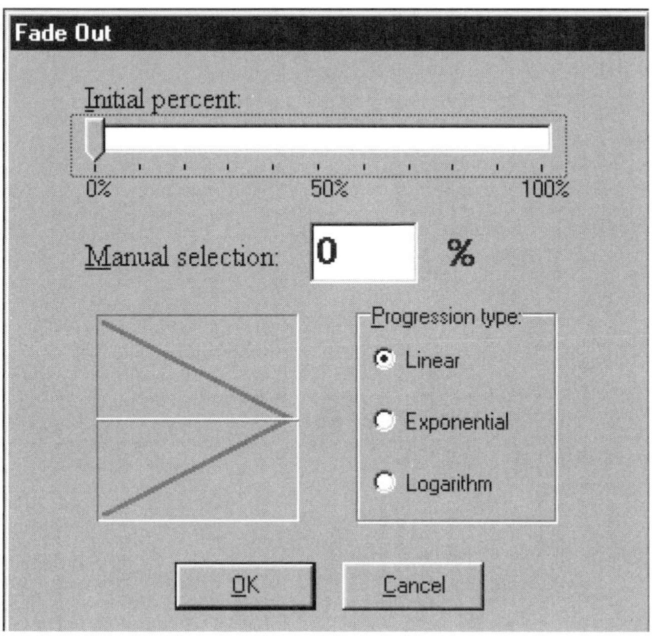

FIGURE 5
Fade-Out effect dialog box.

Common Editing Packages

An audio editing package is very necessary because one rarely uses the audio file as it is recorded in the studio or otherwise in its original raw form. Generally there are some changes that have to be made to the audio file before it can be used. Some of the most commonly used audio editing packages for Windows are:

- COOL EDIT—This is shareware software used to edit audio files. This package supports a variety of sound formats. It has a built-in CD player through which one can convert Red-Book audio (CD audio) into a waveform and save it to any available format. Although this software is shareware, it has enough functions to be used professionally. Being easy to use has made it one of the popular shareware audio editing software packages. It is freely downloadable from the Internet.
- SOUND FORGE XP—It is as powerful as Cool Edit. It is not shareware.
- WAVE STUDIO—It is packaged along with the Sound Blaster Multimedia Kit. It is a powerful aid for editing audio files. This editor supports most of the audio file formats. The only drawback is that this editor works only if you have a Sound Blaster sound card.

EXERCISES

1. Give two reasons why audio editing is required after recording sound at a recording studio.
2. Reverberation is caused by:
   a. Reflection
   b. Absorption
   c. Diffraction
   d. Microphones
3. The sound would be _________ without reverberation in a concert hall.
   a. Strong
   b. Lifeless
   c. Lively
   d. Rich
   e. Pleasant
4. Excessive reverberation will make the sound:
   a. Unintelligible
   b. Intelligible
5. Download an audio editor (such as WaveFlow) and work on some .wav files present in the Windows/Media folder (or its subfolders). Choose a couple of files that play for a relatively long time. Try the following:
   a. Add the reverb effect somewhere.
   b. Concatenate two files.
   c. Add the fade-out effect and fade-in effect where these files are joined.
   d. Add the fade-out effect at the end.
   e. Explore and try out different functions and filters. Note down your observations.

> **Hints**
>
> To concatenate two wave files, use the copy and paste functions of the Wave Flow software.
>
> Always position the cursor of the editor at the desired location in the opened wave file into which you wish to paste the data, before you actually use the paste function.
>
> You can even design your own effects, if you explore the software.

Solutions

1. Audio is recorded in raw format. We must edit audio sometimes to remove unwanted noises, error in recordings, or even unwanted silences. We can enhance audio by adding effects like echoes and reverberations.
2. a
3. b
4. a

CHAPTER 5

Music and Speech

INTRODUCTION

Digital audio has developed in two directions. One direction is where we take analog audio, transform it into digital format, and do various things with the digital file such as add effects, edit it, compress it, play it, or use it in applications. The other direction has developed much less, perhaps because the problems encountered are much harder. This chapter is about the other direction of digital audio—creating or synthesizing sounds using the computer. We have given an introduction to two aspects of audio synthesis, namely generation of music and of speech. For the sake of completeness, we have also given a very brief review of speech recognition.

SYNTHESIZED MUSIC

Synthesized sounds are a set of instructions to the hardware audio device on how and when to produce sound. The MIDI (Musical Instrument Digital Interface) format is the most widely used digital format for generating synthesized sound (Figure 1). Unlike digital audio, the actual data are not recorded. Nearly all software that supports audio can play MIDI files. Half an hour of stereo music takes about 100 KB of disk space in MIDI format. MIDI works by recording the following:

- Keys depressed
- Time when the key was depressed
- Duration for which the key was depressed
- How hard the key was struck

MIDI, like any other technology, has its disadvantages. A MIDI file may sound different on different MIDI synthesizers. This is because the FM synthesizer (an Integrated chip on your sound card which is responsible for producing sound), which simulates the different instrument effects, may be different. The FM synthesizer is, however, good for percussion

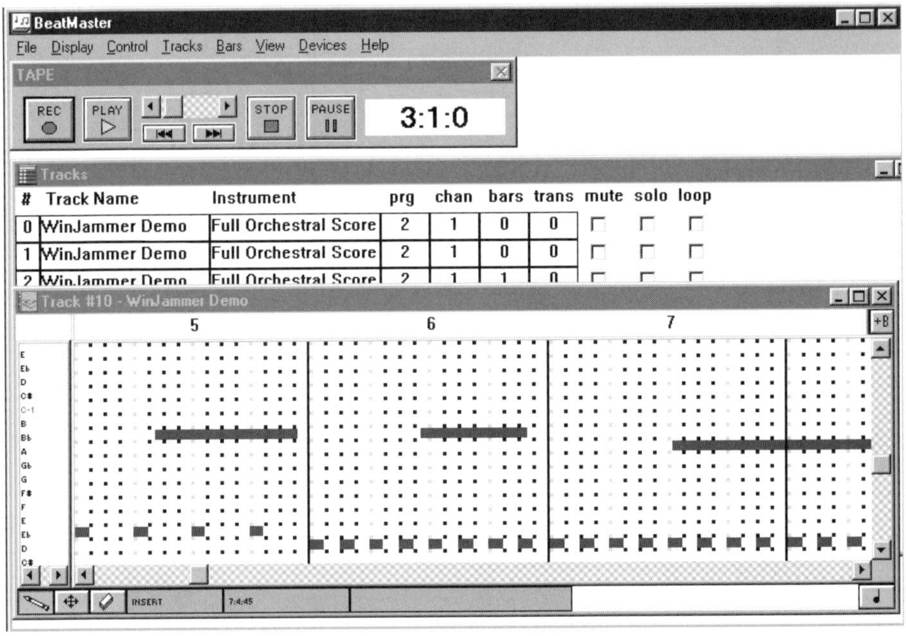

FIGURE 1
A software to ceate MIDI files.

or electronic organ sounds. Thus in a MIDI system, information about the sound is read from a MIDI file and played by the FM synthesizer.

Sampling is a process where an analog signal is sampled over time at regular intervals to councet the analog signal into digital format. The regular interval at which the sampling occurs is called the sampling rate. This sampling obtained at the sampled time is represented by 8-bit or 16-bit values. Sampled sound is represented in Figure 2.

A comparison between sampled sound and synthesized sound is given in Table 1.

When to Use Sampled Sound?

Sampled sounds are used where narration, testimonials, voice-overs, music, and/or sounds are required. They can be used to provide information about animation on the screen, such as a manufacturing process or the function of a device. Narrations are invaluable for self-learning trainings because these take the place of the instructor. These can be used as voice-overs where a short instruction is provided in a multimedia application or to explain what lies ahead in the presentation. Sampled sound is more realistic.

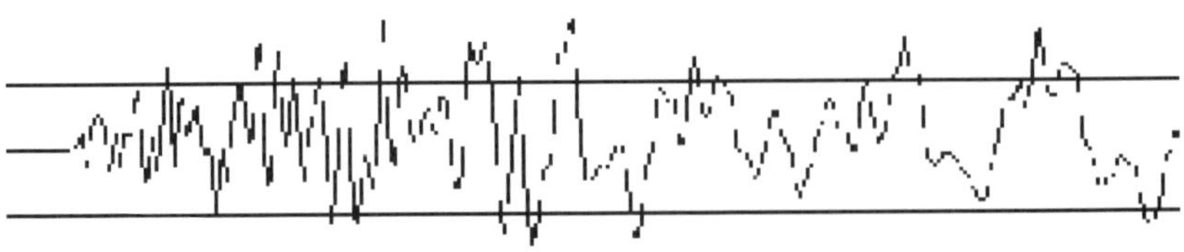

FIGURE 2
Sampled sound.

Table 1 Sampled Sound versus Synthesized Sound

Sampled sound	Synthesized sound
Sampled sound consists of analog signals sampled over time at regular intervals to obtain the amplitude of the analog signal at the sampling time. Sound can be sampled at 44, 22, 11, or 8 kHz. The higher the sampling rate the better the audio.	Synthesized sound is produced by an interaction between hardware and a data protocol that allows musical instruments to communicate with one another electronically. Synthesized sound is not sampled data. It is like a language used by MIDI devices to render sound.
The size of sampled audio files can be very large. For example, a one-minute recording of CD-quality music at a 44 kHz sampling rate and 16-bit resolution will be: $(44 \times 1000 \times 16 \times 60) / 8 = 5.28$ MB.	A MIDI file of half-hour play duration occupies only 100 KB disk space.
If the same sound is recorded in stereo, the amount of disk space taken is double.	
Sampled sound recorded on one machine will sound the same on all machines that support that format.	A MIDI file may sound different on different machines because of the FM synthesizer local to that sound hardware.
It is not possible to play multiple sampled sounds simultaneously because of synchronization problems.	A typical FM synthesizer can play 20 multi-timbral instruments simultaneously.

Synthesized sound can be used to create a soothing atmosphere during a presentation or in a multimedia application. Since these files occupy littre space, they can be used to play music for a long duration. Synthesized sound is rather unrealistic or machine-like because the quality of the sound depends on the rendering capability of the hardware device on the computer.

INTRODUCTION TO SPEECH

Properties of Speech

Human communication is dominated by speech and hearing. Speech is the most natural form of human communication. Speech can be looked at as a part of an interaction in which both participants are usually present, and the speaker has a particular addressee (or several addressees) in mind. Speech is time-bound, dynamic, and transient. The spontaneity and speed of most speech exchanges make it difficult to engage in complex advance planning. The pressure to think while talking promotes looser construction, repetition, rephrasing, and comment clauses. Intonation and pause divide long utterances into manageable chunks, but sentence boundaries are often unclear. Normally, participants in a face-to-face interaction can rely on extralinguistic cues like facial expression and gesture to aid meaning. Remember though that errors once spoken cannot be withdrawn.

Speech is produced by inhaling, expanding the rib cage, and lowering the diaphragm, so that air is drawn into the lungs. The pressure in the lungs is then increased by the reverse process—contracting the rib cage and raising the diaphragm. This increased pressure forces the air to flow up the trachea (windpipe). At the top of the trachea it encounters the larynx, a bony structure covered by skin containing a slit-like orifice—the glottis (vocal cords). The flow of air through the glottis causes a local drop in pressure by the Bernoulli effect. This drop in pressure allows the tension in the laryngeal muscles to close the glottis, thereby interrupting the flow of air. The pressure then builds up again, forcing the vocal cords apart, and enabling the airflow to continue. This cycle repeats itself, producing a train of pulses. The rest of the vocal tract—the oral and nasal passages—then acts as a filter, allowing the harmonics of the glottal waveform, which lie near the natural resonance of the tract, to pass. The acoustic wave so produced is radiated from the lips. Normal voice range is about 500 Hz to 2 kHz—the vowels occur at lower frequencies and the consonants at higher frequencies.

There is an old saying "It ain't what you say, it's the way you say it." The sound system enables us to express meaning in speech in both verbal and nonverbal ways. Verbal meaning ("what we say") relies on vowels and consonants to construct words, phrases, and sentences. Nonverbal meaning ("the way we say it") makes use of such factors as intonation, rhythm, and tone of voice to provide speech with much of its structure and expressiveness.

A commonly used term is "Prosody" or "Prosodic features" of a language and it really refers to the pitch, loudness, and speed of utterance. Different pitch levels (tones) can be used to express a wide range of meaning. To understand this better let us look at a situation. Take a simple question, such as:

"Will you marry me?" The answer could be one of two simple words: "Yes" or "No."

If we look at "Yes" as the answer, then there are at least nine ways of saying, "Yes."

SPEECH EFFECTS

Distortion

Distortion occurs when the speech changes because of a change in the basic speech signal. Say the word "Multimedia." Next, stuff your mouth with some marbles or if you have a bad throat and cold, say "Multimedia" again—the output sounds considerably different. This is because the speech signal gets modified at the source and sounds different.

Noise

Noise gets appended to a speech signal when the sound source and any external noise together produce the resulting sound.

Let us say you are speaking on a long-distance phone call and the phone line is not clear. The person at the other end of the conversation hears the voice mingled with ambient noise. This could also happen when you are talking on the phone and your little dog starts barking because there is a stranger at the door.

Clipping

Clipping is a special case of distortion. The signal here gets chopped off at the higher and lower frequencies and thus sounds flat.

When you say that music sounds flat, the signal has gotten clipped by the sound production mechanism. For example, in a megaphone only a narrow band of the frequencies are allowed to pass through and the speech thus sounds clipped.

SYNTHESIZED SPEECH

Text-to-Speech Synthesis

The ability to communicate by spoken language is unique to humans. Communication among people in speech mode is so natural and effortless that we hardly realize the complex mechanisms involved in this process. We tend to take speech communication for granted, yet many aspects of it are still not completely understood. Communicating with a machine in speech mode has always fascinated computer scientists. Some speech scientists are engaged in basic studies of speech production and perception, the others in designing the machines that recognize verbal messages or individual speakers. Research that seeks to understand how humans produce speech (speech synthesis) and perceive speech (speech recognition) has led to the development of methods for improved communication between humans and machines. This is an attempt towards more effective training and technical aids for those with disorders of communication.

The goal appears to be elusive despite the fact that computer technology has advanced to a level where speed and memory are not likely to be the main hurdles. The whole effort of Speech Technology research is to implement these mechanisms in a machine.

Early attempts at text-to-speech synthesis assembled words or clauses by concatenating recorded words. The system analyzed the text and pulled recordings, words, and phrases out of a prerecorded library and concatenated the digital audio recordings. Unfortunately, if the text included a word or phrase not recorded, the text-to-speech system could not say it. In continuous speech, word durations are often shortened and coarticulation effects can occur between adjacent words. There was also no way of adjusting the intonation of prerecorded words, resulting in a huge word database requiring high storage and choppy speech.

However, true synthesized speech reads text by analyzing the words and having the computer figure out the phonetic pronunciations for the words. These basic phonetic pronunciations or phonemes, as they are called, are passed into a complex algorithm that simulates the human vocal tract or concatenates stored segments and emits the sound. This method allows the text-to-speech to speak any word, even made-up ones like "Tamat" but the voice it produces has very little emotion and is distinctly not human. The intelligibility is, therefore, lower, but the memory required is small. This may seem to be the solution for unlimited speech synthesis.

A phoneme can be defined as the smallest meaningful unit of any language. For example, American English has 44 phonemes defined for the language.

Speech synthesis programs convert written input to spoken output by automatically generating synthetic speech. Speech synthesis is referred to as "Text-to-Speech" conversion (TTS).

There are algorithms which split the speech into phonemes, but combining them to produce fluent speech requires fluent transitions between the elements. The intelligibility is, therefore, lower, but the memory required is small due to a smaller number of basic units. In this case the problem can be broken down into three parts:

- Text-to-Phoneme Conversion—This is the conversion of the textual input message into its corresponding pronunciation, given by a set of phonemes, which are defined for the language being used. The important aspect here is that given that the input text is first analyzed in this module, it should extract information related to prosody.

- PHONEME-TO-SPEECH CONVERSION—This is really the crux of the problem and needs to address the following:
  - The selection of the basic speech units.
  - The generation of the selected basic units.
  - Concatenation of these basic units for unlimited speech synthesis.

There are two main methods for phoneme-to-speech conversion:

- FORMANT SYNTHESIS—Formant synthesizers use a model of the vocal tract and a set of rules to generate speech. The model uses frequencies, energies, pitch, and other acoustic-phonetic parameters as control variables. These systems can achieve high intelligibility, but do not sound very natural since it is very difficult to describe accurately the process of speech generation in a set of rules. This is the principle of the DECtalk digital formant synthesizer developed by the late Dr. Denis H. Klatt, whose work is clearly acknowledged as a milestone in TTS systems.
- CONCATENATION SYNTHESIS—In concatenation synthesis, stored segments from real speech are used. However, the inventory cannot be just a set of phonemes because phonemes are very sensitive to the context in which they are used. The transition from one phoneme to another carries a lot of information necessary for the perception of both phonemes. The inventory here is ideally a set of diphones as the basic units. A diphone is basically a phoneme pair which is cut from the middle to preserve the transition and contextual variations between phonemes. For example, to synthesize the word "street," the diphone sequence /#s-st-tr-re-et-t#/ would be used (# denotes silence).

- If x is the number of phonemes in a language the diphones typically will be x^2 minus the number of diphones that do not exist in the language. These diphones are obtained from recordings of human speech. They contain all coarticulation effects that occur for a particular language. This solves the coarticulation problem, but it is impossible to accurately modify the pitch of any segment. The intonation across a clause is also generally incorrect. Diphone synthesis produces speech that is fairly intelligible, but moving from one speaker to another requires extraction of a completely new set of diphones from the new speaker's voice, which is a very tedious process.
- APPLICATION OF PROSODY—Prosody in very simple terms is the variation of pitch, intensity, and duration of the utterances with time. Proper prosody has to be applied to make speech sound natural or intelligible. For prosody modeling, most TTS systems use linguistic rules to define the prosody parameters. And this to date is an open-ended research problem.

Common Tools for Text-to-Speech Synthesis

Most of the current TTS systems produce an acceptable level of intelligibility, but the naturalness of speech, the ability to control expressivity, speech style, and pseudo-speaker identity are still poor. Here it is important to mention that users' demand vary to a large extent according to the field of application; general public applications such as telephonic information retrieval need maximal realism and naturalness, whereas some applications involving highly motivated persons (for example, visually impaired), demand intelligibility as the highest priority.

A large number of universities and organizations across the world are actively involved and committed to the cause of speech synthesis and recognition. A number of products are being introduced in the market, some programs for the Windows environment are

- AT&T Watson Speech Synthesis
- BeSTspeech from Berkeley Speech Technologies, Inc. (BST)
- Creative TextoLE
- DECtalk: Text-to-Speech from Digital
- Lernout and Hauspie Text-to-Speech Windows SDK
- MBROLA: Free Speech Synthesis Project
- Tinytalk

Speech-to-Text Synthesis

Automatic speech recognition is the process by which a computer maps an acoustic speech signal to text.

Automatic speech understanding is the process by which a computer maps an acoustic speech signal to some form of abstract meaning of the speech.

Speaker Systems

A speaker-dependent system is developed to operate for a single speaker. These systems are usually easier to develop, cheaper to buy, and more accurate, but not as flexible as speaker-adaptive or speaker-independent systems.

A speaker-independent system is developed to operate for any speaker of a particular type (for example, American English). These systems are the most difficult to develop, most expensive, and accuracy is lower than speaker-dependent systems. However, they are more flexible.

A speaker-adaptive system is developed to adapt its operation to the characteristics of new speakers. Its difficulty lies somewhere between speaker-independent and speaker dependent systems.

Vocabulary

The size of vocabulary of a speech-recognition system affects the complexity, the processing requirements, and the accuracy of the system. Some applications require only a few words (for example, numbers only), others require very large dictionaries (for example, dictation machines). There are no established rules for classifying them, but the following estimations can be used to draw a distinction between them:

- Small vocabulary—tens of words
- Medium vocabulary—hundreds of words
- Large vocabulary—thousands of words
- Very large vocabulary—tens of thousands of words.

Continuous Speech and Isolated-Word System

An isolated-word system operates on single words one at a time—requiring a pause after saying each word. This is the simplest form of recognition to perform because the end points are easier to find and the pronunciation of a word does not affect others. Thus, because the occurrences of words are more consistent they are easier to recognize. A continuous speech system operates on speech in which words are connected together, that is, not separated by pauses. Continuous speech is more difficult to handle because of a variety of effects. First, it is difficult to find the beginning and end points of words. Another problem is "coarticulation." The production of each phoneme is affected by the production of surrounding phonemes, and similarly the beginning and end of words are affected by the preceding and following words. The recognition of continuous speech is also affected by the rate of speech (fast speech tends to be harder).

Speaker recognition is the process of automatically recognizing who is speaking on the basis of individual information included in speech signals. It can be divided into Speaker Identification and Speaker Verification. Speaker identification determines which registered speaker provides a given utterance from among a set of known speakers. Speaker verification accepts or rejects the identity claim of a speaker—is the speaker the person he says he is?

Speaker recognition technology makes it possible for the speaker's voice to control access to restricted services, for example, phone access to banking, database services, shopping, voice mail, and access to secure equipment.

Both technologies require users to "enroll" in the system, that is, to give examples of their speech to a system so that it can characterize (or learn) their voice patterns. The following products are available on Windows (including 95, NT) platform for speech recognition:

- AT&T Watson Speech Recognition
- Cambridge Voice for Windows
- Dragon Dictate for Windows
- Dragon Dictation Products
- IBM VoiceType Dictation and Control
- Kurzweil Speech Recognition
- Lernout & Hauspie ASR SDK
- Listen for Windows 2.0 from Verbex Voice Systems
- Microsoft Speech Recognition
- Philips Speech Recognition
- VoiceAssist for Windows from Creative Labs, Inc.
- Whisper

EXERCISES

1. Classify the following as examples of distortion and noise.
   a. You are talking to your friend on the phone and your mother is shouting at you.
   b. You have a bad cold and you are addressing a meeting at the office.
2. You are speaking through a microphone, and the sound comes out clipped. Can you think of another case where the speech signal gets clipped?

Projects

1. Write a 2000 word essay on Fractal Music, by researching the topic on the Internet.
2. Convert a MIDI file present in your computer (in the Windows/Media folder) into a .wav file by using an Audio Editor. Use various sampling rates and bit resolutions. Are there differences in quality?
3. Download an application that uses a text to speech engine (such as "BonziBuddy" from www.bonzi.com), and make notes about the quality of speech generation. What are the strengths and limitations of current text to speech engines?

4. Download an application from the Internet that uses a speech recognition engine. Read the specifications of the speech recognition engine, and summarize it in 50 words using the terminology of this section. Experiment with the system and try to find its major strengths and limitations.

Solutions

1. a. Noise
   b. Distortion

An Interlude: Free for All

When the MP3 music compression standard first appeared in 1998 it caused great consternation in the industry. Here is an article from those times. It is a good example of how a mathematical algorithm can shake the foundations of an industry

If you love music, this is going to be your year. I think the music industry will undergo some soul-searching changes this year. All this is because of the compression standard called MPEG3. You can now have CD quality music for free from the Internet. Sounds incredible? Well, here is how it works.

Let us first recall how we listen to music at the moment. First of all you need a source. This is usually an audiotape player of some kind. The most common is a portable player like the Sony Walkman. If you are a discerning listener, you might have a tape deck. Increasingly, we are keen to use CD players for high-quality music. Some people still have record players, although I have not seen one for many years. Once your source is ready to play, you need an amplifier. The amplifier is actually in two parts, the pre-amplifier that amplifies and cleans up the input signal, and the power amplifier that increases the level so that your speakers can blast the neighbor's cat out of her chair.

If you have a multimedia PC at home, you can do away with the source because the CD drive of the PC will also play audio CDs. In fact, if you carry a multimedia notebook PC, you could do away with the tape player as well and switch to CD music that you can listen to over headphones connected to the notebook. But you still need to buy and carry CDs around. If your notebook has a large disk drive, you could solve part of this problem. You could borrow a CD and record it to your hard disk as a .wav file. If you do this at a sufficiently high resolution (44 kHz, stereo, 16 bit, for example), you will be able to listen to music using the media player of Windows at a quality almost indistinguishable from the original CD. So now, you do not need to carry CDs anymore. But there is a catch. Each 3-minute song that you record will occupy around 40 MB of disk space. As a result, you are unlikely to keep more than a few songs around on your hard disk. This can get very boring indeed. But then came MP3.

MP3 is a method for compressing sound files, using a technique called MPEG1, Layer3 encoding. It reduces the file sizes by almost a factor of ten without loss of data. Now, three minutes of CD quality music can be stored in as little as 3 MB of space. Given the large disks that are common these days, this will allow you to carry dozens of songs on a notebook, or store hundreds of them on a home PC. As soon as the MP3 standard was announced, students all over the world began to put songs onto the Internet. If you are a fellow sufferer of the kind of bandwidth you get from an Internet connection to the Web, you will realize that though it is absolutely impossible to transfer 40 MB from the Internet, downloading up to 5 MB is not such a difficult task.

What about copyrights? Well, the Internet seems to respect no law. Before anyone could react, there were exchange programs created on the Web that would let you download 5 MB for every 1 MB of music you upload. Whatever the law might have had to say, the Internet became full of gigabytes of music.

Here is what you have to do to get on the MPEG3 bandwagon. First, get yourself a player. This is easy. The best MP3 player on the Internet is a player called Winamp. You can download it for free from the www.mp3.com site. Winamp is a marvel of amateur software engineering. It comes along with a graphic equalizer as well and produces the best sound I have ever heard from a 1-inch notebook speaker. Next, you must get some music. Well, there are endless amounts of it on the Web and you will get to it with a little patience. However, you may not necessarily get the music you like. In that case, you have to create your own MP3 files.

The best way to create MP3 files is to convert CD music to this format. To do this, you will first need to create a .wav file out of the piece of music you want to store. You can do this using the controls of the Sound Blaster card, if you are using one. But this can sometimes produce noisy files. A better method is to use a CD ripper. This is a piece of software that will convert the analog signals from an audio CD to a digital file. The best program I have found for this is called WinDac32. It is free, of course.

Once you have a good quality .wav file, you can convert it to MP3 using an encoder. The best free encoder on the Internet is a program called MPEG encoder v0.06 by SoloH. It takes about an hour to do one song, but it is worth the wait. It is absolutely amazing to see a 40 MB song reduced to 3 MB at full CD quality.

In addition to all this, there are dozens of special effects generators you can download that will respond to the music that Winamp is playing and will produce MTV-like special effects. I tried this out one evening and the results are astonishing. A disco in your home for free!

I wonder what the effects of these programs will be on the market. Are we seeing the beginning of the end of the audio CD industry?

Courtesy of Data Quest, April 1998.

CHAPTER 6

Audio: From CD to the Web

CD RIPPING

CD Ripping is a process of converting audio CD into .wav format. This is done using a program known as the CD Ripper or Grabber. The grabber is different from a sampler. The latter reads the analog output signal from the CD player and converts it to digital .wav file. The sampler makes two conversions—from digital data on CD to analog CD output and then from the analog CD output to the digital .wav file on your hard disk. A sampler thus makes a lower quality sound file than the original. On the other hand, the grabber reads the digital data directly from the CD and stores it as a .wav file on your hard disk. So the .wav file that the CD ripper produces contains exactly the same information that is on the CD, without any loss of quality at all. This .wav file being huge (about 10 MB per minute of sound), is difficult to store and transfer.

Rippers use two ways to communicate with your CD ROM drive—ASPI interface and the MSCDEX interface. The following are some differences between them.

- ASPI mode works both with IDE and SCSI drives under both Windows 95 and Windows NT. This mode is supported by almost all audiograbbers available on the Internet. There are, however, some IDE drives that will refuse to work with an ASPI interface, irrespective of which ASPI drivers version you have installed on your computer.
- MSCDEX mode works only with IDE drives, but can be vital for some CD ROM models that cannot be ripped with the ASPI mode. MSCDEX mode is supported only by Audiograbber, CDDA (Compact Disk Digital Audio) 1.7, and CDDA 32. The interface of Audiograbber v1.20 is illustrated in Figure 1.

MP3 ENCODING

MP3 encoding is the process of converting a wave file into MP3 format. The size of the MP3 file is about 12 times smaller than that of the parent wave file. The quality of the MP3

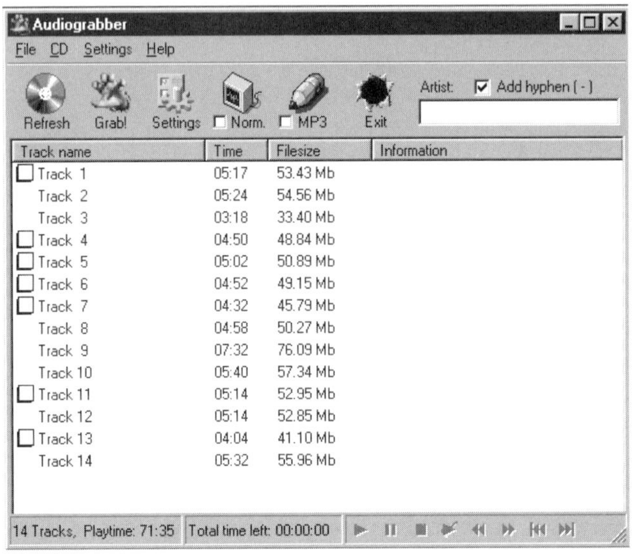

FIGURE 1
Audiograbber v1.20 interface.

file remains more or less the same as the original file. The encoding process removes those frequencies from the wave file that cannot be heard by the human ear (less than 20 Hz and greater than 20 kHz). Sounds masked by other sounds are also removed by MP3 conversion. This reduces the file size to a smaller size than that of the wave file. Most MP3 encoders are written in Visual C++ or Delphi. The source code for some is freely available on the Internet. Encoding a wave file to the MP3 format may take a long time. The duration of converting a single 80 MB wave file to MP3 format on a Pentium takes about 15 minutes, although faster MP3 encoders are being introduced in the market all the time.

Common MP3 Encoders

The MP3 format is based on an algorithm developed by the Fraunhofer Institute. The first program that used this algorithm was L3Enc, written by the same institute. L3Enc is a 16-bit, command line interface encoder. It is a bit slow, but makes high-quality MP3s. But this program is a shareware, and in the trial version encodes only up to 112 Kbps. To make 128 Kbps MP3s (or more) you need to register the software. There are many graphical interface programs that use L3Enc as an encoding engine. These are called Front-ends or GUIs and most of them are free, but yet again, you have to pay for L3Enc.

Fraunhofer Institute released a 32-bit program called CODEC, which is much faster than L3Enc and makes better quality MP3s. CODEC is not exactly a program, but rather a library of functions that other programs use. It is also a shareware with more limitations than L3Enc. Like L3Enc, there many free encoders using the CODEC library as an encoding engine, but again you need to pay for CODECs registered version.

There is an exception to all of this and it is called mpegEnc v0.07 and MPlifier v0.52 (Figure 2). These are really the only freeware MP3 encoders because they use their own engines for encoding.

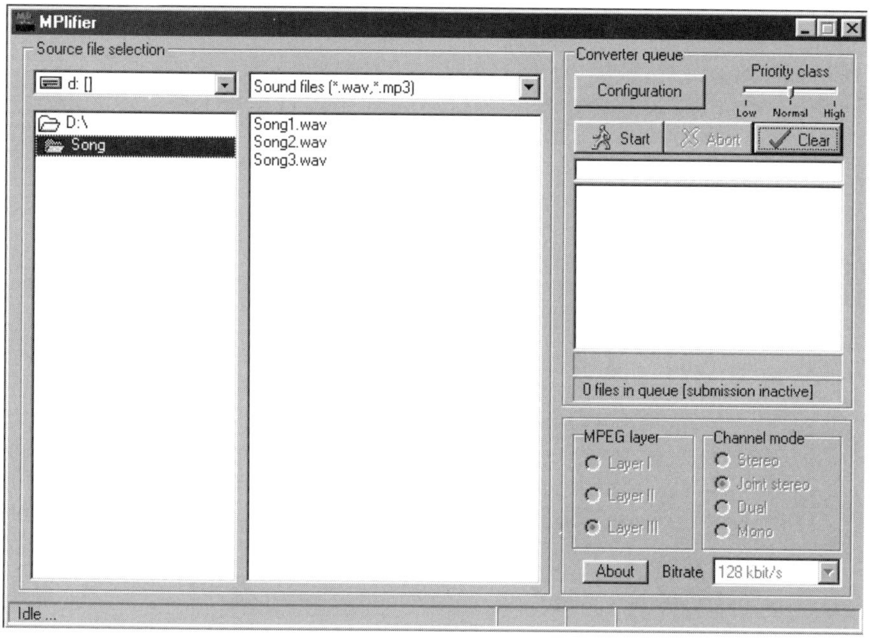

FIGURE 2
MPlifier v0.52.

AUDIO ON THE INTERNET

Streaming Audio

Before the audio streaming technology was perfected, sound had to be downloaded to a hard drive before it could be played, which meant a long wait in many cases. Audio files are tremendously large. Over dial-up connections, the average transfer ratio is 5:1; that is, you have to wait for 5 minutes for every minute of audio playback time.

The term "streaming audio" is made up of two words. The word "streaming" means that you do not have to download an entire audio file before you actually listen to the audio. Continuously streamed audio eliminates download time, thanks to the compression tools employed. The file usually begins playing within a few seconds of clicking on the link. Another benefit is that the clip length is unlimited. Anything from a pop song to a political convention can be recorded and made available on a Web site, even digital sound files, such as .wav (Windows) or .au (Macintosh) files, can be encoded for playback as well.

To listen to streaming audio, you must equip your computer with a sound card and speakers. Then you need audio plug-ins for your Web browser. These are available for free and can be downloaded from the Web.

Some common Streaming Multimedia Players are:

- Real Audio
- Shockwave audio
- StreamWorks
- ToolVox

Using Streaming Audio

Many factors will contribute to the quality of the sound broadcast you create, including the input (original) sound file quality, CPU of the computer, and the CPU of the server on the Web site. Usually both speech and music files transmit well across all bandwidths. The only problem occurs when playing back speech or music encoded for ISDN speed over a 486 PC, with plenty of system resources available. Under repeated testing, it is found that the clip would begin, then start breaking up, and eventually quit (playback with clips encoded for 14.4 and 28.8 Kbps modems execute smoothly). Streaming audio on a Pentium machine causes no problems.

Bandwidth and the Quality of Audio on the Internet

Audio players work adequately with 14.4 Kbps modems, but just like the rest of the Net, the more bandwidth you have, the better. Regardless of the speed of your connection however, you will not hear hi-fi audio. Streaming audio technology has been improving steadily though, and may soon deliver the crisp sound we have come to expect from CDs. In general, speech sounds better than music.

Projects

1. Write a 1000 word report on various MP3 players available commercially. Compare their various features, such as the disk space available for storage, and cost. Include a comparison of costs for operating MP3 players versus regular CD players. Make assumptions for the number of CDs you buy in a month, and then project the costs for a year.
2. Download a good free CD ripper, and convert a few songs into MP3 format. Try various options on the CD ripper and compare the quality of the MP3 and the size of the file in KBs. For a few of the songs, convert to .wav format and figure out the compression ratios obtained. Do this with at least five songs from your CD. Is MP3 really leading to high amounts of compression without loss of quality of the sound? Make a short presentation using MS-Powerpoint and explain the results of your experiments to your friends. Use clips from various music files to add effect to your presentation.

CHAPTER 7

The WAV File Format

INTRODUCTION

Waveform audio is recognized as one of the essential components of a multimedia system. With waveform audio, you can do anything within the practical limitations of memory, disk capacity, sound card capabilities, and so on. The normal functions that you perform on your tape recorder can also be done with waveform audio.

Like CD Audio, waveform audio is a digital medium. However, unlike CD audio, it supports a variety of formats, from 8-bit mono at a sample rate of 11 Kbps to 16-bit stereo at sample rate of 44 Kbps. Also, unlike CD audio, you can read and write it, store and retrieve it, and manipulate it as you like.

DIGITAL AUDIO BASICS

Sound consists of pressure waves moving through a medium, such as air. For each wave pulse there is a traveling zone of compressed air trailed by a zone of rarefied air. When represented electronically, compression is represented by a positive voltage and rarefaction is represented by a negative voltage. The voltage level determines the amplitude of the wave. A pure sine wave would be gradually switching from a positive to a negative value of the same degree and then back again as shown in Figure 1.

The analog waveform stored digitally has the voltage levels of the wave stored at regular intervals as a set of numbers. Audible frequencies range from 20–20,000 Hz. Therefore, to determine a meaningful digital representation, you need to sample the waveform. Sampling is the process of taking a snapshot of the waveform at regular intervals and representing it as a binary number. This process is called PCM (Pulse Code Modulation). To accurately represent any audio signal, we sample at twice the maximum frequency contained in the wave source. This is the reason why CD audio is recorded at 44.1 kHz—which is twice the maximum audible frequency of humans. You need not, however, always stick to this frequency; you may sample at lower sampling rates.

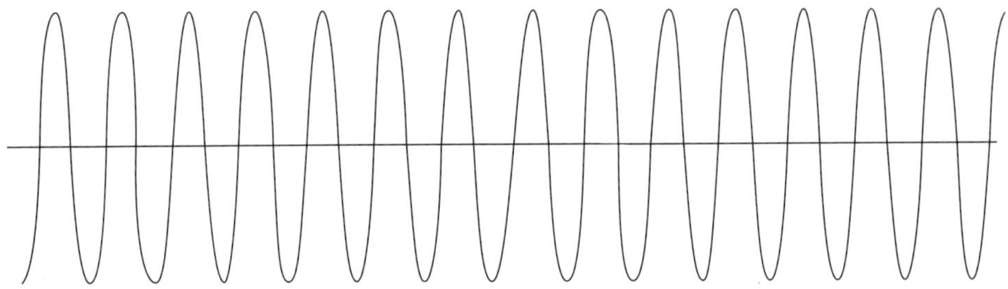

FIGURE 1
A pure sine wave.

Therefore, to record audio at 11 kHz, you need to sample 11,000 times per second.

The format of the data stored is very simple. In 8-bit samples, each byte represents amplitude. If the sample contains two channels of audio, the left channel is recorded in the even-numbered bytes while the right channel is recorded in the odd-numbered bytes. In 8-bit sampling, the baseline of the data is represented by 128. All positive amplitudes have values over 128 while all negative amplitudes have values below 128.

In 16-bit sampling, amplitude values range from –32,768 to 32,767.

THE STRUCTURE OF THE WAVE AUDIO FILE

The wave file not only contains the digital data required to produce sound but also additional information such as the sampling rate, the type of audio data, and other critical data. We can perform tape recorder functions like Play and Pause using the normal MCI (Multimedia functions available in the windows API). However, when it comes to modifying a wave file, we cannot use the MCI functions. Hence, we use the MMIO (MultiMedia Input Output) low-level functions available in the Windows API, for which we need to know the actual structure of the wave file.

Wave data comes in several formats, sampling rates, channels, and resolutions (bits/sample). All we need to know is that the information appears in a format block called the "Resource Interchange File Format," or the RIFF chunk.

Figure 2 represents a file, TADA.WAV which is a standard file packaged with Win95. As the figure suggests, RIFF files have hierarchical structures—chunks which in turn contain more chunks.

The highest level chunk is the RIFF chunk itself. Chunks are identified by labels, known as Chunk Ids. The first four bytes contain the characters RIFF. To read and write RIFF files, the standard data structure called MMCKINFO (MultiMedia ChunK INFOrmation) is used. The structure as defined in Visual Basic is:

- Type MMCKINFO
- Ckid as FOURCC
- Cksize as Long
- FccType as FOURCC
- dwDataOffset as Long
- dwFlags as Long
- End Type

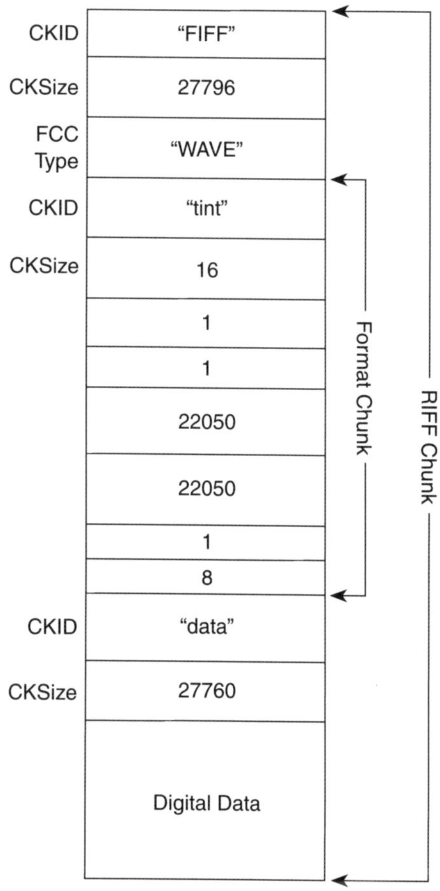

FIGURE 2
Sample waveform structure of TADA.WAV.

where structure FOURCC is defined as:

- Type FOURCC
- Chars as String * 4
- End Type

where:

- FOURCC is a 32-bit code used to identify RIFF chunks, and represented as a sequence of 1 to 4 ASCII alphanumeric characters padded on the right with blank characters.
- Ckid represents the identification of the chunk.
- Cksize specifies the size of the data field of the chunk.
- FccType specifies the form type for "RIFF."
- dwDataOffset specifies the file offset of the beginning of the chunk's data field.
- dwFlags specifies flags giving additional information about the chunk.

To read the WAVE format data the structure is

- Type PCMWAVEFORMAT
- Wf as WAVEFORMAT
- wBitsPerSample as Integer
- End Type

where wBitsPerSample specifies the number of bits per sample, and the structure of WAVEFORMAT is as follows:

- Type WAVEFORMAT
- FormatTag as Integer
- nChannels as Integer
- nSamplesPerSec as Long
- nAvgBytesPerSec as Long
- nBlockAlign as Integer
- End Type

where:

- FormatTag specifies the format types (usually PCM).
- Channels specifies the number of channels, 0 signifies mono and 1 signifies stereo.
- SamplesPerSec specifies the sample rate in samples per second.
- AvgBytesPerSec specifies the required average data transfer rate in bytes/second.
- BlockAlign specifies the block alignment in bytes.

ACCESSING THE WAVE DATA

Why should we use MMIO functions instead of the conventional read/write functions? Well, the answer is simple. Although the structures are the same, they vary in size, which means we cannot read them into or write from them into simple, fixed-length record buffers. To navigate through the wave file we are going to use the following MMIO functions (see Table 1).

We use these functions because we do not need to know the actual size of the chunk. To navigate through the structures, all we have to do is set either the chunk id or the form type (FccType), set a search flag, and then call mmioDescend() or mmioAscend(). The function will search for the next chunk in line and fill in the structure with the details for that particular chunk.

A wave file consists of three chunks—the RIFF chunk, PCMFormat chunk, and the DATA chunk. However, there is another chunk called the LIST chunk, which contains

Table 1 MMIO Functions

Function	Description
mmioOpen()	To open a wave file
mmioClose()	To close a wave file
mmioRead()	To read the chunk data
mmioWrite()	To write the chunk data
mmioDescend()	To navigate through a wave file
mmioAscend()	To navigate through a wave file

details such as copyright and description of the data chunk. Usually it is blank, but in some wave files shipped along with Windows 95, this structure contains some information. Table 2 gives the structure of the TADA.WAV file.

The steps for reading a wave file are as follows:

1. Open the Wave file using the mmioOpen function.
2. Create an instance of the structure MMCKINFO, for example, MMCKINFO Parent.
3. Set Parent.FccType.Chars="WAVE" because the FccType of the RIFF chunk is "Wave"
4. Call the mmioDescend function, passing the structure Parent as one of its parameters and a flag MMIO_FINDRIFF.
   The Parent structure will now be filled with the RIFF chunk data, which means that when you actually print out the values of Parent.Ckid you will find that it contains "RIFF" and the value of parent. Cksize will be (filesize-8) bytes.
5. Create another instance of the structure MMCKINFO, say MMCKINFO Child.
6. Set the Child.Ckid.Chars = "fmt" and call mmioDescend function, passing the structure Child as one of its parameters and a flag MMIO_FINDCHUNK. This will take the file pointer to the beginning of the Format chunk.
7. Call the mmioRead function, passing an instance of the structure PCMWAVEFORMAT to it along with the parameter Child.Cksize that will tell the function how many bytes to read.
8. Next, to reach the Data chunk, use the mmioDescend function. However, before doing that ascend out of the Format Chunk. Therefore, call the mmioAscend function passing the structure Child to it. This will position the pointer to the beginning of the Format Chunk.
9. Descend to the Data Chunk by setting the Child.Ckid.Chars = "data" and calling the function mmioDescend passing the Child structure and flag MMIO_FINDCHUNK as its parameters.

Table 2 TADA.WAV File Structure

Offset position	Size in bytes	Contents	Belongs to chunk	Comments
0	4	"RIFF"	RIFF	Ckid, each byte contains one character
4	4	27,796	RIFF	Cksize, equals the file size minus eight bytes ie. (RIFF's ckid and cksize)
8	4	"WAVE"	RIFF	FccType
12	4	"fmt"	PCMFormat	Next Ckid, ? stands for blank
16	4	16	PCMFormat	Cksize, Wave format chunk is 16 bytes
20	2	1	PCMFormat	Indicates a PCM WAVE format
22	2	1	PCMFormat	Number of channels
24	2	22,050	PCMFormat	Sampling rate
28	4	22,050	PCMFormat	Average bytes per second
32	2	1	PCMFormat	Effective bytes per second
34	2	8	PCMFormat	Bits per sample
36	4	"data"	Data	Ckid id of the wave data
40	4	27,760	Data	Cksize, Size of the digital data

10. Use mmioRead to read the digital data into a byte type buffer. This can be done easily since the size of the data from Child.Cksize is known.
11. You can then manipulate this digital data buffer, such as chop it, add special effects to it, and so on, since it is just an array which contains nothing but numbers.
12. Write the RIFF chunk followed by the FORMAT chunk and the DATA chunk to write the modified file back to the disk.
13. If you have appended some data to the audio data buffer, keep in mind to also modify the respective data in the RIFF structure, such as the Cksize.

Projects

1. The program (in Visual Basic) to read and play a single file is given at the Web site of this book. Change the code so that it appends another file, and add a button to append the code. The program files can be found by following the link to Audio/Projects/WavePlay. Read the code carefully. You will need to modify the code accordingly. Here are a few hints:

   - Use the ReDim Preserve <arrayname> function to increase the size of the data array.
   - Keep adding the chunk size of the newly read file to the previous chunk size.

2. Make an audio presentation on a topic related to your school. Choose a period based on your favorite music, and use clips as a running theme of the presentation. (Classic rock is your favorite? Choose the sixties and seventies as your period.) Add interviews, music, and voice-overs to convey your ideas or the information that you wish to present.

Prelude to Graphics

Graphics have become an integral part of our lives. Pictures, photographs, and mixtures of the two are everywhere. Graphics can be called "good" or "bad" depending on a number of things. Here are some of the things you can do to find out these differences for yourself:

- Compare pictures in newspapers, magazines, TV, and movies.
- Look at a photograph and try to draw it.
- Look at a real object (for example, a cup of tea) and draw it.
- Make a collage by cutting out pictures from magazines and newspapers.

Table 1 will help you think about graphics.

Table 1 Graphics in Various Media

Things to notice	Newspaper	Magazine	TV	Movie	Drawing
Where do you find pictures with more detail?					
Where do pictures look more "real"?					
Where do things look "solid"?					
What kind of picture makes you "feel" something?					

CHAPTER 8

The Paint Shop Pro Interface

> **Learning to Learn**
> A lot of information about Digital Graphics is already contained in the User Interface Design of a Graphics Editor. In fact, the same is true for any software product. Designers of user interfaces try to make sure that their software package is easy to learn by newbies. To become an expert computer user, you should learn how to use this information to learn a package quickly. The chapters on digital graphics are designed to provide you practice on learning to learn a software package.
>
> Before we get into explanations of various terms in digital graphics, you have to conduct some experiments on a graphics editor first. For doing this it is suggested that you download an evaluation copy of Paint Shop Pro (version 5 or above) and install it on your system. While many other bit-map editors also have these features, you will be able to follow the instructions more easily by using Paint Shop Pro.

THE PAINT SHOP PRO INTERFACE

The objectives of the first set of experiments are to get familiar with the interface of Paint Shop Pro and to be able to make simple graphics. Don't worry if you don't understand everything about the software at present. Learning to use a software package is always an incremental process: the more you work on a system, the more you will understand its various features. If you follow the instructions below, you will not only be able to learn about many features of this software, but also get an idea of how you can experiment and learn to use *any* graphics software.

Start Paint Shop Pro and spend a few seconds trying to find icons that are already familiar to you. The icons for new file, open file, save, print, undo, cut, copy, and paste should be familiar to all of you. In the View menu, select Toolbars. Switch off each toolbar one at a time, and figure out the names of all the toolbars. The following toolbars are available:

- Color Palette
- Control Palette

- Histogram Window
- Layer Palette
- Status Bar
- Tool Bar
- Tool Palette

Finally, after you can identify each one, remove the histogram palette, and keep all the rest on the screen. Mark all these toolbars in Figure 1. As you gain more experience with the software, you can experiment and learn about the various functions on each toolbar. Some of them will explicitly be used during the course. Now it is time to make a graphic.

Click on the new icon (or choose File→New . . . from the menu). You will see a dialog box. Make a picture that has width 200 pixels, height 200 pixels, resolution 72 pixels/inch, Background color White, and 13.7 million colors. By looking at various options in the dialog box that come up when you click on the new icon, fill in the following blanks:

1. Possible dimensions of width and height: ____________________
2. Possible units of resolution: ____________________
3. Possible background colors: ____________________
4. Possible image types ____________________

Now you should have a new image window on your screen (Figure 1).

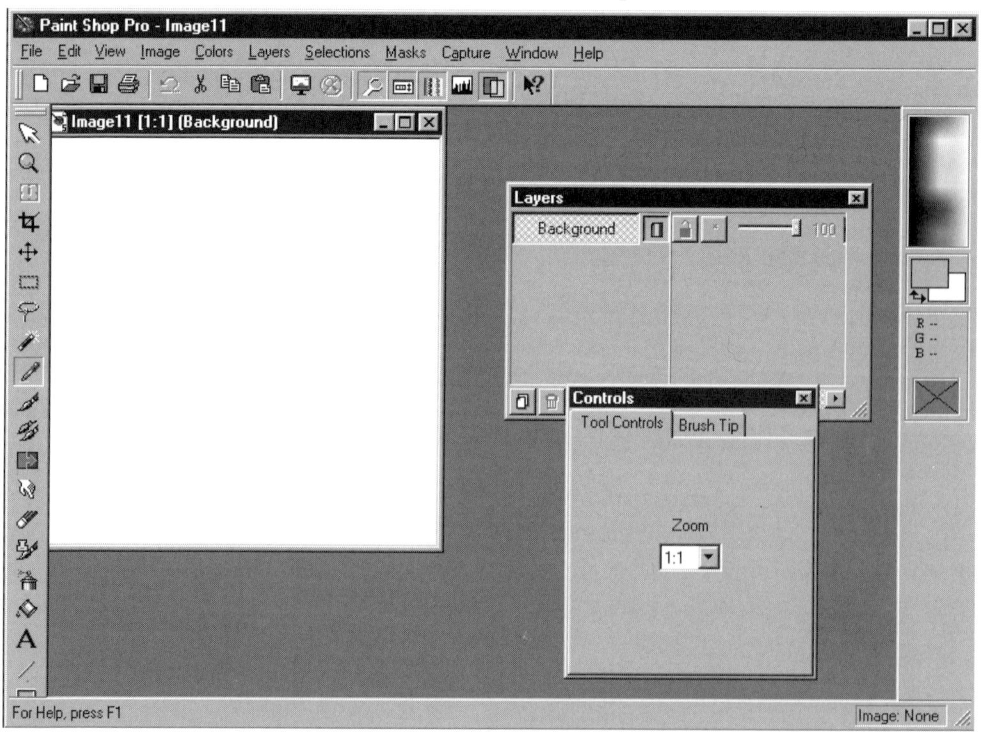

FIGURE 1
The Paint Shop Pro interface.

The image is blank with just the white background.

> **Tip**
> It is a good idea to write down the terms in this chapter that you do not understand. For example, if you do not know what "resolution" means in this context, try to find out its meaning. The meaning of most of these terms will become clear later.

The status bar (the one that says "For Help, press F1" in Figure 1) displays help on various toolbar icons as you move the mouse over these icons or menu items. There is also a context help that comes up, if the cursor stays on an icon for some time. Let us now put some color onto the graphics.

THE FLOOD FILL TOOL

Move your cursor over the Color Palette where you can see a rectangle with various colors. The cursor will take the shape of a dropper as you move over the palette. What does the status bar say when your cursor moves over these colors? Move your cursor onto the blue color, and left-click on it. Now the blue color would be chosen for the foreground. How can you tell? Move it to some yellow area and right-click on it. Now the yellow color is chosen as the background color.

Now locate the Flood Fill icon on the Tool Palette by moving your cursor slowly over various icons and seeing the context help that pops up. It looks like a can of paint. Click on it and record your observations in Table 1.

Table 1 Experiment to Understand Flood Fill

No.	Instructions and questions	Record your answers and other observations
5	Move your cursor over (do not click) the image. What does the cursor look like?	
6	Click on the image. What happens?	
7	Look at the Control Palette. Click on the Brush Tip button. Is there anything active in this palette?	
8	Click on the Tool Controls button. Change various options and click on the image. (Make sure that you press CTRL-z or the undo button to start with a blank screen each time.)	
	Record what you see by changing various options in the Tool controls toolbar, and describe the image that results. Try the following:	
	Change the fill style to Linear Gradient and click on image with white background.	
	Change the fill style to Rectangular Gradient and click on image with white background.	
	Change the fill style to Sunburst Gradient and click on image with white background.	
	Change the fill style to Radial Gradient and click on image with background.	
	Change the fill style to Pattern Gradient and click on image with white background. Can you figure out what this does?	
	What happens when you select one type of gradient, click on the image, and then select another one and click on top of that? Record what you did and what you observed.	
	Now select Solid Color as the fill style. Reduce the Opacity to 20 and click on the white image. What happens?	

By now, you may have found some interesting things about Paint Shop Pro all on your own which are not mentioned in Table 1. Write these down somewhere. Now for all the other tools, you can perform similar experiments, record your observations, and be able to learn about almost all the tools. If you don't understand an option or a tool by doing similar experiments, you can always look at the Help files to understand it. But make sure you experiment first, and then try to read the help (or ask friends).

Record these observations on a piece of paper and staple it to this page. Next, let us go on to the selection tool. Hunt for it in the Tool Palette by moving your cursor over each button and seeing the context help pop up. Select it by clicking and see what kind of selections you can make by looking at the "Type of Selection" menu in the control palette.

In Table 2, record the observations of the experiments suggested on the left. You may have to discover parts of the procedure to do it yourself. Write down the procedure as well as your observations in the right column.

By now you will have figured out "how to experiment" in Paint Shop Pro. To finish the first set of experiments, write down all the tools that we have not considered in the Tool Palette, experiment with them, and fill in Table 3. Make as many images as you wish, but delete them after you are done, and keep only some open at a time.

INTRODUCTION TO DIGITAL GRAPHICS

Computer programs store their pictures as pixel maps (called *bit-maps* or *raster images*).

Table 2 More Tools in the Tool Palette

No.	Instructions and questions	Procedure/comments
9	Make the background blue by using the Flood Fill tool. Select a circle. Now select the yellow color, and Flood Fill inside the circle. Right click on the image to deselect. Similarly make other shapes, and fill them with colors.	
10	Move your cursor over the selection tool button in the Tool Palette, and write down what the Status bar says on the right column.	
11	Over a black background make a crescent to look like the moon. Write down the procedure.	
12	Make a circle and type CTRL-z. What happens?	
13	Find the shapes button in the Tool Palette. Make a few shapes using various tool controls. Record at least three shapes that you can make using this tool.	
14	Click on the select button. Select a small square after making the "feather" value equal to 2. Press the delete key. Do the same after making the feather value 20. (The feather value comes in the control palette.) What does the change in feather do to the deleted rectangle?	
15	Find the zoom tool in the Tool Palette. Now left click on the image to magnify it. Left click again several times. Right click to reduce magnification. How can you tell what the magnification is at any time?	
16	On a blue background image, select a circle with the Antialias box checked. (The Antialias box appears in the tool control.) Delete this circle. Now do the same without antialiasing. Select the Text tool from the Tool Palette, and write some text with and without anti-aliasing. The question: What is antialiasing?	

Table 3 All the Other Tools of Paint Shop Pro

Name of Tool	Your experiment (What you did with the tool, description of image created, and so on.)	Your observations (What you learned via your experiments, what the tool does, and any other remarks you want to record.)
Arrow		
Deform		
Crop		
Mover		
Freehand		
Magic wand		
Dropper		
Paintbrushes		
Clone brush		
Color replacer		
Retouch		
Eraser		
Picture tube		
Air brush		
Line		

The Monitor is divided into a grid of small pixels (short for picture elements). If you go to the display properties control panel (by right clicking on the desktop and choosing properties), you can check the "screen area" of your monitor. Screen areas of 800×600 pixels are quite common on the Windows platform. Each pixel contains values representing a particular color. When a picture is sent to the screen, a graphics *driver* converts the picture data to pixel values on the display. Figure 2 depicts samples of digital images. The large image in Figure 3 depicts how a picture is stored in a PC in pixels.

We can convert a real (analog) picture—such as a photograph—into digital format by using a device called a scanner. Alternatively, we may use a computer to generate a picture. For example, we can easily write a program to draw a geometric figure (such as a straight line or a circle) on the monitor by using a mathematical equation to paint the appropriate pixels. By just using mathematical equations, we can generate quite complicated and realistic pictures.

Thus digital graphics—and graphics editors, too—come in two flavors. Bitmap editors allow you to create and edit graphics as bitmaps. In particular, if you need to retouch a photograph, you will have to scan it and open it in a bitmap editor to edit it. Paint Shop Pro is an example of the bitmap editor. The other type of graphics editor helps you to create graphics using various mathematical tracks. This type of graphics is known as *Vector*

Graphics or *Object-Oriented Graphics*. An example of a Vector Graphics editor is Adobe® Illustrator.

Even in a bitmap editor, many tools exist that allow you to create a geometrical figure. However, once created it is not possible to edit it and change its attributes. For example, if you use your painting program to draw a line, you will not be able to edit that line as a separate object. It becomes part of the image. However, when you create objects in a drawing program, you can still edit them after you have done something else. For example, if you draw a circle in one place, then draw a rectangle in another place, you can still select the circle and change its size and location.

Bit-Mapped and Vector Graphics

Since there are two types of graphics, there are also two types of file formats for digital graphics, bit-mapped (or raster images), and vector formats. They may look the same on the, screen or in print. For example, see Figure 2 for an image created using a Vector Graphics Package and then stored as a bitmap.

If we take the bitmap, and magnify it using Paint Shop Pro, we will see the individual pixels comprising the image, as in Figure 3.

However, if the same picture is stored as a vector graphic, and then enlarged in a vector graphics editor, it will appear sharp on the screen (as in Figure 4). This is because

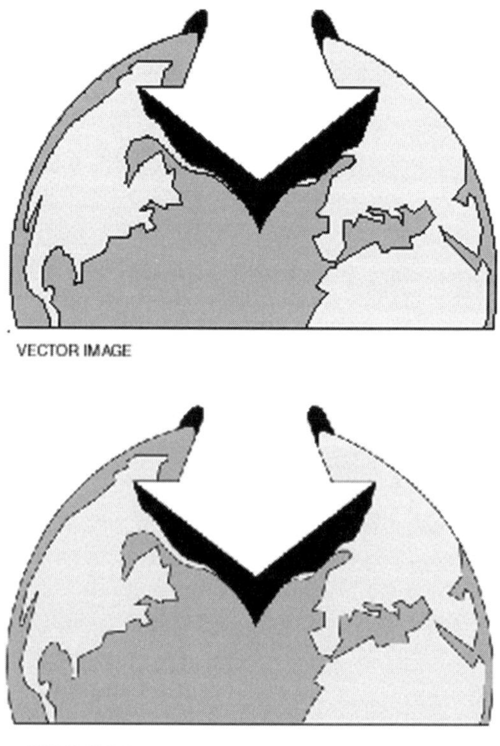

FIGURE 2
The two types of digital images.

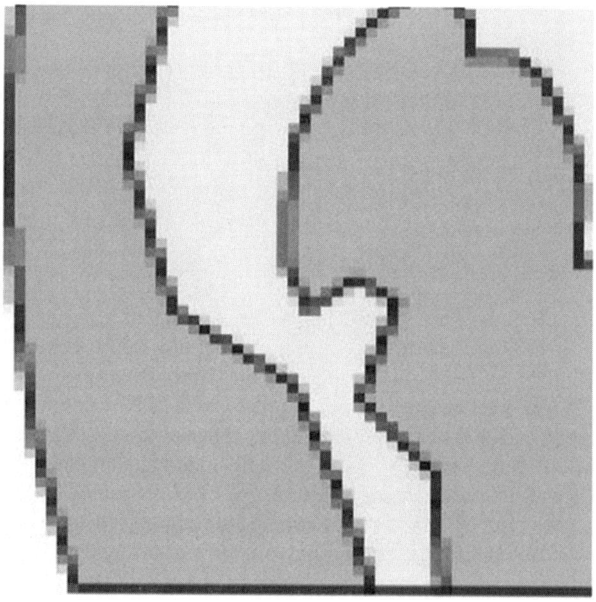

FIGURE 3
A bit-mapped graphic enlarged becomes pixelated.

the data is stored in the form of mathematical equations that describe how the pixels on the screen have to be painted. And when enlarged, the individual values of the pixels are recalculated.

Another concept that is related to whether an image looks pixelated is the resolution. The resolution of an image is the number of pixels in the digital image relative to the physical size of the original material. Resolution is commonly measured in dpi (dots per inch) and can be applied not only to the image but to the input and output devices used to scan or print the image. When it comes to monitors, resolution is often measured a pixels per inch. A common resolution supported by many monitors is 72 pixels/inch.

If the resolution is too low, we will be able to see the individual pixels comprising the image, and we will see a blocky image. The same effect happens when we enlarge a photograph too much. Then we can see the individual dots comprising the picture. Essentially the same effect can be seen when we magnify a picture in a graphics editor. Sometimes when changing the size or enlarging an image using a graphics editor, we also get a pixelated look as in Figure 5.

For the print media, we need a much higher value of resolution. This sometimes creates problems for graphic artists. For example, a 4 × 6 inch photograph scanned at 100 dpi will create an image 400 × 600 pixels in size. If your computer monitor has a dot pitch (dots per inch) of 75 dpi, this image will be displayed at 133% scale or 33% larger than the actual photograph. Consequently, if you print this image on a 300 dpi laser printer it will only measure 1.33 × 2 inches or 33% of the original scale.

The difference between vector and bitmaps also has an implication for graphic artists. A graphic artist prefers to use a vector graphics editor in order to draw cartoons (see Figure 6) and uses raster editors to create or modify more complicated graphics such as photographs or collages made out of many other images. Text editing within graphics is done better by Vector packages, though new versions of bitmap editing programs are also increasingly combining the strengths of both vector and bitmapped images in this regard.

FIGURE 4
A vector graphic when enlarged looks the same.

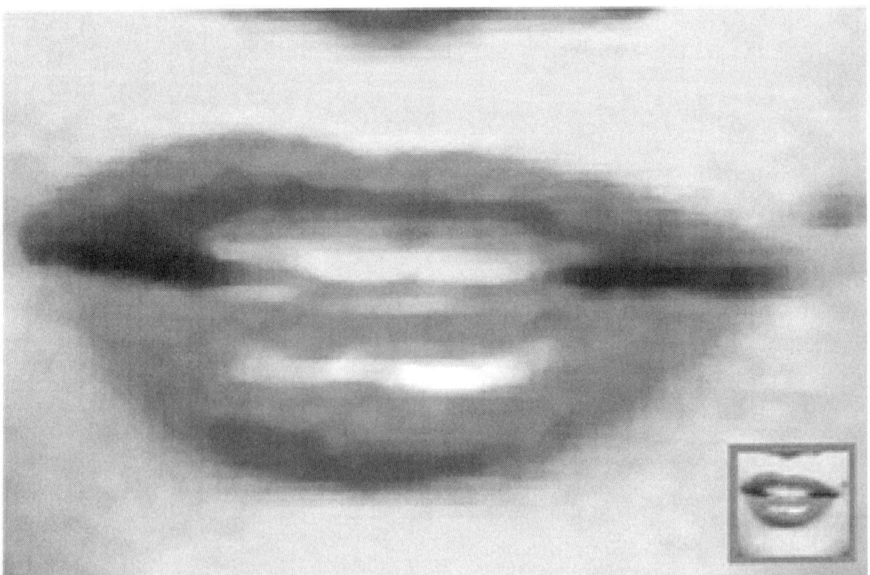

FIGURE 5
A magnified image giving a pixelated look.

FIGURE 11.6
A vector package is better for creating line-art or cartoons.

Common Graphic Packages

Some of the commonly used graphics editors are

- Lview Pro—good conversion/editing, GIF 89a
- Paint Shop Pro—advanced picture editing functions
- xv (UNIX workhorse)
- Adobe PhotoShop
- Fractal Design Painter
- Flash

- Corel Draw
- Corel Photo Paint
- 3D Studio

We are not going to consider a vector image editor in this book. However, if you get familiar with working with a bitmap editor such as Paint Shop Pro it is not difficult to get started with a vector graphics package. Meanwhile, there are many features of Paint Shop Pro that mimic the creation of graphics using a vector graphics editor. As you have seen, there are many functions available in Paint Shop Pro to create simple geometrical figures. There are other mathematical functions used by graphics editors to generate "fill" effects or to transform the image by means of filters. We will discover these as we go along. One of the best things about graphics editors is that they allow people to create interesting graphics, even if they are not very good at drawing or painting—using pencil and paper.

EXERCISES

State whether the following statements are true or false.

1. A photograph is an analog image and a scanner can convert it into a digital image.
2. All digital images are stored in the computer as pixels.
3. A 3 × 2 inch photograph when scanned at 100 dpi will result in an image which is 300 × 200 pixels.
4. A vector image cannot be transformed into a bitmapped image.
5. The "dropper" helps you pick a color in Paint Shop Pro.
6. CTRL-z deletes a circle in Paint Shop Pro.

Projects

1. Make a background for your computer desktop. It should be the same size as the size of your desktop. To figure out the screen size, right click on a free area of the desktop, select Properties and then click on the tab Settings. Hunt for the screen area on this panel.

Solutions

1. True
2. False
3. True
4. False
5. True
6. False

CHAPTER 9

Colors

INTRODUCTION

In this chapter, we learn about colors of graphics. Again, we first present a set of experiments that you can perform on Paint Shop Pro (or any other bitmap editor) to gain some insight into various color models like the RGB (red, green, and blue) and HSL (hue, saturation, and lightness) models.

Open a new image in Paint Shop Pro, which is 200 × 200 pixels, resolution 72 pixels/inch, background color white, and has 13.7 million colors. Let us look at the choice of color in detail. Click on the icon shown in Figure 1 on the color palette. Can you find it? Click all over the color palette until you do. Now you should find the control panel for choosing color. In the Current Color, choose the value R = 255, G = 0, and B = 0. What color do you get in the current color? Similarly choose G = 255 and make the others 0. Experiment with the following RGB values and write down the corresponding colors and HSB values in Table 1.

Now perform your own experiments and answer the following questions concerning HSB (hue, saturation, brightness) values. You may need to look at Table 3 for some answers or perform some new experiments.

COLORS OF LIGHTS—THE RGB COLOR MODEL

By now you should have gained some insight into thinking about colors in RGB and HSL. In the rest of this chapter, we explain various color models in some detail. Newton discovered that if a thin pencil of sunlight passes through a prism, the light spreads into an array of colors called a spectrum. Newton deduced that white light is a mixture of colored lights and these colored lights can be put back together to make white light again.

However, a strange thing is true for colors. For example, we know how to get an orange light by simply taking the orange part of the spectrum. But is there any other mix of wavelengths that also produces orange light? The answer is yes. Indeed, if we shine a light of red color over a green light, it produces a light that is yellow. If we change the proportions

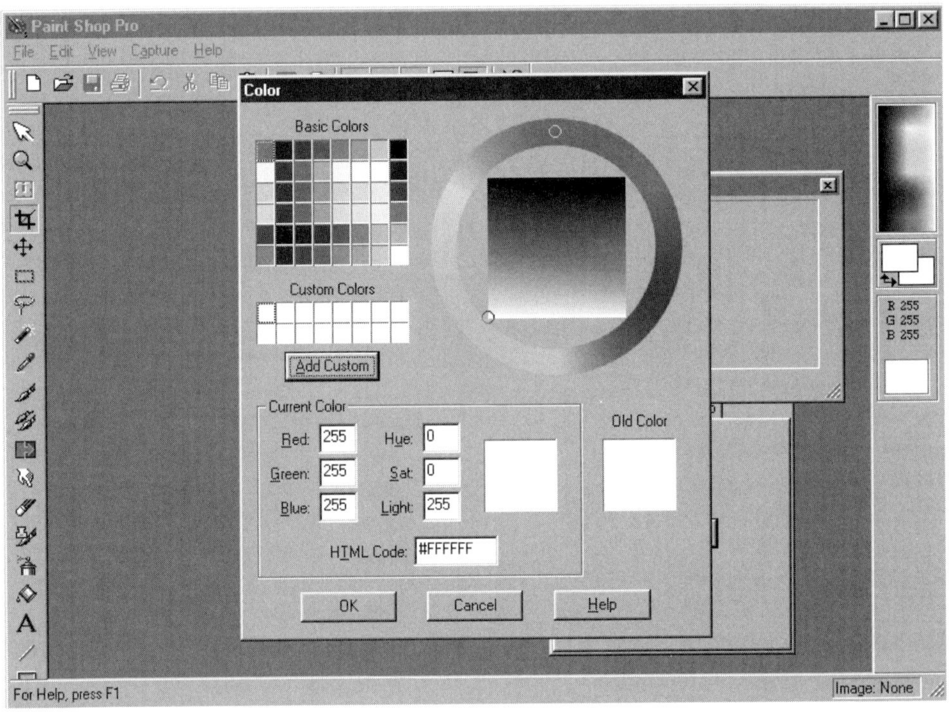

FIGURE 1
The Color Palette and choosing colors.

Table 1 Experimenting with RGB Values

No.	RGB value			Observed color	HSB values	Remarks and other observations
1	R = 255	G = 0	B = 0			
2	R = 0	G = 255	B = 0			
3	R = 0	G = 0	B = 255			
4	R = 255	G = 255	B = 0			
5	R = 255	G = 0	B = 255			
6	R = 0	G = 255	B = 255			
7	R = 0	G = 0	B = 0			
8	R = 20	G = 20	B = 20			
9	R = 50	G = 50	B = 50			
10	R = 100	G = 100	B = 100			
11	R = 150	G = 150	B = 150			
12	R = 200	G = 200	B = 200			

of the red and green colors, we can get through various shades of orange. In fact, the strangest thing about light is that if we mix various intensities of just three lights, we can get all the colors of the spectrum! The only stipulation is that we should also be allowed to *subtract* colors (by means of filters). Moreover, if we choose the three colors red, green, and blue, we will get quite a large spectrum by just adding colors.

So far we have just considered the colors of light. What about the color of paints? The colors in paints are also subtractive in nature. That is to say, when light falls on a colored opaque object, part of it is reflected and part of it is absorbed. When the reflected light reaches our eyes, it produces the sensation of color due to the remaining wavelengths. For example, when light strikes the surface of blue paint, the paint absorbs most of the light of long wavelengths (red, orange, and yellow) and reflects the remainder that appears blue to our eyes. Now if we mix yellow paint in blue, the yellow pigment absorbs most of the light of short wavelengths (blues and violet). Thus when these two paints are mixed together, we obtain (after reflection) only light of the medium wavelengths that appears green to us.

Finally, what about the colors in a transparent object. Here the colors are based on the wavelengths that the object allows to pass through and reflect.

COLORS IN PRINTING

In our considerations of color, we have seen that colors are lights of different wavelengths. We also know how to generate them by adding appropriate intensities of the three *primary* colored lights—Red, Green, and Blue. If we mix all these three lights in equal intensities, we will get white. In the case of paints, the primary colors are red, yellow, and blue, and we can get all colors by mixing appropriate quantities of these three colors.

The printing industry does not use any of these color schemes for printing. The printing industry tried to find a middle ground between the computer screen and the usual paints. They use Cyan (blue-green), Magenta (purplish-red), and yellow. Further they also use a special black (denoted by K) called *carbon black,* because of the special role black has to play in the printing industry. What is remarkable is that on a computer screen, Cyan is obtained by mixing Blue and Green lights, Magenta is obtained by mixing Red and Blue light, and Yellow is obtained by mixing Red and Green lights. Further, these three colors are very close to the three primary colors of paint, since Cyan corresponds to Blue, and Magenta is close to Red. Thus the printer can mix these colors just like paint and get all the colors that can be created by the computer.

Printers have an interesting way of printing color. As the paper passes in front of the roller in the printing press, it collects a certain amount of colored ink (say, Cyan) on the paper. From the next roller it collects a certain amount of Magenta, and then Yellow and Black. The measure of C, M, Y, or K needed to obtain a particular color is measured as a percentage of the total amount of ink that can be put on the paper as it passes the roller. For example, suppose the image has a green circle. Then it will pick up 100% yellow, and 100% cyan.

THE CLASSIFICATION OF COLOR—HUE

In this section, we will describe a classification of colors, called the color circle. This classification of colors rests upon three attributes of colors, called *Hue*, *Brightness* (or *Lightness*), and *Saturation*. We will describe what each of these terms mean, and list the units used to measure them. But before reading the description, perform the experiments in Table 2.

We have seen that when sunlight passes through a spectrum it spreads into lights of different colors. Each part of the spectrum may be named a *hue*, such as red, orange, yellow, blue, green and violet. Not all hues are observed in the spectrum of the sun. For example, the purples are formed when lights of short and long wavelengths are mixed together. Moreover, some hues may not have been given a special name such as red.

Table 2 Hue, Saturation, and Brightness (or Lightness)

No	Question	Procedure and answer
13	What are the Hue values corresponding to Red, Yellow, Blue, Green, Violet?	
14	What happens when Lightness becomes 255? When it becomes 0?	
15	What happens when S = 0? When S = 255?	
16	For a gray color, what are the values of H, S, and L? How do you get a deeper gray?	
17	What happens when you keep H and L fixed and change S from 0 to 255? (Say, H = 0, L = 130, change S and see what happens.)	
18	What happens when S and L are fixed, and H changes?	

In order to classify all the colors that we perceive we will do a thought experiment. We follow the ideas of Deane Judd (see *College Physics* by Weber, Manning, White, Weygand, and Tata, McGraw Hill, Fifth Edition, 1977) in our exposition below. First imagine there is a box full of colored papers containing a paper for every color. We first sort our papers into two piles: those that have hue (the *chromatic* colors) and the grays (the *achromatic* colors). Then we place the chromatic colors in a circle by hue as red, yellow, and so on. Next, we place the intermediate papers in between the colors. For example, orange will come between red and yellow. We will find that we can arrange them in a continuous circle. (Actually, we will find later that we need only about 20 million papers, but they are so many, that they will appear to be continuous, if the paper size is small enough!) As expected, the colors in the circle will be organized much like the colors on the spectrum of sunlight. Except, of course, that purple (which is a combination of lights of short and long wavelength) will take its place between violet and red.

Some numerical values for popular hues are noted in Table 3. The hue is measured as the angle of the circle where that particular color lies. This numerical value helps graphic artists in choosing a particular hue. Note that many packages also measure hue as percentages, and some (like Paint Shop Pro) measure hues from 0–255. Table 3 indicates some colors and their hue values in various units.

BRIGHTNESS OR LIGHTNESS

We now place the grays in a straight line, from white through the grays, all the way to black. Note that white paper will reflect all the incident light on it, and black none. A gray

Table 3 Colors and Their Hue Values

Color	Hue (degrees)	Hue (0–255 as in PSP)
Red	0/360	0
Orange	30	21
Yellow	60	43
Green	90	64
Blue	230	164
Violet	290	206

paper simply reflects less light than a white, but the proportion of wavelengths is the same as in the incident sunlight. In other words, by placing the grays in the manner described, we have classified the nonchromatic colors based on the intensity of the reflected light. Now, suppose we pick all the samples of a particular hue, say red. We will find that some of the samples are lighter than the others. We match the papers of a particular hue with the grays, and classify the color by "lightness." This lightness of a color is usually measured in percentages. 100% lightness would mean that the paper reflects 100% of the incident light, and is matched with white, 0% indicates that the color absorbs all the incoming light (thus matched with black). The grays come in the middle.

When we are talking about a light source—a computer monitor, for instance—the term brightness is often used in place of lightness. The words *value* and *luminosity* are also used in talking about lightness and brightness.

SATURATION

Finally, we introduce the term saturation, which means concentration. Saturation is a measure of the difference from a gray of the same lightness. We use such adjectives as vivid or strong to describe high saturation. For the grays, saturation is zero. In a mixture of grays and a chromatic color, saturation is increased by increasing the concentration of color.

Another term used as a measure of saturation is chroma. Usually, chroma is measured as a percentage of gray in a color. Zero percent chroma will be gray and 100% will be fully saturated.

Another example of saturation in the case of paints is as follows. Suppose you mix red paint in two glasses of water. In one glass put a half spoonful of paint, and in another glass put two spoonfuls. The red in the glass with two spoonfuls of paint will appear deeper, or more saturated.

EXERCISES

State whether the following statements are True or False:

1. If you mix Red, Green, and Blue lights in equal intensities, you will get white light.
2. Magenta is blue-green in color.
3. Match the following:

a. Hue	(i) Amount of color
b. Saturation	(ii) Intensity
c. Brightness	(iii) Name of color

4. Match the following:

a. Artist	(i) Cyan, Magenta, Yellow, Black
b. Computer Monitor	(ii) Red, Yellow, Blue
c. Printer	(iii) Red, Green, and Blue

Projects

1. Find five images in .bmp format on your computer. Try the various options in the "Image" and "Color" menus and try to come up with modifications to the original

images that you like. Save the images with another name to keep them for use another time. Keep track of what modifications you made.

2. Using Paint Shop Pro, make diagrams in Figures 1 and of Chapter 3 in color.

Solutions

1. True
2. False
3. (a)-(iii) (b)-(i) (c)-(ii)
4. (a)-(ii) (b)-(iii) (c)-(i)

An Interlude: The Properties of Light

INTRODUCTION

In his book *Surely You're Joking Mr. Feynman!*, the famous physicist and Nobel laureate Richard Feynman wrote about the time he was in a restaurant and was talking to a painter about how a painter learns a lot by being in the business. In his book, Feynman describes what happens later as follows:

> The guy seems to know what he was doing, and I was sitting there, hanging on his words, when he said, "And you also have to know about colors—how to get different colors when you mix the paint. For example, what colors would *you* mix to get yellow?"
>
> I didn't know about how to get yellow by mixing paints. If it's *light*, you mix green and red, but I knew he was talking *paints*. So I said, "I don't know how to get yellow without using yellow."
>
> "Well," he said, "if you mix red and white, you'll get yellow."
>
> "Are you sure you don't mean *pink*?"
>
> "No," he said, "you'll get yellow"—and I believed that he got yellow, because he was a professional painter, and I always admired guys like that. But I wondered how he did it.
>
> I got an idea. "It must be some kind of *chemical* change. Were you using some special kind of pigments that make a chemical change?"
>
> "No," he said, "any old pigments will work. You go down to the five-and-ten and get some paint—just a regular can of red paint and a regular can of white paint—and I'll mix 'em, and I'll show how you get yellow."
>
> At this juncture, I was thinking, "Something is crazy..."

The upshot of this argument was that Feynman went to the store and bought the paints. Of course, the painter could not mix red and white paints to get yellow, and Feynman won the argument. The restaurant owner, who witnessed the entire argument, summed it up by saying: "That guy (the painter) has his nerve, arguing with a guy who has studied light all his life."

In the case of multimedia too, we will find that if we understand the properties of light and colors, and the properties of our vision, we will be able to understand various features of digital graphics too.

A BRIEF HISTORY OF THE STUDY OF LIGHT

Plato, the Greek philosopher, knew in the fourth century B.C. that light bounces from certain surfaces. This property is called *reflection*. In the second century B.C., the Greeks studied *refraction*, the property that light bends when passing from one medium to another. The rectilinear nature of light—light rays appear to travel in straight lines in a medium—was also known to the early Greeks. In the seventeenth century, two theories came up to explain the various properties of light.

One theory was circulated by the famous scientists Newton and Laplace. This theory held that light was propagated by particles of matter emanating from luminous objects such as a candle flame, or reflecting from nonluminous surfaces, much like balls bouncing off walls. Another explanation for these properties came from considering light to be a special form of wave. The wave theory was given by the English physicist Robert Hooke and published in 1690 by Huygens. None of these theories is considered to be the final word in our understanding of light. The wave theory does not explain the rectilinear motion of light very well. In the case of the particle (or corpuscular) theory, Newton predicted that the speed of light in water would be more than in air. This last prediction was finally disproved in 1850, when Foucault provided convincing proof that the speed of light is in fact *less* in water than in air. This was exactly what was predicted by Huygens.

The modern theory of light, stemming from Planck's word on Black Body Radiation finally combined some aspects of both these theories of light. We have to understand light as having a dual nature, as both a particle and a wave. To take this dual nature into account, the term *photon* was invented. A photon is one "particle" of light (and in general of *electromagnetic radiation*). It is also a wave. While we will not use this term often, many authors talk about the "photons of light" having various properties, so it is an important term to remember.

For us it is not important to delve deeply into the nature of light. Nevertheless, we should know about some of the properties of light so that we are able to understand what happens when we see colors, how our eyes see, and the principles of digital graphics.

PROPERTIES OF LIGHT

Perhaps the most fundamental property of light is that it appears to travel in straight lines in a medium. In addition, we have seen that the speed of light in media such as water and glass is observed to be less than in air. When light meets surfaces, part of it is reflected, part is absorbed, and part is refracted (if the material of the surface is not opaque).

When light hits a shiny surface like a mirror, it bounces off uniformly. In mathematical terms, we say that the angle of incidence is equal to the angle of reflection.

Refraction is the property of light to bend as it goes from one medium to another. The direction of the bend is determined by the speed of light in the two media. An interesting principle that explains the direction of this bend is called Fermat's (pronounced *Fur-Ma*) principle or the principle of least time. Fermat's principle may be stated as follows: out of all possible paths that it might take to get from one point to another, light takes the path that requires the shortest time.

For example, to explain the process of refraction, consider that you are a lifeguard on a beach and have to save a person from drowning. You know that you can run faster than you can swim. So how will you make sure that you reach the person drowning in the shortest possible time? Do you go in a straight line? A little thinking should convince you that you should go along a slightly longer path, where you run a little more, and try to swim a little less.

This is essentially the same problem that light faces in going from a point A in the air, to a point B in a glass. The speed of light in glass is observed to be less than in air. According to Fermat's principle, it will tend to travel a little less in glass than in air, so it bends a little (Figure 1).

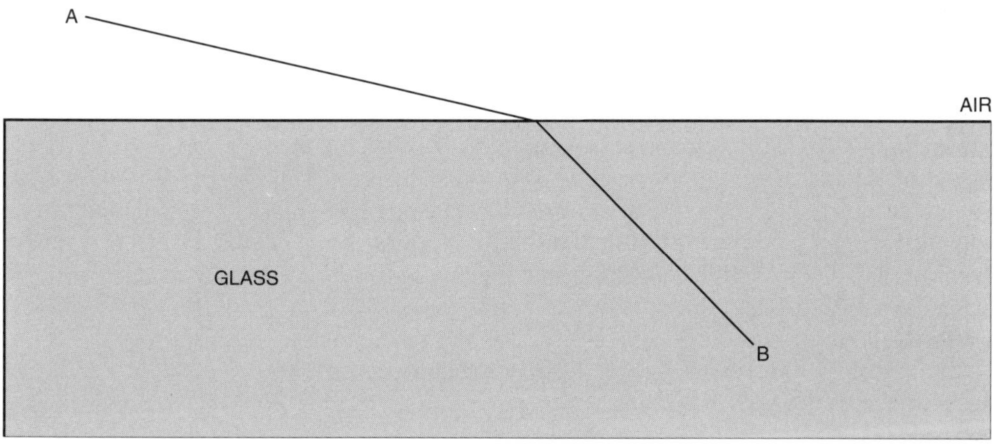

FIGURE 1
Refraction.

Our statement of Fermat's principle is a simplified version of the principle of least time, but it helps in understanding some of the properties of light. A more detailed exposition is given in *The Feynman Lectures in Physics, Vol. 1,* by Feynman, Leighton, and Sands. We have mentioned that light also has wave character, just like sound. Thus, there are various parameters associated with it, such as wavelength, amplitude, frequency, speed, and so on. In fact, just as not all frequencies of sound are audible to us, there are only certain frequencies in radiation that are visible to us.

COLORS

Newton also discovered that if a thin pencil of sunlight passes through a prism, the light spreads into an array of colors called a spectrum. This is represented in Figure 2. Newton deduced that white light is a mixture of colored lights and these colored lights can be put back together to make white light again. The separation of colors is called *dispersion.* This happens because the light is a mixture of waves of different wavelengths. The speed of different wavelengths of light in a glass is related to the speed of the light of that wavelength.

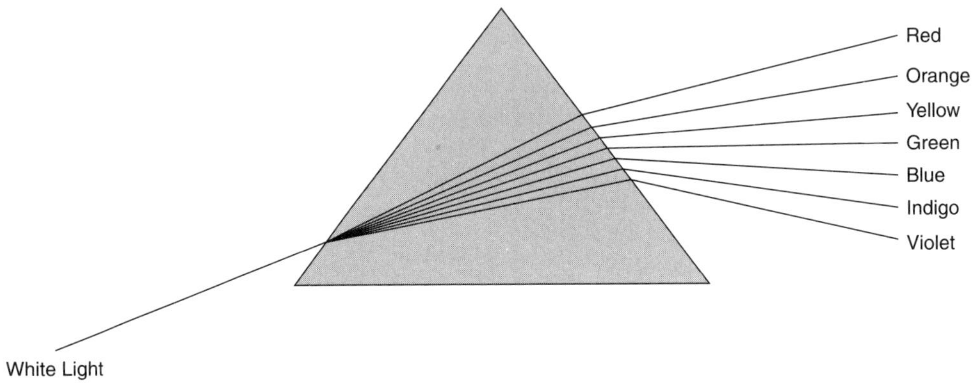

FIGURE 2
Dispersion of light.

The shorter the wavelength, the slower the speed, and the more that wavelength will have a tendency to bend. In addition, the prism is made in such a manner that it increases the spread of various wavelengths as light comes out of the prism. Thus, since colors are spread out in passing through a prism, we can conclude that colors have something to do with the wavelength of the light wave. Indeed, the shorter wavelengths are associated with the violet and blue end of the spectrum, and the longer wavelengths are associated with the red end of the spectrum. Sunlight also contains some ultraviolet and infrared rays that are not visible to us.

To summarize, we have seen that light of different colors corresponds to the different wavelengths of the light wave.

INTENSITY

The analog of "loudness" of a sound wave in the case of light is called the intensity of light. We know that sunlight is a mixture of lights of various colors. When we speak of intensity of a particular colored light, we think of the amount of a particular wavelength, or how big the incoming wave is. Mathematically speaking, intensity is proportional to the square of the amplitude. Intensity gives a sensation of brightness. Just like the sounds of loud music played on our car stereo can drown out the sounds of the noise of traffic, the intensity of particular colors coming from a light source can drown out the other colors in the light.

Intensity has much to do with our perception of colors. Sunlight is an equal mixture of all the wavelengths and appears white to us. If we go into a dark room lit with a candle, we can see only shades of gray, and black and white. As the light in a room increases, we can see the colors. In the case of colored objects that we see around us in a reasonably lit room, we often notice that an object is looking brighter than the others. This is because of the intensity of the reflected light.

Polished surfaces will tend to reflect more of the light in a particular direction, than a rough object. To understand why this happens, consider again our example of bouncing balls. If we throw a bunch of tennis balls on a rough patch of ground, they will undoubtedly scatter in all directions. Light also will scatter when it reflects off a rough surface, and the surface will appear dull.

The intensity of light falls with the distance of the light source. The decrease is fairly dramatic: If we double the distance between a source and us, the intensity is reduced by four times. If the distance between the source and destination is tripled, the intensity is reduced *nine* times. The same is true of objects that reflect light. Thus the brightness of an object fades as we move away from it. This principle is known as the "inverse square law."

EXERCISES

State whether the following statements are True or False:

1. When light passes from one medium to another, the angle of incidence is equal to the angle of refraction.
2. A photon may be considered both a "particle" and a "wave."
3. Wavelength is defined to be the color of the incident light.
4. Sunlight contains ultraviolet rays that are not visible to us.
5. If the distance between the source and destination of light is quadrupled, the intensity is reduced eight times.

Projects

1. Make a multimedia presentation using MS-PowerPoint, explaining how Fermat's principle shows the process of refraction. Add text, graphics, and audio appropriately.
2. Make a multimedia presentation using MS-PowerPoint on the theme of the history of the study of light. Download pictures of the various scientists involved by searching the Web. Add some interesting vignettes about the life of the scientists involved.

Solutions

1. False
2. True
3. False
4. True
5. False

CHAPTER 10

File Formats and Web Graphics

INTRODUCTION

In this chapter, we will learn about the size of graphics. The size can mean two things. One is the actual physical size of the graphic on the monitor or on the printout. The size of a digital graphic also refers to the size of the file on the computer. The file size of the bitmap is determined by the physical size (height and width in pixels), and the amount of color information stored in each pixel. In addition, we can compress the image and store it in another file format. The quality and size of the picture is dependent on the amount of compression we use. When graphics are used on the Web, we try to use compression to reduce the file size without compromising too much on the quality of the graphics.

GRAPHICS FILE FORMATS

Start Paint Shop Pro and create a new image with a width of 640 pixels and height of 480 pixels. Keep the resolution at 72 pixels/inch, and make sure it has 16.7 million colors. Spend about 5 minutes on this picture and make whatever you feel like making, using various paintbrushes, colors, and any other tricks you may have learned. In the colors menu, there is function: Count colors used. Use that to see how many colors there are in this file. Keep adding more things until the number of colors becomes close to 60,000 or more. These are the actual colors used in this image. Now perform the following experiment, and keep recording the data asked for Table 1. Save this file (call it experiment.psp) in a directory created by you, which can be deleted when you finish the experiment.

In all these experiments you will have to select Save Copy as in the File menu of Paint Shop Pro. Make sure you choose "save copy as" and not "save as" in the next experiment. If the particular format has any options, look at the options given as default, and change them to some other value. Record the options used in the Observations/comments column in Table 1.

Table 1 Various File Formats and Sizes

No.	Save copy as in the following format	File extension	File size (in KB)	Observations/comments
1	Compuserve Graphics interchange format	.gif		
2	Encapsulated Postscript			
3	JPEG–GIF compliant			
4	Paint Shop Pro Image			
5	Photoshop			
6	Portable Network Graphic			
7	Tagged Image File format			
8	Windows meta file			
9	Windows or OS2 Bitmap			

These are some of the popular formats supported by Paint Shop Pro. Note in some of them, the file size is remarkably small. In particular, the .gif and .jpg files are quite small. Also note that when you saved as a .gif, the picture must have been "reduced to 256 colors." The last set of experiments is about this concept—the concept of color depth (Table 2)

In each of the following you will start with the image you made earlier (if you have closed it, you can open it again from the .psp file you saved earlier). In each of the later observations you have to decrease the color depth. This is an option that comes under the colors menu. After you reduce the color depth, observe any change in the picture, save a copy as a .bmp (call them 28, 29, and so on) and observe the file sizes again. The first row is for the original picture.

> **Quiz**
> Can you figure out how to calculate (approximately) the file size given the bit depth and the height and width of the image? For a hint see the bottom right corner of the status bar whenever you reduce the color depth of the picture.

The next set of experiments is on the topic of Web graphics. The idea in the case of Web graphics is that the smaller the file size, the faster is the download from the Web. As a general rule, you can assume that a standard 28.8 Kbps (kilobits per second) modem, with a good connection to the Internet, allows data transfer at the rate of about 2 KB per second.

Table 2 Color Depth, Bit Depth, and the Size of Graphic Files

No.	Number of colors	Bit depth	File size (in KB) of saved .bmp file	Quality of picture and other observations or options chosen, while reducing color depth
10	16 million	24		
11	64 K			
12	32 K			
13	256			
14	16			
15	2			

This figure is based on average download speed calculated by many Web designers, and is just a rough guideline to be used while making Web pages.

The two most popular formats for Web graphics are .jpg and .gif. Both give good compression of pictures but one may be better to use than the other to reduce file sizes. The following experiments can help you judge this issue.

Finally, the file size may be really small, but what if it does not convey its message? The trick is to reduce file size but still ensure that the quality is acceptable.

In the following experiments, find the files mentioned (by following the Graphics/Exercises link on this book's Web site), estimate download time according to the calculations above (2 KB/second in a 28.8 Kbps connection). Record your observations in Table 3.

Now after doing these experiments, what do you conclude? Is file size dependent on the number of elements in the image? For photographs, is it better to use GIFs or JPEGs? For cartoon characters, is GIF or JPEG better? We answer these questions in this chapter.

Bit Depth and File Sizes

Consider first a bit-mapped graphic. The entire image is broken up into a grid of pixels, and each pixel stores some color information. Since information on computers is stored in the form of bits, the color information of each pixel is stored in a specified number of bits. For example, if we allow only one bit per pixel, we can represent only two colors using this bit. In particular, we can represent black by 1 and white by 0, and get a graphic that is black and white. The term *bit-depth* is used for the number of bits used to represent the color information in each pixel. To take another example, when the bit-depth of an image is 24 bits, we can use 8 bits for the intensity of each of the three Red, Green, and Blue colors. Thus 2^8 or 256 possible values of R, G, and B are possible for each pixel. And the number of colors that can be used in the graphic is $256 \times 256 \times 256$ (approx. 16.7 million colors).

In the case of .gif files, the color information is stored in a table. GIF files support 8-bit representation, so there are 256 possible colors. Each of these 8 bits are mapped onto a color table used in displaying the graphic. So each string of eight 1s and 0s corresponds to a particular color, and there is an index present that indicates the mapping. This is why you will encounter the term *indexed colors* when dealing with GIFs. Table 4 indicates the maximum number of colors possible for a given image type and bit-depth.

Table 3 Graphics for the Web

No.	File name	Size of file (in bytes)	Estimated download time in a 28.8 Kbps connection	Remarks and observations on quality and content of images
16	Example1.gif			
17	Example2.gif			
18	Example3.gif			
19	Example4.gif			
20	Example5.gif			
21	Example6.gif			
22	Example7.gif			
23	Example8.gif			
24	Example9.gif			
25	Example10.gif			

Table 4 Maximum Number of Colors Possible for Image Type and Bit Depth

Image type	Color depth	# Colors possible
24 bit (True Color)	24 bits/pixel	16.7 million colors
16 bit (Hi Color)	8 bits/pixel	65 thousand colors
Indexed 256 Color	8 bits/pixel	256 colors
Indexed 16 Color	4 bits/pixel	16 colors
Gray Scale	8 bits/pixel	256 shades of gray
Scale	4 bits/pixel	16 shades of gray
Monochrome	1 bit/pixel	Black or white

For a .bmp file (the bit-map format for windows), we can easily calculate the size of the file if we know its bit depth and dimensions (in pixels). Suppose the graphic is *x* pixels wide, and *y* pixels high. Then,

A = The number of bits in the graphic = [(x • y pixels) × (bit-depth)]
B = Number of bytes = A/8 and
C = Number of kilobytes (KB) = B/1024

For example, the file size of a 640 by 480 picture of 256 colors is calculated as follows:

A = (640 × 480)•8 = 2,457,600 bits
B = 2,457,800/8 = 307,200
C = 300 KB

Some more examples of sizes of graphics files are as follows:

- 640 × 480 — 8 bit/256 color image — 300 KB
- 640 × 480 — 24 bit/16 million color image — 900 KB
- 1024 × 1024 — 1 bit/black and white image — 128 KB
- 1024 × 1024 — 8 bit/256 color image — 1024 KB
- 1024 × 1024 — 24 bit/16 million color image — 3072 KB

To appreciate the difference between image files and text files, note that a 250-page novel saved as a text file is only about 300 KB!

Compression—JPEG and GIF

Just as in the case of audio files, using appropriate compression technologies is important in the context of digital graphics. This is especially true for graphics used on the Internet, since download time goes up drastically with increasing file size. Again, it is important that while the image is compressed, the quality of the image does not suffer.

While many compression algorithms are available, we will only discuss two common compression methods that are widely used on the Internet—namely, JPEG and GIF. While JPEG compression works well with 24-bit images, GIF is a format that only supports 8 bits of color information. Thus for images that contain many colors (such as photographs), JPEG is desirable, and for cartoons containing at most 256 colors, GIF is useful.

Both JPEG and GIF support an interesting feature that is especially useful when they are used in Web pages. For example, GIFs can be saved so that they appear "interlaced." Essentially the image is shown in stages in interlaced GIFs. First every 8th row is shown, then every 4th row, and so on. In effect, the viewer sees a low-resolution image quickly, which slowly comes into focus. Similarly, we can use the "consecutive" GIF format that shows the image from top to bottom as it downloads. Thus the user does not have to wait for the entire image to load, before seeing something on a Web page. Progressive JPEGs also appear from top to bottom.

Next, we note some of the strengths and weaknesses of the two formats.

Strengths of JPEG Compression

- It provides support for full 24-bit color images. In contrast, GIF only supports 8-bit images.
- The compressed image size and image quality trade-off can be user determined.
- It is ideally suited to images of real-world scenes or complex computer-generated images.
- It is platform independent for displaying 24-bit images.
- It is quite good for compressing photographs.

Weaknesses of JPEG Compression

- JPEG compression is a trade-off between degree of compression, resultant image quality, and time required for compression/decompression. Blockiness results in high-image compression ratios.
- Bad quality is obtained when compressing an image with sharp edges or lines (as in text).
- It is not suitable for 2-bit black and white images.
- The degree of compression is greater for full color images than it is for gray scale images.
- It is not intended for moving images/video.

Strengths of GIF Compression

- It is lossless for 8-bit images.
- It is ideally suited to images such as line drawings, those containing a limited number of colors, and for images containing text.
- It is preferred for Vector Graphics over the Internet.
- Animated GIFs are easy to make by using GIF constructing packages such as Animation Shop (this comes packaged with Paint Shop Pro).

Weaknesses of GIF Compression

- GIF is not suitable for 24-bit images. When compressing such images, much of the color information is lost due to the reduction of color depth. Good algorithms can still optimize this process so that the resultant image still has reasonable quality.
- The compression ratios are low.

Web Palettes

Making graphics that look great on your own computer is one side of the coin. When you are making graphics to be displayed on other systems, you have to consider what they will look like at the viewer's end. If you are making graphics for a stand-alone system, you have to worry about what kind of computer and display standards your client's computer supports. For example, you may decide to make a small graphic (300×200 pixels) that is displayed on a screen which has size 1024×768 pixels. This graphic will appear very small. Similarly, when you have an image with millions of colors to be displayed in just 256 colors, the quality will be quite bad. When you are making a graphic for the Web, the problem gets even worse, since the number of potential viewers increases tremendously.

Both Windows and Macintosh platforms support a set of 256 colors (called the default palette) that do a good job of representing 24-bit images, even if the system is set to 256 colors. Thus, when we use the .jpg file format, the millions of colors in a 24-bit image are approximated by combinations of colors from these palettes. Usually when we use the JPEG compression, the quality of the resulting image is much the same on all platforms.

When Web browsers such as Netscape and Microsoft Explorer detect an 8-bit display system, they will change the image (by a process called *dithering*) as necessary into their own 8-bit palettes, which are different from the host palettes. The Windows and Mac browser palettes are slightly different—they share only 216 out of 256 colors. This means that if, for example, you use the Mac system palette for an image, any of the 40 nonshared colors you use will be dithered when the image is viewed on an 8-bit Windows browser. The difference is not monumental, especially when viewing photograph-like images, but it is something to be aware of when working with flat-color areas and elements. For instance, areas that have solid color such as backgrounds, type, and line art such as cartoons—dithering can be very unattractive.

The 216 colors shared between the two palettes will not dither from platform to platform. Therefore, you could use these colors for all the flat-color areas of your Web graphics. These colors are obtained by taking R, G, and B values to be 0, 51, 102, 153, 204, or 255. Since there are six possible values for each of Red, Green, and Blue, the total number of colors is $6 \times 6 \times 6 = 216$ as expected. Thus, if you are using colors on your Web page (whether in the HTML file, or in graphics saved as GIFs) it is a good idea to use only these colors.

Reducing the Size of Graphic Files

As we have seen, the size of graphic files is dependent on three things:

- The dimensions of the graphic
- The bit depth of the graphic or the number of colors used in the graphic
- The compression used

You have already conducted a few experiments in reducing the color depth (the number of colors in a graphic). If you play around with various options of Paint Shop Pro, you can find many other ideas that are used to reduce the size of the file. For example, you can check the number of colors you actually use in the graphic. If that happens to be 16 or less, you may as well reduce the bit depth to 4 and compress it into a .gif. Note that if you have 17 colors, you still need an 8-bit image. A 17-color image file is substantially bigger than a 16-color file!

You can reduce the dimensions of the graphic by resampling or resizing the image. Many times, there is little or no loss of clarity in the graphic in reducing the actual dimensions of the image. Often the number of objects in the image also have something to do with the compression. You may be able to break down a large image into small pieces and get a better compression on each. At the client end, your Web page can put those pictures back together. Web designers usually break up an image bigger than 30 KB into smaller parts, because errors in downloading happen less frequently when a smaller size of data is being downloaded.

Finally, we should mention that solid experimentation can lead to substantial savings in file sizes, when it comes to graphics. Further, many free or shareware utilities are available that use very good algorithms to save files for the Web. They sometimes do a much better job at reducing the file size while maintaining quality of the image.

Tips for Handling Text in Images

Text is often a part of graphics. In working with text or geometrical figures in Paint Shop Pro, you must have noticed the concept of "anti-aliasing." This paints a few pixels near the line with a color that is interpolated between the color of the line and that of the background. So some shades of gray are added around the black pixels, if a black line is drawn on a white background (see Figure 1).

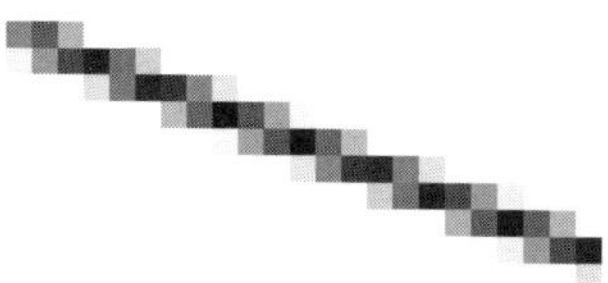

FIGURE 1
Anti-aliasing.

Some text-tips that are useful to keep in mind are

- When working with text smaller than 14 points, turn off anti-aliasing for text. Using anti-aliasing with text of such small size will result in a "fuzzy" appearance on the text edges.
- When working with text greater than 20 points, turn on anti-aliasing in the text rollup. Generally, text greater than 20 points will look jagged without anti-aliasing.
- The quality of text between 14 and 20 points will vary, depending on the resolution setting of your monitor. Lower monitor resolutions will result in jagged text at smaller font sizes.
- When the image is 256-colors, you will not be able to toggle the anti-aliasing check box. Convert the image to RGB Color (24-bit) to get the option to anti-alias the text.
- Due to the nature of its compression, JPEG is not always a suitable file format to use for images that contain text; if the results are unsatisfactory with JPEG, use GIF instead.

Some File Formats on the Web

You are already familiar with some file formats such as those that appear in Table 1. Most of these are raster files (bit-mapped image files), except for Windows meta-file format, which is used by MS-Word when it incorporates pictures in text documents.

While the file formats in use currently on the Web are .jpg and .gif, newer formats keep coming up, which are currently under development or are developed but haven't yet gained popularity. The most likely contender to join .gif/.jpg files on the Internet is *portable network graphic* (.png) which improves upon some of .gif's features. Currently, Web-browsers require plug-ins for .png. Some of the other formats to watch out for are PNP, Wavelet, Art, FIF, Bravo, and Flashpix.

EXERCISES

1. Which format would you use for graphics in the following applications:
   a. Multimedia kiosk
   b. Corporate Web site
2. Which format allows higher compression—JPEG or GIF?
3. State whether the following statements are true or false:
   a. 1-bit color is capable of displaying 2 colors.
   b. The higher the bit depth, the larger the size of the picture.
   c. An animated GIF contains multiple frames.
   d. If you reduce an image from 24 to 8 bit prior to JPEG compression, the compression ratio will worsen as will the overall quality.
   e. 24-bit color is also called hi-color.
   f. There are 216 colors that are common between the standard Windows and Macintosh palettes.
   g. It is better to anti-alias text used in a graphic if the font size of the text is less that 14 points.
   h. GIF stands for "graphics indexed file."

Projects

1. Make a graphic that can serve as an advertisement to sell your school bag (even if it is old and tattered!), some old sweatshirts, and your last pair of shoes. You should spend some time thinking about your potential audience, how you can attract them, what should be the "copy" in the advertisement. The advertisement would be for the print media, so it should be static.
2. Make a banner (in GIF format) to advertise your school Web site (assuming it has one). Look at banners that keep popping up when you browse the Internet, and decide on what the file size should be, and also the dimensions of the banner.

Solutions

1. a. JPEG, BMP—depending on the software compatibility.
   b. GIF for text and drawings, JPEG for photographs.
2. JPEG

4 a. True
   b. True
   c. True
   d. True
   e. False
   f. True
   g. False
   h. False

CHAPTER 11

Layers and Filters

INTRODUCTION

The objective of this chapter is to learn about using layers in Paint Shop Pro, and also to use various options for deforming the images that exist in Paint Shop Pro. You will also experiment and use various filters in Paint Shop Pro. In practice, these options often allow programmers with some "graphics sense" to be able to create interesting images without knowing anything about drawing. Very often, multimedia programmers have to be able to modify images previously made, and knowledge about filters, layers, and deformations comes in handy.

SCREEN GRABS AND LAYERS

One of the common tasks of multimedia and Web designers is to take screen grabs. Paint Shop Pro is very useful for that purpose. To take a screen grab using Paint Shop Pro, the steps are:

1. Start Paint Shop Pro.
2. Select Setup from the Capture menu.
3. Select Window in the Capture dialog, and note the hot key used for capture. By default it is F11.
4. Click on "Capture now." Paint Shop Pro minimizes on its own, and you can press the hot key to capture the screen as an image. Now you can edit the image in Paint Shop Pro.

Capture the entire screen using this method. Now do the activities listed in Table 1 to continue your experiments with Paint Shop Pro.

As you can see, layers are a very useful idea. Every new thing that you do can be done in layers. So if you do not like a part of the graphic, you can just delete the layer and make

Table 1 Screen Grabs, Layers, and Buttons

No.	Activities and questions	Procedure, observations, and answers
1	Take a Screen Grab of the main screen of your computer.	
2	Select the area around the My Computer icon. Press CTRL-C, so that area is copied. Go to the Edit menu, select Paste and click on "Paste as a new layer." What happens? Do you see any changes on the Layer Palette?	
3	The Layer Palette should show two buttons labeled "background" and "Layer 1." Move your cursor so that it lies over each of these buttons. What do you see? (Wait until an image pops up.)	
4	Right click over the button that says Layer 1. Go to view and select, "Current only." Move your mouse over the Layer Palette until you find a context help that says "Layer Visibility Toggle." Click on this toggle. What do you think a layer is?	
5	Double click on the Layer 1 button. Make Opacity = 50, and change name of Layer to "My Computer Icon." Press OK. What happens when Opacity is reduced?	
6	Click on the background button on the Layer Palette to make it active. Select the Network Neighborhood icon. Copy it and paste it as another layer. Rename the layer as Network Neighborhood Icon, and place it somewhere other than you placed the earlier icon. Make the Background invisible using the layer visibility toggle. Now right click on the My Computer Icon layer button and the other layers, go to "Merge" and Click on "Merge Visible." What happens?	
7	Select another icon from the Background, and now Paste it as a new image. Use the "resize" option in the Image menu to make it 200% of its original size. Now Go to Image → Effects → Buttonize. Experiment with various options and make a button out of this icon. Where do you think this kind of feature will be most useful?	

it again! It is a great way to undo anything you do. You can copy layers by dragging the button in the Layer Palette onto the new layer icon. You can delete a layer in the same manner, by dragging it to the Delete Layer Icon. (Try it!)

TRANSFORMATIONS

You can copy a layer and use some transformations and filters. By making some layers opaque, and some a little transparent, you can make a collage of existing pictures. In the next activity, work with all the options and try to generate a picture on your own. You can make many images in the same file, with an image in each layer. Give names to layers so that the names reflect what you did at each step. When the image represented by a few of the layers becomes final, you can merge them by making only these layers visible, and then merging the visible layers. It is a good idea to keep text in separate layers so you can edit it and keep the same backgrounds. For example, when you make buttons for a Web page, keep the background in a separate layer, duplicate the layer, and add the text of the buttons. Later you can change the text and make more buttons.

Working efficiently with layers requires lots of practice. In the next activity, try to understand how to do so, while experimenting with various deformations and filters available in Paint Shop Pro. You are free to make whatever image you wish, but keep different layers for each thing you try out, and in Table 2 note every change that you made, as well as what the effect was. Finally, cut and paste pieces of each layer and make a collage on another layer. Write your name in the corner and ask your friends to view and comment on your work. Spend at least 15 minutes on this activity. Attach a paper if the table is too small to describe what you have done. Make sure you use as many options from the Images and Colors menu as you can. And make sure you write down what you did.

For example, you can begin by opening an image. Use Flood Fill to fill in an image. Now copy to another layer and begin deforming it in various ways. Record your observations in Table 2.

By now you should have learned enough about how to use Paint Shop Pro to be a good

Table 2 Layers, Deformations, and Filters

No.	Layer name	What you did (used which deformation, filter, paintbrush, fill effect, and so on), what it accomplishes, description, and comments.

graphic designer capable of designing complicated two-dimensional graphics for multimedia systems and Web pages.

Projects

1. Design a counting book for children, teaching them 1, 2, 3, up to 10. Each layer should be a page, which has various shapes. Use options in paintbrushes or picture tubes, or make your own geometrical figures. Write numbers in a large enough font. A sample is given on this book's Web page.
2. Copy one of the layers in the counting book you nede and paste the entire graphic into Animation Shop as a new animation. Animation Shop is a software that is currently packaged with Paint Shop Pro. Note down things about animation that you did not understand. Perhaps the chapters on Animation and Video may provide some of the answers.

An Interlude: Vision

THE EYE

Introduction

We have seen some physical properties of light. In particular, the spreading of light by a prism indicates that the colors of light are determined by the wavelength of the light wave. However, the sensation of color only partly depends upon the physical properties of light. It also depends upon the eye and what happens behind the eye when the brain interprets the signals the eye sends it.

In this chapter we will look at the structure of the eye to understand how we perceive colors. We will also look at the properties of vision that we should keep in mind as we think about the design of our multimedia systems.

The Structure of the Eye

The eye is covered by a tough fibrous coat called the *schlera*, a portion of which is transparent (see Figure 1). The schlera is the white portion of the eye. In the middle, there is a transparent membrane called the *cornea*. The eye contains a *lens*, a variable diaphragm called the *iris*, and a sensitive screen called the *retina*. The iris is opaque and has a central opening called the *pupil*, which expands or contracts to control the amount of light entering the eye. Light enters through the cornea. It is bent by the lens and forms an inverted image on the retina. Different parts of the retina receive light from different parts of the visual field. The retina has different kinds of *photoreceptors* that undergo some changes when light falls on them. The retina receives the incoming light signal, processes it, and sends it off to the brain (via the *optic nerve*). The brain is largely responsible for collating the images from the two eyes and interpreting the signal as the three-dimensional view that we see.

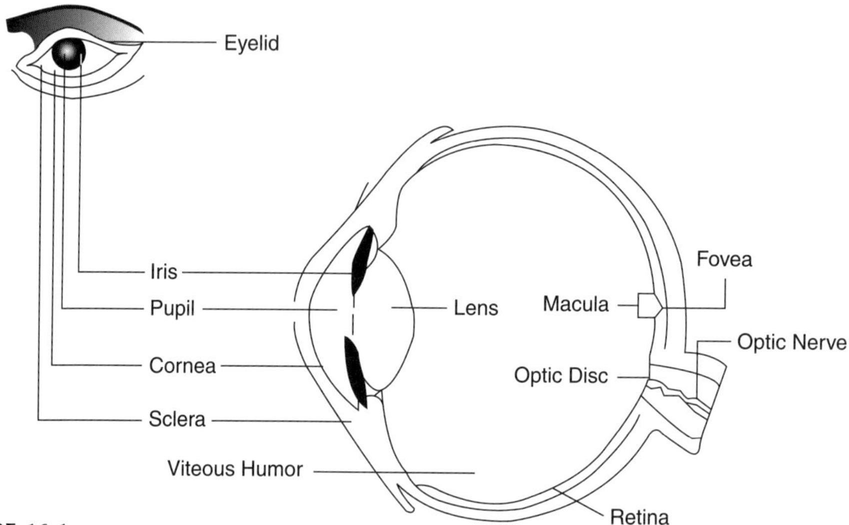

FIGURE 16.1
The structure of the eye.

VISION

Photoreceptors—Rods and Cones

There are two types of photoreceptors called rods and cones. The distribution of rods and cones is not uniform in the retina. There is a spot, called the fovea, or the macula, which we use for the greatest acuity of vision. This spot is somewhere in the middle of our visual field, and the image is formed near the fovea when we are trying to look at something very carefully. The sides of the eye are not very good for seeing detail, but are quite good at detecting motion and for seeing in the dark. There is also a blind spot in the eye at the place where the optic nerve meets the eye. There are no rods and cones at the blind spot.

Locating Your Blind Spot

An interesting thing the brain does is that it often "fills in" for the blind spot of our eye. The spot where the optic nerve meets the eye is known as the blind spot for the eye. No message is sent to the brain for any light falling on the blind spot.

To locate the blind spot in your right eye, close your left eye and look at the plus sign in Figure 2. Bring your face close to the picture and move it slowly backwards, all the while looking at the plus sign. When you are about 6 inches away from the picture, the circle will disappear!

FIGURE 2
Locating your blind spot.

Remember that you have to keep looking at the plus sign. If you come closer or move farther away, you will see the round spot again. What happens when the spot disappears is that the light coming from the black spot falls right at the blind spot of the eye. As you can see, it is a pretty big spot! Now locate the blind spot again a few times and observe what you see in place of the spot. What you see is just continuous white space. So the brain received no signals from the blind spot, but shows you something anyway. Now you know that the brain can perceive something even if the eye sends no signals to it!

Rods are used to see at night or under very low illumination. They are very sensitive but color blind. The photoreceptors responsible for color vision are the cones. There are three types of cones in the retina:

- L-receptors—Most sensitive to light of long wavelength (red light).
- M-receptors—Most sensitive to light of middle wavelengths (green light).
- S-receptors—Most sensitive to light of short wavelengths (blue light).

Thus, we see that when it comes to color, our eyes also follow the RGB system!

Color vision depends on the intensity of light, or rather the illumination of the objects. When the illumination is very low, our cones are not activated. However, the rods are activated even when there is very little illumination. Thus in a room with very dim lighting, we just see objects as black and white. If we increase the illumination slowly, we will notice that at some illumination we begin seeing colors in objects. As we have mentioned earlier, the distribution of rods and cones in the eye is not uniform. Indeed, the concentration of cones is greater in the center of the retina, and the rods are more numerous than the cones on the sides. Thus, we are better at perceiving colors in the middle of our visual field. To see if this is true, look at a particular fixed direction, and ask a friend to hold some colored cards and walk from the periphery of your visual field to the center. Try to decide what colors the cards are before your friend is right in front of you. You will find that you can determine that there are cards in your friend's hand long before you can see their colors.

On the other hand, in a dark room, if we want to see an object, we would do better to look at it from the side of our eyes. This is because the rods are used for vision in the dark and are concentrated more on the side of the retina. The sides of our eyes are quite good at perceiving movement also.

Tip

People with normal color vision have all three receptors. However, we should keep in mind that about 8% of the male population is *color blind*, or have *color variant vision*. People with color-variant vision are missing one or more of these three receptors. Due to genetic reasons, most color variant people are male.

Thus, use colors judiciously while designing your multimedia systems. For example, it is not a good idea to place crucial information (such as warning messages) in red or green!

The Color Resolution of the Human Eye

An important consideration in working with digital data is the importance of knowing the limits of human perception. For example, in the case of sound, when storing sampled sound, we do not need to store the parts of the sound file with frequency beyond 20 kHz. This is because human beings cannot perceive frequencies beyond this number. Indeed, the MPEG Layer 3 compression standard achieves such a large amount of compression by taking into account (to a large extent) the limitations of human hearing. Similarly, in the case of graphics, understanding how many hues human beings can perceive has an important bearing on digital graphics.

The human eye can make subtle distinctions in hue within the entire spectrum of colors. To measure the color resolution of the human eye—or the power of human beings to distinguish different colors—scientists perform the following experiment. Scientists project lights of different wavelengths onto the two halves of a screen. When the difference in wavelengths is very small—for example, 5 angstroms—no difference in colors is perceived. As the difference between wavelengths is slowly increased, a point is reached when we can see different colors. It turns out that the resolution between different colors depends on where we are in the spectrum. For example, in the blue-green and yellow it is as low as 10 angstroms, but in the deep red and violet it may be 100 angstroms or more. (An *angstrom* is a unit of length. About 10 billion angstroms make up 1 meter!) The wavelengths of visible light range from about 7600–4000 angstroms. Since the visible spectrum is about 3600 angstroms long, the eye can distinguish at most 360 different spectral band. The calculation becomes more difficult if we also consider the fact that many hues are formed only by mixing lights of different wavelengths. The calculation becomes still more difficult when we factor in the possibilities of obtaining different hues by adding quantities of white light to a given mixture of light. Research in this area still does not give a definitive answer to this question, but it is estimated that the eye can distinguish between 20 million colors. At any rate, the capacity of the human eye to distinguish colors is finite, though a huge number.

The Resolution of the Human Eye

Visual acuity is a term that is used to describe the resolution of the eye. If a paper has two dots, and that paper is taken farther away from us, at some point we will be unable to distinguish between them. Thus, to measure the resolution of an eye, we need a measure that takes into account the distance between the dots, as well as the distance between our eyes and the dots. If the eye sees two objects, it will see them at a certain angle. If this angle gets too small, the eye cannot distinguish them from each other. The smallest angle which still allows the eye to see that there are two objects is called the *resolution angle*. When an optician checks the vision of a person, he shows him a chart that is attached to a wall at a specific distance. The letters are arranged so that in each successive line, they subtend smaller and smaller angles at the eye. The visual acuity is defined as the inverse of the resolution angle (under certain specified conditions of lighting), measured in minutes of arc. (A minute of arc is 1/60 of a degree.) The "typical" or normal resolution angle is 1/60 of a degree.

CONCLUSION

Application of Vision Research to Design

We have already seen some properties of the eyes such as the fine resolution and the millions of hues that our eyes can distinguish between. Before we end this session, we will review some of the properties and see where these may be applied in the design and construction of multimedia systems.

We have learned that human beings are quite good at perceiving colors in the middle of our visual field. Thus if our multimedia presentation is projected on a big screen, we should make sure that a colorful graphic is kept in the middle of the screen. On the other hand, since we are quite good at seeing movement through the corner of our eyes, we can use a small animation in the corner to attract the attention of our user. At the same time, this very strength of our visual system means that too many animations will irritate our user! Remember also that using some colors to communicate an important idea is not good, since one in 10 persous has color-variant vision.

The fact that human beings can distinguish between so many different hues causes many problems for the graphic artist. We will see later that digital images using a large number of colors (so they appear more realistic) can take up huge amounts of disk space, or may take a long time to load if used on the Web. Clearly, there has to be a trade-off between size and quality.

The resolution of the eye also has important connotations for graphics. This is true of analog systems as well. For example, when newspapers are printed, the printer must make sure the individual dots that make up a letter are close enough for our eyes to see only the breaks that should be seen. Similarly, if we enlarge a picture to a big poster size, our eyes will be able to see the individual dots comprising the picture. In other words, the picture will appear grainy. However, since the angle is what determines our visual acuity, we can get a sharp picture by putting it far away.

Finally, we should say that there are many areas where our physical and our biological circumstances play a role in what we see. For example, when we see a building through a fire, the heat makes the building seem hazy. Similarly, if we are driving over a long stretch of a straight road on a very hot day, we will see what seems like water ahead of us.

There is another important reason for us to keep track of the research being done on vision. Answers to questions such as how many and which colors a human being sees sets biological goals for technology. At the same time, generating more colors than our eyes can see is not of much human use. So, biological research even sets some limits to technology.

EXERCISES

State whether the following statements are True or False:

1. If we say somebody has blue eyes, the color of the iris must be blue.
2. If you suddenly move out of darkness into a brightly lit area, the pupil in your eye will expand.
3. An inverted, three-dimensional image is formed at the back of the retina.
4. Photoreceptors are types of rods and cones.
5. The rods are responsible for night vision and cones for seeing colors.
6. There are three types of cones: each sensitive to Red, Green, and Blue kinds of light.
7. We cannot see colored objects in the dark, since the cones are not activated in the dark.
8. A human being can distinguish between 20 million hues.
9. A normal human being (with 6/6 vision) has visual acuity 1.
10. Since human beings are quite good at noticing animations, we should try to put many animations on each screen of our Web page.
11. Since the color "red" denotes danger, the most important warnings in our multimedia system should be colored red.
12. An enlarged picture may appear grainy because you can see the individual dots comprising the picture. If we see a picture with half-closed eyes, it will appear sharp. (Try it!)

Projects

1. Use Paint Shop Pro and draw a diagram of the eye. Make sure the labels are printable. Use this graphic and make a simple Web page (in .html format) which explains the structure of the eye.

2. Research and write a short essay (with pictures) on "Optical Illusions." Be sure to search for the artist "Escher" who has made many interesting lithographs that seem contradictory when viewed carefully.

Solutions

1. True
2. False
3. True
4. False
5. True
6. True
7. False
8. True
9. True
10. True
11. False
12. True

CHAPTER 12

Process of Animation

PERSISTENCE OF VISION

In 1877, Eadweard Muybridge was said to have made a bet that a horse's legs leave the ground at full gallop. When Muybridge set up his twelve cameras, he equipped each one with a thin, harmless tripwire to trigger each camera. After developing these photographs, Muybridge lined them up sequentially and noticed the first illusion of still pictures: Motion.

This illusion can be attributed to persistence of vision. The term *persistence of vision* describes the way an image "burns" itself onto our retina so that it remains with us for a small fraction of time after the source of the image has been removed (also called persistence of motion). This phenomenon is the basis of the cinema film, enabling the succession of projected images to be assimilated without interruption, thereby producing an illusion of continuous and natural movement.

MAKING MOVIES

The eye can detect extremely small amounts of luminous energy. A dark-adapted eye can detect light equivalent to that received from a single candle at a distance of approximately 30 km, in which case the retina receives only a few quanta of light.

The visual system lags a bit in its response to a stimulus, and the sensation lasts an even greater fraction of a second after the stimulus ceases. This retention of the mental image, referred to as the persistence of vision, prevents the appearance of any "flicker" when a motion-picture film is projected on a screen at the rate of at least 16 screen illuminations per second. Commercial motion pictures use 24 frames per second or 72 screen illuminations per second, although the screen is completely dark while the film is in motion. The illusion of movement in a motion picture is becouse of a fortunate propensity of a moving object intermediate between those imaged discretely and successively upon the retina.

Typically at the speed of 15 frames per second, the eye sees smooth motion.

ANIMATION

Animation is the art of creating an illusion of movement from a series of still drawings. The pioneers of animation are Muybridge, Emile Cohl, Earl Hurd, and Walt Disney.

TRADITIONAL METHODS OF ANIMATION

Before the advent of computer animation, all the frames in animation had to be drawn by hand. Considering that each second of animation contains 24 frames (film), one can imagine the tremendous amount of work that had to go into creating even the shortest of animated films! Different techniques were developed for creating animation by hand, These are:

- Key frames
- Cel animation
- Rotascoping

Considering the immense amount of work that has to go into the making of an animation sequence, the drawing or painting is usually done by more than one person. After a storyboard has been laid out, the senior artists go and draw the major frames of the animation, known as *key frames*. These frames are then reviewed and modified. These are the key points of the animation. Later, a bunch of junior artists draw in the frames in between. This way, the workload is distributed and controlled by the key frames. By doing work this way, the time in which animation can be produced is reduced dramatically, depending on the number of people working on the project. Work can be done simultaneously by many people, thus reducing the time needed to get a final product out.

Cel animation is another process of creating animations. In creating animation using this method, each character is drawn on a separate piece of transparent paper. A background is also drawn on a separate piece of opaque paper. When it comes to shooting the animation, the different characters are overlaid on top of the background in each frame. This method also saves time in that the artists do not have to draw entire frames, but rather just the parts that need to change such as individual characters. Sometimes, even separate parts of a character's body are placed on separate pieces of transparent paper.

In classic animation (what you see in old Disney films) each moving element is drawn on a transparent sheet of celluloid. The cel is placed over the background and is repositioned during the course of an animation sequence to simulate movement.

Rotascoping is the process of copying images from moving video to create animation. For example, assume that you want to animate a pig running. It is a lot easier to draw the motion and shape of the pig in different parts of the animation when you have some reference, such as video, as opposed to imagining it. With the help of rotascoping, one can animate some complex scenes that would be very hard to visualize. One disadvantage of rotascoping is that you have to get the exact video you want to animate. For example, if you want a pig running across the screen, video of a pig running from the top of the screen to the bottom of the screen will not do.

All these animation techniques are great, but when they are most useful is when they are all used together. Cel animation by itself would not help much if it was not for the key frames and the ability to distribute the workload across many people.

PROCESS OF ANIMATION

In general, an animation sequence is designed with the following steps:

1. Story board layout—Give the outline of the action. Define the motion sequence as a set of basic events (it can also contain rough sketches).
2. Object definitions—Define the movement for each object.
3. Key frame specifications—Give the detailed drawing of the scene of animation at a particular time.
4. Generation of in-between frames—Define the number of intermediate frames between key frames.

Animator Pro is used to create 2-D animation, and 3D Studio is used for 3-D animation.

QUALITY VERSUS SIZE OF ANIMATION

As it stands for images, the compromise between size and quality holds for animation also. An animation would run faster if it is smaller in size. The playback speed of the animation also depends on the configuration of the machine. Animation can be in any of the following formats:

- Flic format (FLI/FLC)
- MPEG (.mpg)
- Quicktime (QT/MooV)

The Flic format (FLI/FLC) is the animation format used by 3D Studio and many other DOS-based graphics software packages. FLCs are 256-color animations of any image resolution (Animator Pro) and FLIs are 256-color animations at 320 × 200.

The MPEG (.mpg) format is a special animation format that can be up to 40 times smaller in file size than a Flic. This format is very popular for use on the Internet since it allows for a much faster file transfer because of its reduced file size. Like JPEGs this format is considered very lossy because depending on the type of compression the quality of the image is greatly reduced.

The Quicktime Movie (QT/MooV) format is the standard Macintosh animation format, which allows for many types of compression and resolutions and can contain audio tracks. Quicktime movies vary a great deal in quality and file size depending on the color depth and compression.

FILE FORMATS—A COMPARISON

This example illustrates the image quality and file sizes for a 100-frame animation at a resolution of 240 × 160.

- FLI/FLC—3.8 MB
- MPEG—430 KB
- QuickTime (8 bit, JPEG Compression, Medium Quality)—280 KB

- QuickTime (8 bit, JPEG Compression, High Quality)—1.7 MB
- QuickTime (8 bit, Video Compression, High Quality)—1.8 MB
- QuickTime (16 bit, No Compression, High Quality)—7.68 MB

ADDING AUDIO TO ANIMATION

Packages like Aawin, Animator player, and Adobe premier can be used to attach audio to animation. The steps for adding audio to animation are:

1. Creating the animation.
2. Selecting audiofile (midi, wav, or any other).
3. Editing audiofile (to fit the animation).
4. Linking the audio file to the animation by using either a package (for example Adobe Premier) or a programming language.

LOOPING

Looping is the process of playing the animation continuously. It can be used if the animation requires just a basic few frames to be created. These few frames played in a loop give the appearance of a long animation. This can be used to show, for example, a man walking in 2–3 frames. If these frames are put in a loop, it would appear that the man is walking a long distance.

You can loop animations not just from the beginning, but from any frame you want to. For example, if you want an animation to run once and then repeat itself from the fifth frame, you can set the option in the player and manage this. Again if you wish to show the logo of a company during the entire presentation, a small animation of the logo can be put in a loop.

MORPHING

The term "MORPH" (derived from the greek word "morphe," meaning "shape") has, in recent years, acquired the meaning of "shape-changing." Computer graphics has adopted this term in at least two very distinct forms. The first form, of which most people are aware of, is the two-dimensional (2-D) MORPH. Typically, in 2-D morphs, control points are placed in two images at locations that correlate between the two. A 2-D morph algorithm then calculates intermediate images. Viewed in succession, the first image is smoothly changed into the second.

Morphing, thus, is the transformation of one image to another. It involves taking two elements—the one that needs to be changed and the other to which the original element has to be changed. The idea is to make it appear as if one item is physically changing into the other. The animators select points, which are similar on the two elements. For example, eyes, ears, hair, and other such features work well for faces. When moving from two objects that are very similar, a car to a car, or a person to a person, it is easy to find points that can shift well. But on other objects, you need to stretch a little. Shadows should always be matched.

3-D MORPHING

Morphing comes from the word metamorphosis that means a physical change in form or structure. Animated sequences, which use morphing techniques, are commonplace today in movies—for example, "Terminator 2: Judgement Day," television advertising, and music videos.

Morphing software allows for the generation of in-between images from a given pair of images to serve as the "before" and "after" for the animation sequence. A set of control points correlating features in the two images is chosen for the morphing process and played back at several frames per second. These images depict a smooth transformation from one state to the other. If control points are chosen properly, animation can be quite convincing.

Fundamentally, this type of morphing is a blend of two simple yet interesting computer graphics techniques:

- Warping
- Cross-dissolving

Warping exerts unseen forces at precise points in the image, stretching and shrinking it like a reflection in a fun-house mirror. Algorithmically, warping is accomplished by dividing an image into polygon-shaped pieces like a jigsaw puzzle and distorting the polygons by moving their vertices. Knowing the coordinates, before and after each of the vertices of the polygon, the computer can determine the intermediate shapes of the polygon through simple interpolation.

Cross-dissolving is a technique used for shifting smoothly from one color to another. For a single pixel, cross-dissolving is accomplished by incrementally changing the red, green, and blue values of the pixel. If the colors of the pixels within the polygons are cross-dissolved as the polygons themselves are warped, the result is a morph.

Atomizing describes an effect that shatters a 3-D object into small pieces, usually spheres.

IMAGE MORPHING VS 3-D MORPHING

Image morphing, the construction of an image sequence depicting a gradual transition between two images, has been investigated extensively. For images generated from 3-D models, there is an alternative to morphing the images themselves: 3-D *morphing* generates intermediate 3-D models, the morphs, directly from the given models; the morphs are then rendered to produce an image sequence depicting the transformation. 3-D morphing overcomes the following shortcomings of 2-D morphing as applied to images generated from 3-D models:

- In 3-D morphing, creating the morphs is independent of the viewing and lighting parameters. Hence, we can create a morph sequence once, and then experiment with various camera angles and lighting conditions during rendering. In 2-D morphing, a new morph must be recomputed every time we wish to alter our viewpoint or the illumination of the 3-D model.
- 2-D techniques, lacking information on the spatial configuration of the model, are unable to correctly handle changes in illumination and visibility. Two examples of this type of artifact are

- Shadows and highlights fail to match shape changes occurring in the morph.
- When a feature of the 3-D object is not visible in the original 2-D image, it cannot be made to appear during the morph. For example, when a singer needs to open his mouth during a morph, pulling his lips apart thickens the lips instead of revealing the teeth.

Michael Jackson's video of "Black or White" and movies like Mask and Terminator implemented morphing.

Some of the common processes of morphing are

- Morphing with lines
- Point morphing

In morphing with lines, morphing between two images is done as: Let A and B be two images. Lines are defined on the two images A and B. The mapping between the lines is specified. Depending on the number of intermediate frames required, a set of interpolated lines is obtained. The steps for obtaining intermediate frames are:

1. The lines in the image A are warped to the lines corresponding to the intermediate image.
2. The lines in the image B are warped to the lines corresponding to the intermediate image.
3. The two warped images are now combined proportionately, depending on how close the frame is with respect to the initial and final frames.

POINT MORPHING

Point morphing is based on a forward mapping technique, where each pixel from the input image is mapped to a new position in the output image. Since not every output pixel will be specified, we must use an interpolating function to complete the output image. We specify several *control points*, which will map exactly to a given location in the output image. The neighboring pixels will move somewhat less than the control point, with the amount of movement specified by a weighting function consisting of two separate components, both dependent on the distance from the pixel to each control point in the image.

RENDERING

Rendering is the process a computer uses to create an image from a data file. Most 3-D graphics programs are not capable of drawing the whole scene on the run with all the colors, textures, lights, and shading. Instead, the user handles a mesh that is a rough representation of an object. Satisfied with the mesh, the user then renders the image.

Let us understand this by using the example of projectile motion—if an object is thrown in the air, it will fall in an arc. The position can be calculated for this object at every point. Now, if these calculations are given to a rendering package, it would create the 30 frames, which will result in animation, representing the realistic motion of the object.

THE PROCESS OF RENDERING

Rendering is the process of producing bitmapped images from a view of 3-D models in a 3-D scene. It is, in effect, "taking a picture" of the scene. An animation is a series of such renderings, each with the scene slightly changed.

A camera is placed at a location in a 3-D coordinate space pointing in a given direction. Those polygons that fall within the field of view of the camera are mathematically projected onto a plane, just as a real camera projects an image onto film. The rendering process necessarily involves some means of determining whether another surface closer to the camera obscures a given surface of a model.

Once it is determined what surfaces are visible to the camera, and where they project to on the viewing plane, the color of each pixel must be determined. Depending on the sophistication of the process in a given case, this result is the combination of the surface properties assigned to the object (color, shininess, or any other) and the lighting in the scene.

As an animation requires as many as 30 renderings for every second, the rendering time is an extremely important consideration in all 3-D animation. Rendering time is a function not only of the power of the computer used, but also of the number of polygons in the scene, the complexity of the lighting, and the presence of computationally intensive elements such as transparency and reflective surfaces.

Some common methods of rendering are:

- Wire frame
- Flat shading
- Gourad
- Phong
- Ray tracing
- Radiosity

Wire frame is not really a rendering method by definition. Most 3-D graphics programs represent objects as meshes. What happens in wire frame rendering is that every section of the mesh gets colored in with the average color of the texture. This is useful for special effects and quick previews. To take wire frame rendering one step further, some programs a undertake process called hidden line removal. It is just like normal wire frame rendering, except the parts of the mesh that would not be visible if the mesh were a solid area are not rendered.

Flat shading is the quickest rendering method. Some programs are able to render flat shaded objects in real time. When rendering using flat shading, the computer creates an average color for an object and then renders each face with different amounts of black or white added to simulate shading. Objects look flat and unrealistic. No textures are applied in this mode.

Gourad rendering takes flat rendering one step further. The computer figures out values of a color on vertices of a face and then applies a gradient to the face to simulate shading. This mode is slower than flat shading, but not much, and can also be rendered in real time on some of the more powerful computers.

Phong rendering takes rendering one step further. It actually probes every pixel in the visible area and tries to determine a correct color for it. It takes into account all lights and textures. Phong rendering is often as good as that achieved by low-end programs. The results are pretty good, and the time it takes to render is not extremely long.

Ray tracing is the best rendering method in terms of quality. It also takes a very long time, but the results are good. Everything is rendered, including shadows, lighting, reflections, and transparencies. Unlike other rendering options, it gives light a physical attribute. For example, the rendering of a pencil in a glass of water would give you the same refraction effect that nature does: the pencil will appear broken. When a computer ray traces an image, it simulates a beam of light going out of every pixel on the screen. It reflects and deflects the beam of light in a similar fashion as nature would. Finally, it displays the outcome on the screen.

Radiosity is a new method of rendering. It does something the other rendering methods do not: it figures out the relationship of the objects in a scene. For example, in real life, if you take a bright colored ball and place it in a white room, the walls of the room will reflect a little bit of color from the ball, making them look a little reddish. This is not possible in ray tracing, since it does not bounce rays off matte objects, such as a wall.

Radiosity produces extremely good results, but unfortunately, there is a trade-off—rendering time. Before the computer even starts rendering, it has to solve a certain "radiosity model" which is the relationship of one object to the others in a scene. Then it can start rendering.

TOOLS FOR ANIMATION

Computer animation can be done on a variety of computers. Simple cel animation requires nothing more than a computer system capable of simple graphics with proper animation software. Unfortunately, most of the computer animation you see on television and in other areas is done on extremely sophisticated workstations. In this section, we will discuss the different hardware platforms for computer animation and the software used for it. Because there are so many, only the most popular and most well-known software will be explained.

The various platforms used for animation are:

- SGI
- PCs
- Macintosh
- Amiga

The SGI (produced by Silicon Graphics, Inc.) platform is one of the most widely used hardware platforms in professional or broadcast quality computer animation productions. SGI computers are extremely fast, produce excellent results, and operate using the wide spread UNIX operating system. There are many types of SGI platforms ranging from the general purpose Indy®, to the high power Indigo2 Extreme® used to produce animations, to the mule of the horde, the Onyx®, which is especially suited to do the complex calculations involved in rendering. A number of major production studios use SGI's state-of-the-art software like Wavefront, Alias, and SoftImage on SGI machines.

PCs are very versatile computers. Because of their combination of flexibility and power, PCs have proven to be very useful for small companies and other businesses as platforms for making computer animation. Applications such as 3D Studio and Animator Studio are used on PCs to make animations. PCs are relatively cheap and provide good quality for their price.

Macintoshes were originally designed to be graphic and desktop publishing machines. Macs did not become widely known until recently, when newer faster models came out.

Many people consider Macs slow and inefficient, but that is not necessarily true. Right now with the advent of the Power Macintosh, it has become a useful tool of small-scale companies for making good multimedia applications. Many companies are producing computer graphics and animation software for the Macintosh. Some of these are Adobe with products such as PhotoShop and Premiere and Strata with Strata Studio Pro. There are also a few applications that were ported to the Macintosh from the SGIs such as Elastic Reality and Alias Sketch (a lower-end version of Alias). Lately, a lot of production studios have begun using Macs because of their ability to produce good graphics for small-scale projects.

Originally owned by Commodore, Amiga computers have held a position in the computer animation industry for a number of years. There are two software packages that Amigas are basically known for: Video Toaster and LightWave 3D. The Amiga is based on a Commodore, but it has been greatly customized to be a graphics machine. Many television shows use Amigas for their special effects and animations.

SOFTWARE

There are hundreds of computer animation and graphics software packages out there. Only a few are, however, considered industry favorites. The software mentioned here is only the tip of the iceberg. These are some of the most popular software packages used by companies, schools, and individuals around the globe:

- 3D Studio Max
- 3D Studio
- Light Wave 3D
- Adobe PhotoShop
- Adobe Premier
- Alias Wavefront
- Animator Studio
- Elastic Reality
- SoftImage
- Strata Studio Pro

The successor to 3D Studio 3.0, 3D Studio Max runs on Windows NT. It is entirely object oriented, featuring new improvements such as volumetric lighting, spacewarps, and an all new redesigned interface.

3D Studio is a 3-D computer graphics program that runs on PCs. It is relatively easy to use. Many schools and small production studios use 3D Studio. It is created by Autodesk. 3D Studio consists of a 2-D modeler in which shapes can be drawn, a 3-D Lofter, in which 2-D shapes can be extruded, twisted, or solidified to create 3-D objects. Then there is a 3-D modeler in which a scene is created. Finally, there is an animator in which key frames are assigned to create an animation and a material editor in which a great variety of textures can be created.

LightWave 3D is another high-end PC 3-D computer graphics software package. Originally developed for the Amiga platform, LightWave 3D is now also available on the PC. LightWave 3D is used in quite a few television productions such as Babylon 5 and SeaQuest. Many people argue that LightWave3D is the best 3-D product for the PC.

Alias is one of the topmost computer animation packages. Alias was produced by the company that used to be Alias, but it joined with Wavefront and is now known as Alias Wavefront. It runs on SGIs. Alias is well known for its great modeler which is capable of modeling some of the most complicated objects. Also, this software package is very flexible, allowing for programmers to create software that will run hand in hand with Alias.

Animator Studio is a cel animation program from Autodesk. Its predecessor was Animator Pro for PC DOS. Animator Studio runs on Windows. It has a multitude of features that minimize the animation creation time.

Elastic Reality is one of the top of the line morphing programs. Elastic Reality runs on Macs and SGIs. One of the great features of Elastic Reality as opposed to other programs is that it uses splines as opposed to points to define the morphing area. Elastic Reality allows one to morph video as well as still images.

SoftImage is one of the topmost computer animation software packages. It is used in many top production studios around the country and the world.

Strata Studio Pro is probably the most well-known 3-D graphics application on the Mac. It is created by Strata, Inc. Strata Studio Pro is mainly a still-graphic rendering application, but it does have animation capabilities. Graphics for some games such as Myst were created in Strata Studio Pro.

EXERCISES

1. Name two packages that use the flc format for animation.
2. In which format does 3D Studio Max create animations?
3. What are the key things to remember while morphing two faces?
4. What is the quickest form of rendering?

Projects

1. Design a storyboard for an animation of hatching of an egg.
2. Make a "looping GIF" that serves as an animated banner, to advertise your school Web site. Use Animation Shop (or any other GIF animator) to animate two or three graphics. Try to keep the size of the file to a minimum.

Solutions

1. Animator Pro and 3D Studio.
2. Avi.
3. The two faces should have the same background. Each feature should be mapped properly (eye to the eye, nose to the nose, etc.).
4. Flat shading.

CHAPTER 13

Video

INTRODUCTION

Video is a medium of communication that delivers more information per second than any other element of multimedia we have considered. We are used to seeing analog video on TV and are well aware of its impact on our life. Nowadays, a lot of video we see on TV and in movies has a digital component. For example, many of the special effects that you see in movies are digitally generated using the computer.

The DVD (Digital Video Disk or Dynamic Video Disk) makes it possible to distribute large videos in a compact form, much in the same way as the Compact Disk made the move from analog sound to digital sound easy.

Digital Video has a substantial contribution in not only movie making, but also in the gaming and IT industry. For example, using the techniques of digital video, real-life video is mixed with computer-generated effects for maximum impact.

In this chapter, we will first learn the advantages of using digital video as to analog video. Since video is such a data-intensive medium, Codec (Compression/DECompression) techniques are very important, and it is therefore necessary to gain an overview of these algorithms. Associated with various compression algorithms are the file formats used for digital video. Finally, we look at some issues regarding video on the World Wide Web.

First, let us contrast the two worlds of analog and digital video.

ANALOG AND DIGITAL VIDEO

Currently only analog video is used as a broadcast medium. The video that you see on TV, on Cable TV, or a VCR is broadcast in analog format, even though specific movies that you see may be in digital format prior to broadcasting. There are three standards worldwide for broadcasting analog video. They are NTSC, PAL, and SECAM.

NTSC is a standard devised by the National Television System Committee and is used in the United States and Japan. This standard displays 30 (29.97 to be exact) frames per second. Each frame can contain 16 million different colors. Each full-screen frame is composed of 525 lines.

PAL stands for Phase Alternation by Line and is used in Europe and India. It displays 25 frames per second. Each full-screen frame is composed of 625 lines.

SECAM stands for Sequential Couleur Avec Memoire and is used in France. This standard displays 25 frames per second. Each full-screen frame is composed of 625 lines.

Occasionally, a video expert needs to convert video between formats to make it compatible with the respective video players.

While these systems are currently in wide usage, there is a distinct trend towards digital video, even in the case of consumer electronics. For example, digital TVs are being sold now by many large TV manufacturers. The main advantages of the digital medium are

- Random Access allowed by the digital format enables us to quickly jump to any point in a movie. In analog format, we have to wind the tape backward and forward to reach a point in the movie.
- Digital format also allows us to quickly cut, paste, or edit video in other ways. It also allows easy addition of special effects.
- It is easy to duplicate digital video without loss of quality. In the analog tapes, video producers lose some quality after the first time they edit the video. This loss in quality is known as generation loss. Now video producers can convert real-life video that they have shot into digital format and edit it without losing the original quality of the film.
- Finally, digital video allows for interactivity. Currently this is not widely available, but once we get digital TVs it should be possible for us to have interactive TV.

EDITING VIDEO

As mentioned earlier digital video is easy to edit. Editing videos typically involves: removing frames, inserting frames, mixing audio with video, giving special effects on video, adding transitions between two clips, superimposing clips and adjusting transparency, applying filters to the clips, and adjusting volume of audio. We can also fade-in and fade-out the audio in various frames.

In order to edit videos, it is helpful to understand the concept of timecode. Timecode, a unit of measurement, can be used as an address of a frame, and it can also be used as a unit to measure the duration of a video clip. The timecode used by SMPTE (Society of Motion Picture and Television Engineers) has become a standard and is in the form hrs:mins:secs:frames. For example, a clip with a duration of 00:02:31:15 plays for 2 minutes, 31 seconds, and 15 frames. At the rate of 30 frames per second (fps), 15 frames will take half a second (0.5 seconds) to play. This clip will, therefore, play for 2 minutes and 31.5 seconds. Thus, a fraction of a second is measured in frames, and to know the time with millisecond accuracy, we need to know the fps of the clip.

The same code can be used to address a particular frame. For example, 00:1:30:12 is the address of the 12th frame that comes after 1 minute and 30 seconds of playing a clip.

There are many software packages which support such editing. Some that are well known among these are Adobe™ Premiere, Adobe™ After Effects, Strata™ Avid Video, Asymmetric ™ Digital Video.

DIGITIZING ANALOG VIDEO

The process of digitizing analog video (in PAL, NTSC, or SECAM formats) is called video capture. Video is generally captured using plug-in cards called video capture cards. Nowadays digital cameras are also available that directly store full-motion video in digital formats that can directly be copied onto a computer's hard disk. A video capture card accepts a video input from an input device such as a VCR or a video camera. Note that the audio has to be sampled through a separate cable which attaches to the sound card. The software with the video card synchronizes the two channels of audio and video.

There are some important considerations to keep in mind as you capture video. To understand these, think about what happens as you digitize video in real-time. The video player plays the video at the rate of 30 fps. Each of those frames has to be converted into digital format and stored on the hard disk. The computer is doing several jobs in a very short interval. Thus, it is a good idea to have as much RAM as possible so that the computer is fast enough to do this large amount of processing.

In addition, you should ensure that your video capture card supports capturing at the rate of 30 fps (the maximum rate used in analog formats). Otherwise, some frames will not be captured and you will get sudden breaks in the picture when you play it back. This phenomenon is known as frame dropping, which may also be caused if the RAM is insufficient because of the large amount of processing required. You may also get better quality by compressing the information to be processed by reducing the size of the video window. Playing full motion video on the entire screen requires a lot of memory, and only a small window may be required for your purpose.

The type of input socket used also determines the quality of the grabbed video. The two common types of input sockets available on most video cards are Composite and S-Video connectors.

Composite video is the standard that connects most consumer video equipment such as TV sets, VCRs, laser disc players, and camcorders. Normally, the cable used for this port has a male RCA plug on both ends. The composite format carries a combination of three basic elements of a video picture—color, brightness, and synchronization data. These three are transmitted together in a single, composite channel.

S-Video (Y/C or component video) is carried on cables that end with 4-pin DIN connectors. A video signal transmitted using S-Video format is separated into color and brightness and transmitted over two separate channels. This makes for better looking and less granular pictures on the receiving end.

Normally, for a higher quality of video, S-Video is used rather than Composite video. However, S-Video sockets are only available on high-end video equipment, such as Betacam, Umatic, and Camcorders/Video Cameras.

After deciding on the video input equipment, connect the two using either of the above-mentioned connectors (S-Video or Composite), and also connect the audio out from the video equipment, with the audio in socket of the sound card. Now with the software that comes along with the digitizing card, we can begin the video capture process.

COMPRESSION

Compression is the process of removing or restructuring data to reduce the file size. Since digital video files are extremely large, these not only take a large amount of disk space, but also require high data transfer rates (from hard disk to screen) for playback. It is, therefore, recommended that during video capture, some lossless compression technique be used. As a compressed video file is played, it is decompressed.

Compression and decompression is even more important if the movie is to play off of a CD-ROM drive, since the reading of data is comparatively slower from a CD than from the hard drive.

Several compression/decompression (codec) algorithms are available for Compressing digital videos. Codecs can be software-based, hardware-based, or both. Hardware-based compression is significantly faster than software compression, because the hardware is dedicated to compression. The codec you choose affects the visual quality of the movie as well as the speed with which it plays on the monitor.

An important feature of codecs is whether they are Asymmetric or Symmetric. A Symmetric codec takes approximately the same time to compress as it takes to decompress data. On the other hand, an Asymmetric codec usually takes longer to encode video than it does to decode. An Asymmetric codec generally delivers significantly better playback performance than a symmetric codec.

WINDOWS-BASED COMPRESSORS

The following software compressors come packaged with MS-Video for Windows (VfW):

- Microsoft Video 1 codec—This compressor is best used in converting analog video into digital format. This is a lossy compressor and supports color depth of 8 bits (256 colors) or 16 bits (65,536 colors).
- Microsoft RLE codec—This compressor is used often for compressing animation and computer-generated images. It supports only 256 colors.
- Cinepak codec—This compressor is used for compressing 24 bits (or 16 million colors) for playback from the CD-ROM disk. This codec attains higher compression ratio, better image quality, and faster playback speeds than Microsoft Video 1 codecs. For best results, this codec is used on data that has not been previously compressed with a highly lossy compressor. A feature of Cinepak is that decompression is much faster than compression since it is asymmetric.
- Intel Indeo Video R3.2 codec—This compressor is very similar to Cinepak, and is used for digitizing video using Intel's video digitizing card.
- Intel Indeo Video Raw codec—This is used for capturing uncompressed video. That is to say it results in lossless compression.

It is also possible not to use any compression if enough disk space is available and the data transfer rate allows it.

THIRD-PARTY COMPRESSORS

For many applications, it may be desirable to use specialized codecs, which are mostly hardware based. Some of these are:

- MJPEG—Motion JPEG (MJPEG), a digital video compressor, is an extension of the JPEG standard. It is used for compressing digital videos.
- MPEG-1—MPEG-1 is a standardset by the Motion Picture Experts Group and is primarily used for CD-ROM video playback. It uses an extension of the lossy compression

techniques involved in JPEG by predicting interframe motion. For compact storage and distribution, MPEG-1 attains a compression ratio as high as 200:1 and creates small consumer quality data files. MPEG-1 can be transmitted through narrow bandwidth networks as it supports data rates of 0.4–1.5 Mbps at a quarter of TV resolution. In order to achieve fast playback at low cost, the standard is asymmetric, requiring much more computing power to compress than to decompress. It is very useful in consumer applications where low network bandwidth is the predominant factor.

- MPEG-2—MPEG-2 has high resolution for excellent quality and requires data rates of 4–8 Mbps. Since infrastructure costs (storage, network bandwidth) have fallen, these bandwidths are becoming available, encouraging multimedia applications that will make video playback a reality on the corporate desktop.

FACTORS AFFECTING COMPRESSION

There are many factors that affect the performance of the compressor in terms of the amount of space required to store the compressed video, the quality of compression, and the quality of video playback. These factors are:

- Frames per Second (fps)—Naturally, the more frames that are flashed in front of our eyes per second, the better and smoother the motion will appear. However, the fps rate used should be the maximum playback rate of the computer system on which you intend to run the finished movie. The maximum rate of the playback system depends on the speed of its components: the CPU, the hard drive, and the display card. If the fps rate is higher than the maximum rate of the playback systems, it will result in jerky motion at the time of playback since the system will not display certain frames. This is known as frame dropping.
- Key Frames—A key frame is a baseline frame against which the following frames are compared for differences. The intervening frames are called delta frames. The compressor saves the entire key frame but only the differences between the delta and the key frames. Greater compression and playback speeds can be achieved using key frames. Most compressors provide a key frame option which allows us to specify the rate at which the video is sampled for key frames. For example, if the playback rate is 30 fps, and the key frame is set to 10, then it implies that the compressor will select one frame for every 10 frames as a key frame. If we do not provide any value for the key frame option, the compressor treats every frame as the key frame. In general, the more frequently the key frame is displayed, the better is the quality of the video. However, more key frames will result in a bigger file size. Normally, the key frame value is the same as the fps value, or it is a multiple of it.
- Data Rate—This option is available only for certain compressors, such as Cinepak and Indio, for CD-ROM playback. In the single-speed CD-ROM drive the data rate limit should range from 90–100 KB per second. For a double speed CD-ROM drive, it should start from 150–200 KB per second. On triple speed, a rate as high as 300 KB per second works, and for quad speed 550–600 KB per second may be given.

To summarize, some of the factors that affect compression are the choice of fps, the number of key frames used, and the data rate specified for playback.

The foregoing guidelines are good theoretically, but an accomplished expert in digital video often experiments to figure out what compressor should be used for a particular movie, and also experiments with the various codecs used by the compressor.

For example, if the subject of a movie is that of a person sitting at a table, as in a news broadcast where the motion is largely limited to some head and facial movements, then a higher key frame number (key frames shown at longer intervals) may be desirable. We may also increase the amount of compression by decreasing the quality of the compression of the delta frames, if that is allowed by the compressor.

FILE FORMATS FOR VIDEO

After a digital video is edited, it is time to save it in a particular file format. For the PC, the AVI format is used, and for the Macintosh, the Quicktime format is used. We may also choose to use the file format associated with various codecs used, as described in the previous section. There are also specialized file formats associated with the MPEG compressions, but we will not consider them here. More information about the AVI and Quicktime formats follow.

AVI

The AVI format was developed by Microsoft to play videos in the Windows environment. The greatest advantage of this standard is the support provided by Microsoft.

AVI supports color resolutions from 256 colors to millions of colors. It can support sound from 5 kHz Mono to CD quality stereo sound. It can deliver video at rates as low as 0.03 MB/sec and as high as 0.3 MB/sec. An editing suite or conversion programs available on the Internet can be used to convert between .AVI and other video and graphics formats. Table 1 summarizes the requirements for the AVI file format.

QUICKTIME

Quicktime was developed and supported by Apple Computers and was one of the first digital video formats for the Macintosh computers. This was the first format available for PCs and the Macintosh. It is similar to the AVI format. Both use similar strategies for compression and decompression of video information. However, Quicktime is not limited to just the Macintosh platform and can be viewed on almost every platform available

Table 1 Essential Requirements for the AVI Format

Extensions	avi
Platform(s)	Windows 3.x – Windows 98/NT
Hardware requirements (MS/Intel)	386/33 processor at minimum, at least 125 MB hard disk space to store AVI files, at least 4-MB RAM.
Software requirements (MS/Intel)	In MS Windows environment Video for Windows is distributed along with Windows 95 but you need to get other players if you use another environment.

today. Programs are available for converting Quicktime to other standards and vice versa. Table 2 summarizes the requirements for using the Quicktime format.

VIDEO ON THE INTERNET

A live camera Web site broadcasts video captured in real time from a live source. It takes audio/video input from a TV or a video camera and enables it for the Internet by compressing it to a size that can be delivered over the Internet. Many sites offer the Web surfer the facility to tilt and pan the camera. As capture and compression is done simultaneously the color intensity and the number of frames captured per second is reduced to maximize the encoding speed to match the rate of capture. For example, Figure 1 shows the broadcast of a heart surgery live on the Internet.

Live video camera on the Internet is an inexpensive and powerful surveillance tool. This could be installed in hospitals to monitor patients. Imagine being able to view a loved one in a hospital bed by browsing on the Internet, sitting thousands of miles away. Working parents could check on their children left at day care with such a system installed. A security manager at a sensitive establishment could keep an eye on any breach even while being away physically. Do you want to avoid traffic jams? Choose a clear route by going through the traffic police site having such cameras placed at strategic points on all heavy traffic routes. The list of possible applications is endless.

The technology that makes video on the internet possible is the concept of Streaming Video. Another useful concept is Surround Video. We will now discuss streaming video.

STREAMING VIDEO

Streaming video is a term applied to compression and buffering techniques that allow you to transmit real time video via the Internet, enabling a user to watch the video as it downloads. In case the transmission slows for a moment, a reserve of video is available to the client user's computer memory to enable uninterrupted viewing. This is done by giving the file a few seconds to load before starting the image. In case the transmission speed does not improve the buffer gets exhausted and the video appears jerky.

Many products are available to implement streaming video. Some of the popular products are: VDOLive, RealVideo, Web Theater, and Stream Works.

Video quality over the Internet mainly depends upon the following factors: available bandwidth, sound intensity/frequency, and difference in information between two successive video frames. Suppose we have to put a clip of an action movie on the Internet. In encoding

Table 2 Essential Requirements for the Quicktime Format

Extensions	mov,movie,qt
Platform(s)	Any PC or major Workstation platform.
Minimum Hardware Requirements (MS/Intel)	4MB of RAM or greater VGA or SVGA video card and monitor
Software Requirements(MS/Intel)	Windows 3.x, Windows 98, Windows NT Quicktime for Windows

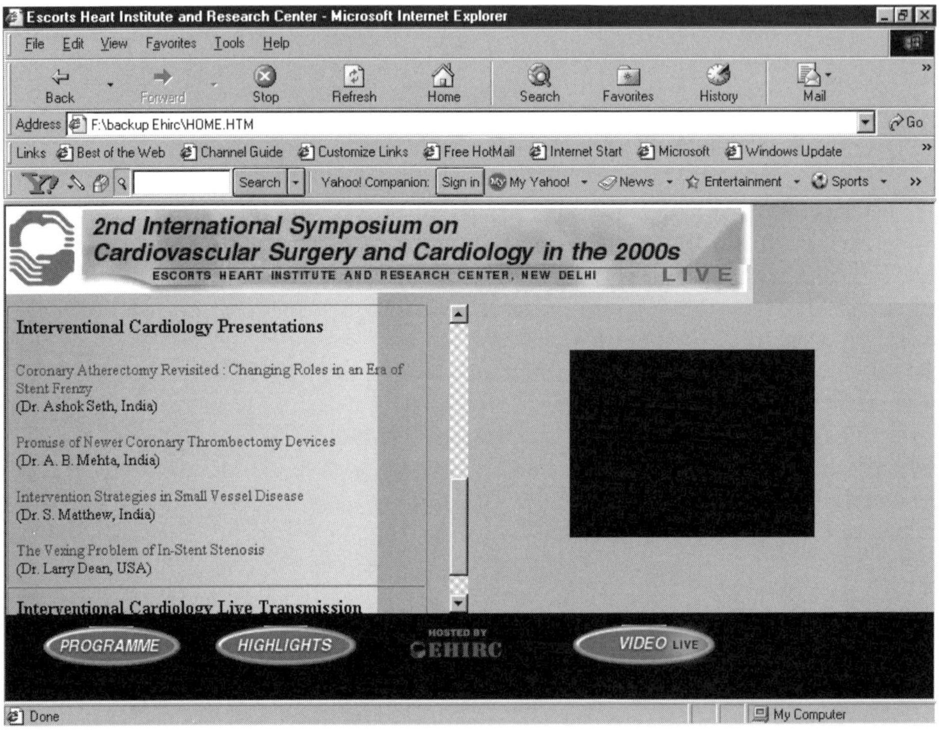

FIGURE 1
Live broadcast of video on the internet.

it, the video bit rate has to be considerably high since there are a lot of changes in the scene. For example, to cater to a 64-Kbps ISDN Internet connection, the suggested audio-video bit-rate could be 8.5 Kbps for audio and 36.5 Kbps for video, with a frame rate of about 10 fps. On the other hand, in the case of a video of someone's speech as the key frame, the delta frame difference is quite low, the bit-rate combination could be 8.5 Kbps for audio with 12.5 Kbps for video. Hence depending upon the available bandwidth and the input video content, a combination of audio and video bit rate has to be applied to get the ideal output.

SURROUND VIDEO

Surround video is a way to allow real time navigation and give photo-realistic visuals in Web pages by adding seamless 360 degree panoramic images. In other words you can turn the image around in your Web page and interact with it from every angle. This can be very handy to display products as the client can zoom in to any point or click on hotspots with image and URL links.

EXERCISES

1. What does Codec stand for?
2. What is the exact fps display of the NTSC Standard?

3. Suppose the SMPTE timecode of a video clip is 00:1:30:12 and has 15 frames per second. What is the total number of frames in this clip?
4. Suppose we are digitizing a video that is 640 × 480 pixels wide, with 24-bit color depth, and 30 fps. How much space will one second of this video take if put uncompressed on the hard disk.
5. State whether the following statements are True or False.
   a. Composite video is better than S-Video in terms of visual quality.
   b. A symmetric codec takes approximately the same time to encode as it does to decode video.
   c. MPEG is the default Windows based codec.
   d. In general, the smaller the value of key frame, the bigger the size of the video.
6. Suppose the fps is 30 and key frame is 5, then how many key frames appear in one second?
7. State whether the following statement is True or False:
   Streaming video allows you to transmit real-time video via the Internet, enabling a user to watch the video as it downloads.

Projects

1. By researching the Internet, write a 1000 word report on this topic: The use of video on Web sites. Include, as case studies, ten sites which use video. Describe in detail the purpose of the site, the formats they use, and the purpose of the clips. Download a few of the videos, and make notes on how easy and fast it is for users to download and view the videos.

Solutions

1. Compression/DECompression
2. 29.97 fps
3. 1362 frames
4. 26.37 MB = 640 × 480 × 3 × 30/(10242) MB
5. a. False
   b. True
   c. False
   d. True
6. Key frames = 30/5
7. True

An Interlude: The Term Dimension

DIMENSION

The term "dimension" is defined as the number of pieces of information required to locate a point in a space. This is rather an abstract definition, which describes many situations, so it would be worthwhile to understand it well. For example, consider a line segment, marked at one end with a symbol "a." For any point on that line, we can describe its location by means of just one number, the distance of that point from "a." Since for all points of the line, one number suffices to locate it, we say that the dimension of the line segment is one.

As another example, we saw that any color can be found by mixing appropriate quantities of three colors, red, green, and blue If we use the new term we have just learned, we would say that colors are three-dimensional, since three numbers are required to locate a color. Indeed, our classification scheme of colors also depends on some values for the three attributes, hue, saturation, and brightness.

The computer monitor or a printed page is two-dimensional. To specify a particular pixel on the screen, we need to specify two coordinates, the horizontal and vertical distance from the top-left corner of the screen. For example, to reach the pixel (3, 5), you start at the top-left corner of the screen, turn your face toward the top-right corner, take three steps to reach (3, 0). Now turn right, and go five pixels down to reach (3, 5). Paintings, photographs, and sketches are also two-dimensional.

The painter perceives the three-dimensional world around us, and represents it in two dimensions on paper, canvas, or the computer screen. On the other hand, a sculptor will construct a three-dimensional structure.

2-D AND 3-D GRAPHICS

Since a computer graphic appears on a two-dimensional monitor screen, it has to be two-dimensional itself. However, the artist represents depth in a two-dimensional image in various ways. For example, look at Figure 1, which demonstrates the notion of perspective.

FIGURE 1
Perspective helps us to see depth. (From PhotoDisk, 1997.)

Perspective is a technique where the same objects shown further away are shown proportionately smaller.

There are other subtle things we can do to show whether one object is farther away from another one.

For example, look at Figure 2 and try to see what makes you think that some of the objects are in front of the others.

Note that:

- The person is obscuring the view of some flowers behind him.
- The objects at the back appear hazy to us.
- The objects in front seem brighter than the others.
- The flowers appearing at the bottom of the picture appear closer than the ones above them.

FIGURE 2
What gives you the perception of depth in this picture? (From PhotoDisk, 1992.)

In summary, perspective, variations in intensity, and the visibility of some objects and obscuring of others, all give us an impression of depth.

There are 3-D packages and programs (such as POV-Ray and VRML) that allow for modeling in three dimensions. There are also virtual reality environments, where a user accomplishes interactive input using a data glove, which is capable of grasping and moving objects displayed in a virtual world. The virtual world is displayed through a head-mounted viewing system, that sends different signals to each eye, and the brain makes a three-dimensional picture of the virtual scene. Three-dimensional packages also allow for projection into a two-dimensional scene. These use the above-mentioned ideas of indicating depth and map the scene onto a two-dimensional image. On the other hand, these could be viewed using the 3-D viewing devices indicated earlier. Such packages involve visualizing several different views of the object being constructed.

EXERCISES

State whether the following statements are True or False:

1. A line is one-dimensional.
2. An array is two-dimensional.
3. A 5×2 matrix is 10-dimensional.
4. The computer screen is two-dimensional.
5. When we see a picture of railway tracks, they seem to meet at the horizon. This is due to perspective.

Solutions

1. True
2. False
3. False
4. True
5. True

CHAPTER 14

3-D Graphics

INTRODUCTION

There are two types of 3-D packages. One is written for use by programmers and the other is for use by graphic artists. POV-Ray (Persistence of Vision Raytracer) is of the first type. It gives us a language to describe 3-D scenes in terms of geometric objects, lighting, textures of objects, colors, etc. Then it uses a technique called ray tracing to render the 3-D scenes into a bitmapped file. It produces quite high-quality photo-realistic images and can even generate 3-D animations.

The second type are packages such as 3D Studio Max that are designed for graphic artists. These allow users to make a "sculpture" digitally and render the scenes using their algorithms. These packages hide the details of how the scene is rendered from the graphic artist, and provide a front end for graphic artists to design their scene. An example is Breeze Designer, which is a front end for POV-Ray.

Some of the fundamentals of POV-Ray can be learned by going through the sample programs and examples provided by various people. A CBT (Computer-Based Training) package is available on the Web site of this book. This CBT, under development by Manish Sinha, is adequate for getting started with POV-Ray. It uses all the sample programs that are available from the POV-Ray Web site and structures them to explain features one at a time. This CBT, and also the images/sample programs, are all freeware and designed to help newcomers get started with POV-Ray. In this chapter, we will give a brief introduction to some of the principles that are required for understanding POV-Ray. We will also mention briefly how to get started with Breeze Designer. How much you learn about making 3-D graphics depends to how much more you can discover on your own, by looking up sources on the Internet and by experimenting with the software on your own.

POV-RAY

The interface of POV-Ray for Windows is very similar to any Windows program.

POV-Ray files have the extension .pov. These are text files that contain a description of the scene, lighting, etc., that all go into generating a particular scene. Figure 1 shows the opening interface of POV-Ray for Windows.

THE POV-RAY COORDINATE SYSTEM

To define the attributes of a scene we use a 3-D coordinate system. We have to specify the exact position of an object in a scene and, therefore, we use 3-D coordinates. The usual coordinate system for POV-Ray has the positive *y* axis pointing up, the positive *x* axis pointing to the right, and the positive *z* axis pointing *into the screen* as in Figure 2.

This kind of coordinate system is called a left-handed coordinate system. If we use our left hand's fingers we can easily see why it is called left-handed. We just point our thumb in the direction of the positive *x* axis, the index finger in the direction of the positive *y* axis, and the middle finger in the positive *z* axis direction. We can only do this with our left hand. If we had used our right hand we would not have been able to point the middle finger in the correct direction.

The left hand can also be used to determine rotation directions. To do this we must perform the famous Computer Graphics Aerobics exercise. We hold up our left hand and point our thumb in the positive direction of the axis of rotation. Our fingers will curl in the positive direction of rotation. Similarly if we point our thumb in the negative direction of the axis our fingers will curl in the negative direction of rotation.

POV-Ray takes the origin <0, 0, 0> of the coordinate system as the center point of the computer screen. The positive *x* coordinate is toward the right of the screen and the negative *x* coordinate is toward the left. The positive *y* coordinate is toward the top of the screen and the negative *y* coordinate is toward the bottom. The positive *z* coordinate will

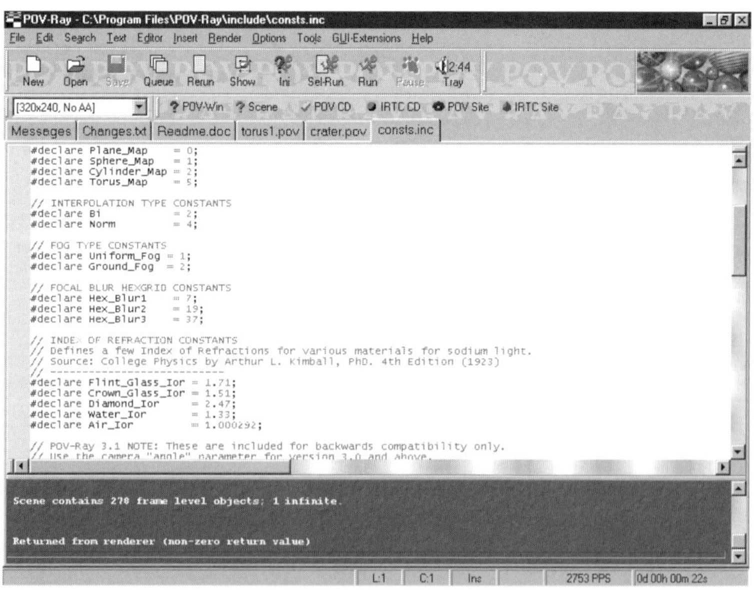

FIGURE 1
The POV-Ray interface.

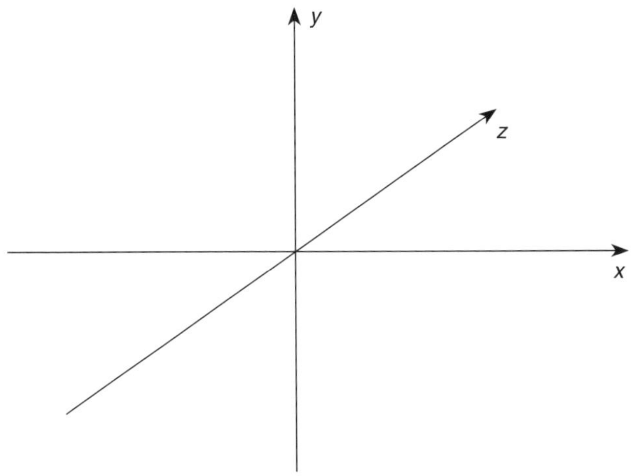

FIGURE 2
The left-handed coordinate system—the *z*-axis is pointing away.

be into the screen and the negative *z* coordinate will be moving away from the screen. For example <4, –3, –3> will refer to a coordinate 4 units to the right on the *x* axis, 3 units toward the bottom of the screen and 3 units away from the origin at <0, 0, 0>.

GETTING STARTED WITH POV-RAY PROGRAMMING

POV-Ray provides some standard-include files. These files are included at the beginning of any POV-Ray program. For example, if you want to use colors in your scene you have to write the following statement:

```
#include "colors.inc"
```

If you want to use textures the following statement has to be written:

```
#include "textures.inc"
```

Some of the standard-include files are:

```
#include "colors.inc" // The include files contain
#include "shapes.inc" // pre-defined scene elements
#include "finish.inc"
#include "glass.inc"
#include "metals.inc"
#include "stones.inc"
#include "woods.inc"
```

Any POV-Ray scene consists of a minimum of the following three attributes (see Sample Program 1):

- At least one object (like a plane, sphere, or box)
- A light source (to light the scene)
- A camera (viewing point of the scene)

Spend some time reading the comments in the sample program. These will help you become familiar with the mathematical descriptions of the scene.

Sample Program 1

```
#include "colors.inc"

plane {   // Plane
   y, 0   // The equation of the plane is y = 0. So this is the xz plane, formed by
          // the x and z axes. Think of the plane as the floor.
   texture {
      pigment {Green} // Green color given to the plane
       }
   }

   sphere { // An Object
      <0, 2, -2.5>, 2 // Center of the sphere is 2 units above the origin on y axis,
         // and coming out of the screen 2.5 units (negative z-axis direction)
         // The radius is 2 units so the sphere is 'resting on' the plane above.
   texture {
         pigment { Red } // Gives the sphere a red color.
      }
   }

   light_source { // Light source to light up the scene
      <20.000, 20.000, -20.000> rgb 1 //coordinates and color of light rgb 1 = rgb <1,1,1>
                                      // = white light
   }

   global_settings { // Global lighting in the scene to bring a pleasant effect
   ambient_light <2.0,2.0,2.0> } //Ambient means 'all-over'

   camera { // Camera to set the viewing point (Or our eyes!)
      location <0, 2, -10> // So Camera is 2 units in y direction, and
         // 10 units outside the screen. About 10-2.5 units
         // from edge of sphere. So a Red Sphere should rest on a green
         // plane and be
         // 7.5 units away from viewer.
   look_at <0, 0, 50> // Looking 50 units inside the center of the screen.
}
```

The output is as expected, a red sphere resting on a green plane, some distance away from us (Figure 3). Note that the sphere is in the center of the image and also how the shadow was calculated automatically by POV-Ray.

To create and compile a POV-Ray program, the steps are:

1. Create a new file by clicking on the "Create new file with internal editor" icon (see Figure 4).
2. Write the program code (see Figure 5).

FIGURE 3
The output of Sample Program 1.

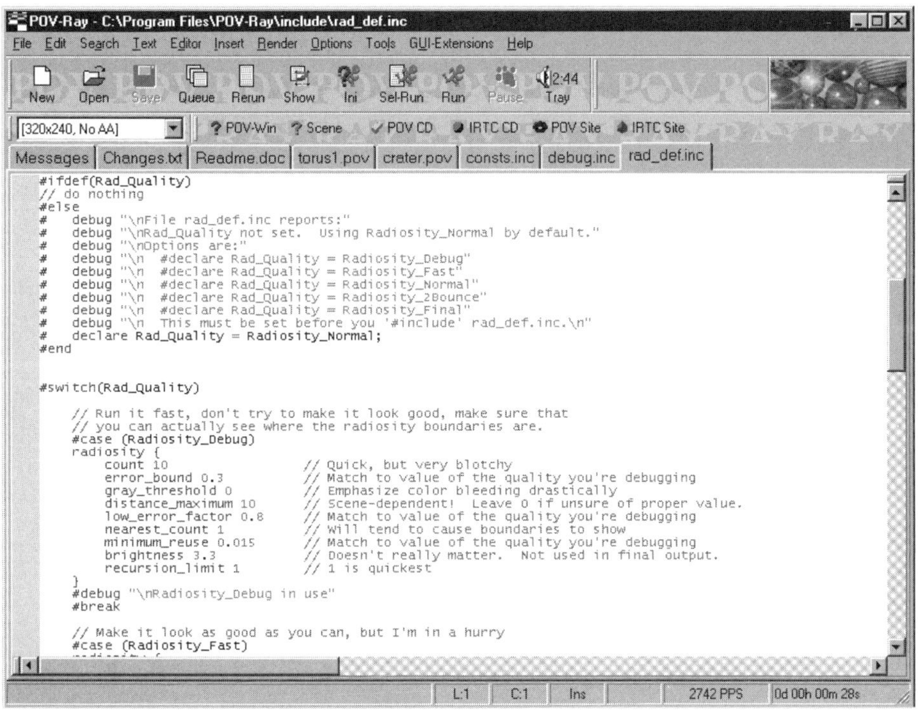

FIGURE 4
POV-Ray interface.

3. Select the resolution of the image to be compiled. The "AA" refers to the antialiasing switch. Use AA for the final image, since the antialiased images take longer to render, even though they are of better quality (see Figure 6).
4. Click on "Run" icon (see Figure 7).
5. The program is compiled (see Figure 8).

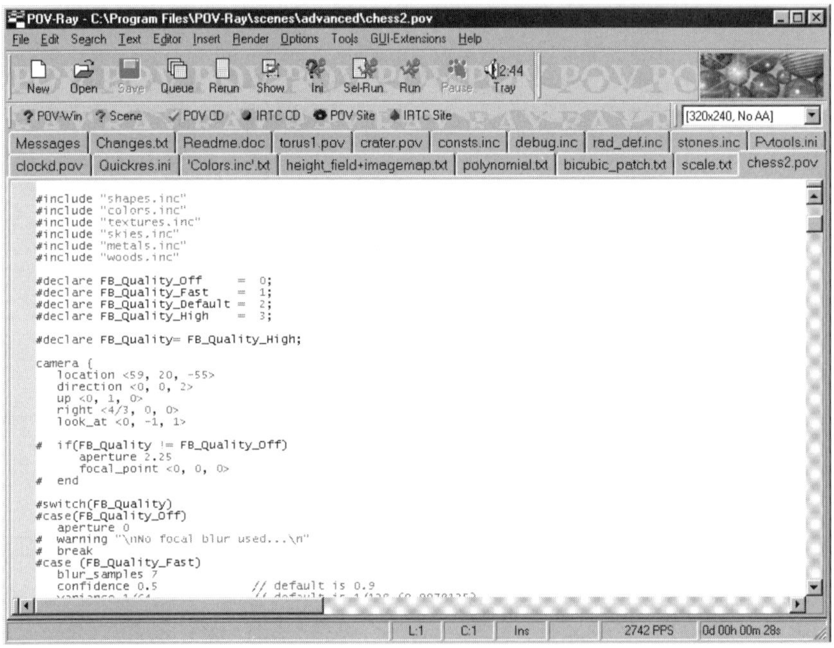

FIGURE 5
POV-Ray program code.

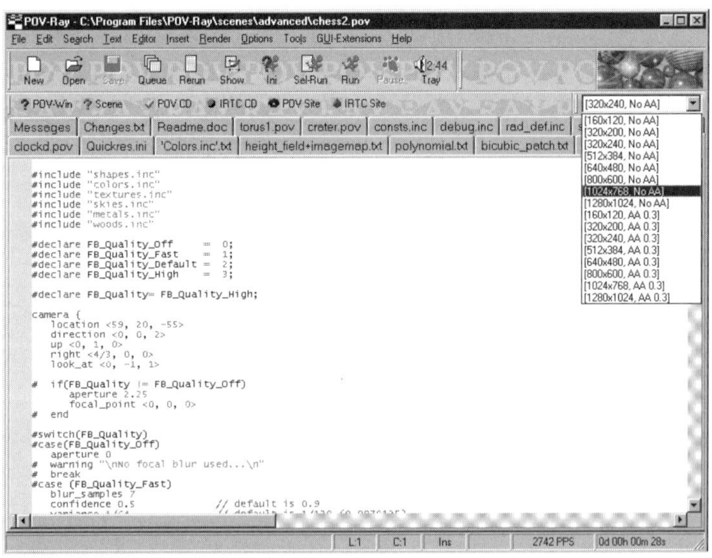

FIGURE 6
Selecting the resolution.

A 3-D MODELER—BREEZE DESIGNER

Breeze Designer is a 3-D modeling and design tool for creating scenes for a number of ray-tracing and rendering programs. Breeze Designer may also be used to develop simple key frame animations by combining a succession of scenes.

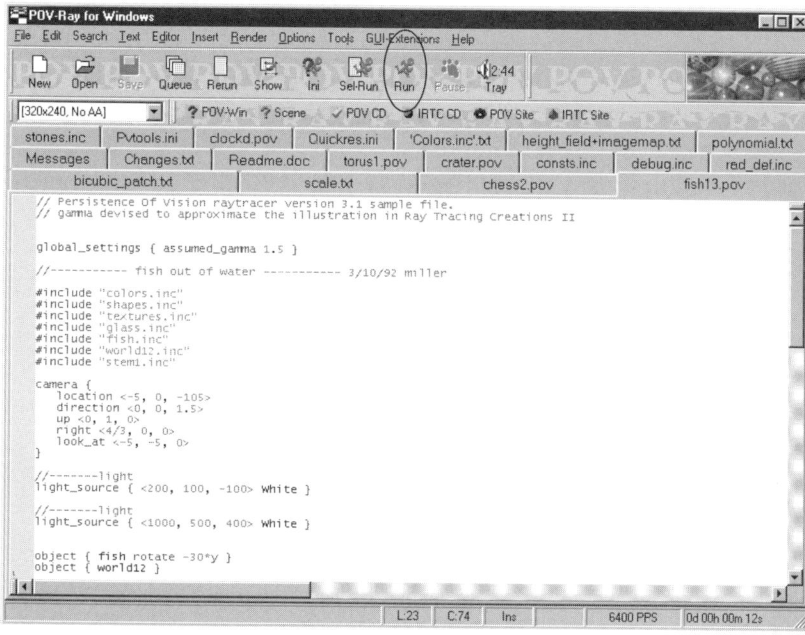

FIGURE 7
Rendering icon.

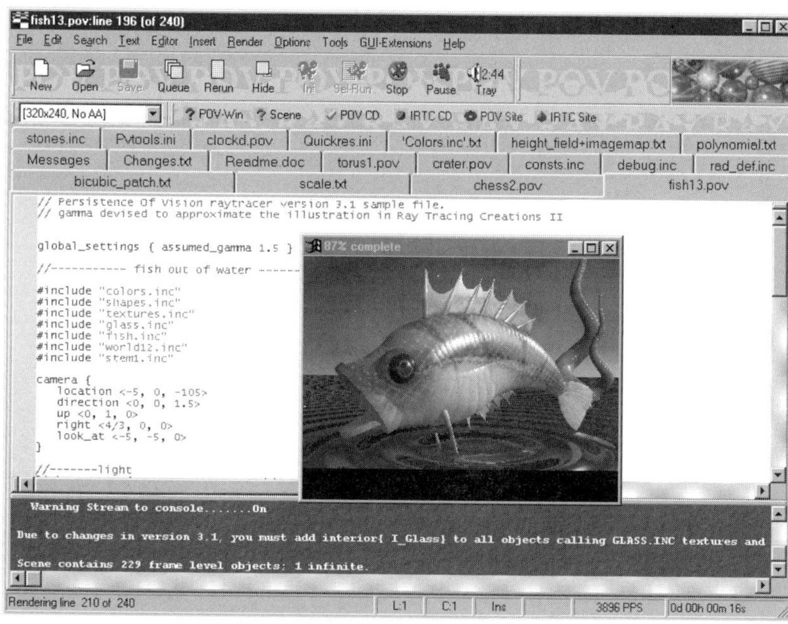

FIGURE 8
Compiling a POV-Ray program.

Breeze Designer provides a mostly modeless modeling environment. Creating scenes, animations, and rendering may all be done through the Breeze interface. Placing objects with the mouse or keyboard in front, side, and plan construction views creates scenes. A number of construction views may be used simultaneously for object placement. A preview window, showing the scene from the camera perspective, may be used during scene creation. The perspective view may be used to show the scene in wire-frame or shaded views.

There are a number of floating palettes found under the Tools menu option. These may be used to select and edit objects and to control the scene animation. These palettes may be left active at all times, allowing quick access to key program features. Figure 9 shows the Breeze interface.

- The toolbar on the left is used for creating images.
- The four windows show the different views of the scene.
- The perspective window shows the partially rendered scene.
- The selected object is shown in a wire mesh.
- By right clicking on the selected object a menu pops up through which properties of the object can be set.

To render the scene created by Breeze Designer, the steps are:

1. Select the Export option from the File menu to export the scene as a POV-Ray file.
2. Assign the scene a file name and save it as "POV Raytracer (*.pov)."
3. Start POV-Ray and open the file exported from Breeze Designer.
4. Click on the rendering button to start rendering the image. The image is rendered (see Figure 10).

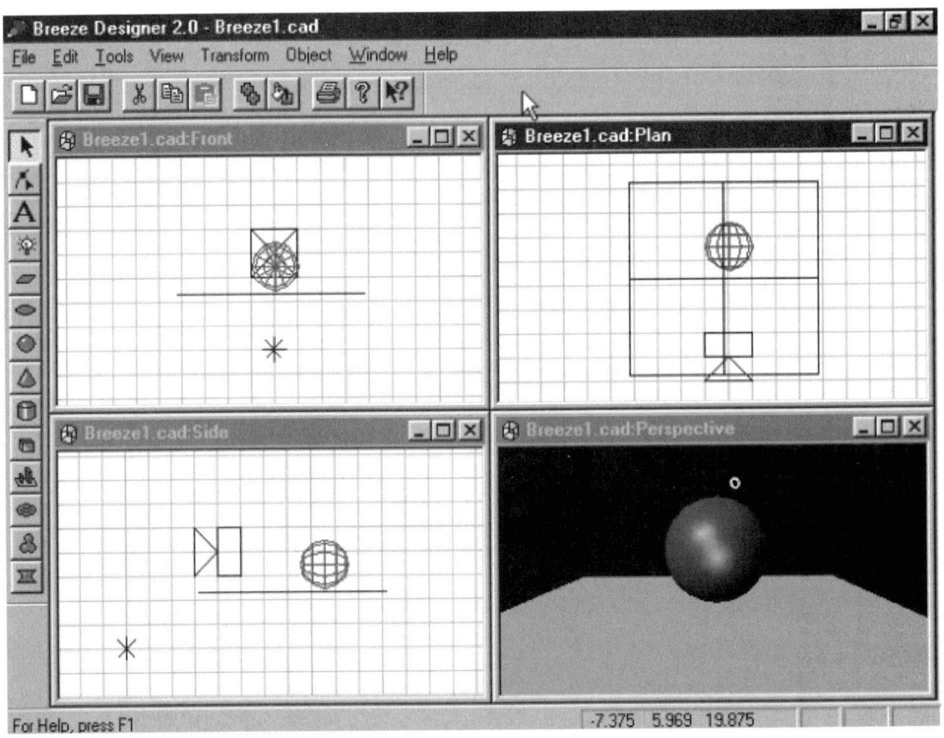

FIGURE 9
Breeze designer interface.

FIGURE 10
The rendered image.

POV-Ray is a good modeling language and hides many concepts from the properties of light from the programmer. But in order to really understand how to program in this language, it is necessary to understand some essentials of 3-D geometry and also some fundamentals of physics aside from the principles of digital graphics. Languages like VRML are also similar in that these are modeling languages. Three-dimensional graphics and animation are now commonplace in movies, but are largely made by professional 3-D graphic artists using more sophisticated packages. Rendering 3-D scenes also takes a large toll on computer resources and requires large amounts of RAM on the rendering packages. However, an interested beginner can get started using POV-Ray very quickly. Further, its ray-tracing algorithms seem to do a quick job with rendering most images.

EXERCISES

State whether the following statements are True or False.

1. The statement "plane {*z*, 0}" will create a plane containing the *x* and *y* axes.
2. The distance between the points <0, 10, 0> and <0, –10, 0> is 20 units.
3. The point <–1, 0, 0> is one unit inside the center of the screen.
4. Any POV-Ray program scene consists of a minimum of at least one object, some ambient lighting and a camera.
5. Rendering an antialiased image takes longer in POV-Ray.

Projects

1. A free tutorial on POV-Ray is available on the Web site of this book. Go through the various programs in it. Modify each of the programs in some manner to understand the various concepts of 3-D geometry used in POV-Ray. Now cut and paste from various programs and create a 3-D image on your own.
2. Use POV-Ray and/or Breeze Designer to create graphics of various 3-D objects, such as a cone, cube, cylinder, sphere, etc. Also make some common 2-D shapes using

Paint Shop Pro, such as a circle, rectangle, square, various polygons, etc. Use the images created and make an electronic book for children (1–4 years old) explaining these shapes. The "e-book" can be in electronic format. Use bright, primary colors and big graphics because babies like to see such colors. If you have access to a color printer, you can also design the entire book in MS-Word and print it out (and maybe send it to a publisher who prints children books!).

Solutions

1. True
2. True
3. False
4. False
5. True

CHAPTER 15

Text in Multimedia and the Internet

A BRIEF HISTORY OF WRITING

The words *Internet* and *Multimedia* conjure up images of videos, animation, pictures, and colors. At first, it appears that writing plays a small role in multimedia and that we no longer have to read page after page of text. However, text continues to play a part in multimedia and the Internet although it is a more limited part and often a different one. In multimedia, text is used for four major purposes:

- Titles
- Menus
- Navigation
- Content

Imagine that you have to design a multimedia product for a wide audience who does not read English very well. It would be possible for you to design a multimedia product that does not use any English text—the titles are graphics, the menus and navigation buttons use clear symbols, and the content is video animation. This is possible but it is exhausting on the normal user; it is easier to read and browse through text than it is to listen and watch. Thus, text is still important in multimedia and the Internet. In fact, text is still the predominant medium on the Internet.

However, we should not treat text in multimedia the way we treat writing with traditional paper-and-pen technology (Table 1). We have become so used to the traditional printed page that we cannot begin to change our way of thinking about new technologies. To break this mindset, let us look at some of the differences between the traditional printed page and the newer multimedia.

Paper-and-pen technology conveys information through a single medium—text. In multimedia, we are not limited to text and can use other ways to convey information. So, text may have a more limited role to play. At the same time, text in multimedia has to work together with other modes of communication, such as sound and graphics. Because of this,

Table 1 Printed Page versus Multimedia

Paper-and-Pen Technology	Multimedia and the Internet
Linear: We turn pages	Nonlinear: We can jump back and forth
Single mode: Written	Multiple channels: Writing, pictures, sound, animation, and so on.
Black text on white paper	Color

text in multimedia should add to the information and not merely repeat it or present something entirely different. Text should be used sparingly but effectively. In this chapter, you will come across ways to make text work for you. This is important because text remains the easiest option for technology.

In multimedia and the Internet, information comes in from several modes—pictures, sound, and text. Humans cannot handle so much information. We are built to take in a small amount of information at any one time. We can absorb about seven pieces of information one time. Beyond this level, we get confused or forget what we are viewing. This is called cognitive overload. It is a very common problem in working with multimedia and the Internet, where sound, pictures, and text compete for attention. In such a situation, text has to be short and to-the-point.

WHERE DID WRITING COME FROM?

In the history of the human race, writing is very recent; it was invented only 5000 years ago. It was used to keep records; it helped administrators keep track of which farmer had how many cows. In this way, administrators could keep permanent records and inform other officials in far-off places. Writing had two advantages over speech: it was more permanent and could be used for distant communication.

In the beginning, writing was very simple. A drawing of a cow along with a specific number of lines was enough for record-keeping. However, as demands became more complicated, the writing system had to expand. Pictures were replaced by ideographs, which are still used in the Chinese language. Another approach to developing a writing system was to work with the spoken language. Spoken language has a limited number of sounds that are combined in different ways to provide an enormous set of words. In such systems, a written symbol or grapheme is associated with a sound, which can be either a syllable (as in Japanese) or a single phoneme (as in English). For example, in English the *p* sound is linked to the letter *p*.

Over the years, writing has been standardized so that everyone agrees on the meaning of the written word. For example, we had to standardize English spelling. Earlier, a word like *fellow* could be written as *felow*, *felowe*, *fallow*, or *fallowe*; now, we have all agreed on a standard spelling—*fellow*. In the same way, standard formats have developed—newspapers have one format, an article in a learned medical journal has another, and textbooks follow their own style. Texts have a standard format or grammar that readers become used to and expect in any new material. When we read a novel, for example, we expect a setting, some complication, and a conflict that finally gets resolved. Informative material too has a clear format: it has a beginning, a body, and a conclusion. A newspaper report is designed as a series of concentric circles; the main point is summarized in the headline; the first sentence or paragraph expands the information in the headline, and the remaining report provides further details.

FONTS

Words

Words

Words

The words above do not look the same. This is because their typefaces or fonts are different.

A typeface is a set of characters or letters that has a similar look. *Times* is a kind of typeface. Other common typefaces are *Courier* and *Arial*.

When a style and size are added to a typeface, it is called a font. For example, Times New Roman 10-point bold is a font. In most applications, you can choose the font for your text. In addition, you can download additional fonts (such as fonts for the Indian languages) from the Internet.

Typefaces are divided into two broad categories: Serif and Sans Serif. A serif is the decoration at the end of a letter stroke (Figure 1).

On paper, serif fonts are easy on the eye because the flags at the end of the letter stroke guide the eye along the line. So, serif fonts, such as *Times*, are used when there is a lot of text to be read. Sans Serif typefaces, such as *Arial*, are used for titles and headlines.

On computer screens, the situation is different. Screen resolution is poor which makes the flags on letters difficult to read. Therefore, serif fonts are difficult to read on-screen.

STYLE

You can change the look of your text by altering the Style. The most common style effects are **Bold** and *Italic*. Bold is type with very thick strokes whereas italic characters slope to the right.

SIZE

The easiest change you can make to your text is to change the size. Size is expressed in points. It is the distance between the highest point (that is, the top of the capital letters) to the lowest point (that is, the bottom of letters such as *p* and *g*).

SCREEN DISPLAYS

What you see on the screen is a pixel display. You want to watch out for "jaggies" in which

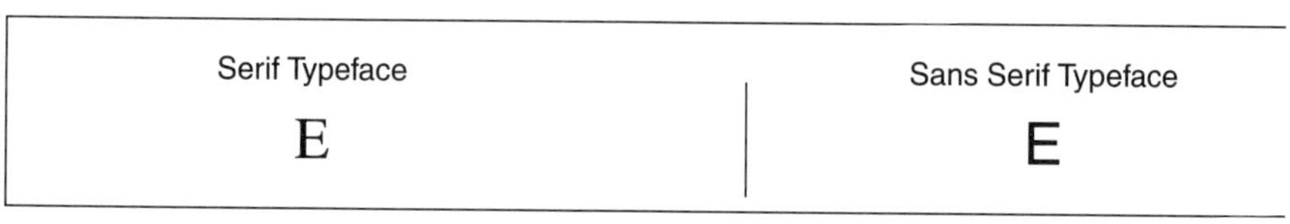

FIGURE 1
Categories of typefaces.

the letters appear rough and jagged because the diagonal and curved lines are displayed as a series of tiny horizontal and vertical lines. This is aliasing.

To smooth out this pixelation, antialiasing is used. In antialiasing, the jagged edges are made smooth by shading the pixels along the edge. This can be done only on screens that have more than 256 colors. Antialiasing makes text look neater, but curiously it becomes more difficult to read!

What you see may not be what you get. Text displayed on the screen may differ from the printout. When you use TrueType fonts, what you see on your screen is what you get on paper. However, with PostScript, there may be a difference between the screen display and the paper version. For example, with PostScript if you type text in a script like Devnagiri, your screen may display the text in the Roman script but PostScript will allow you to print out the Devnagiri characters.

SELECTING FONTS

The selection of fonts should be made based on:

- Readability
- Focus

READABILITY

The text should be easy to read. To ensure readability, keep the following points in mind:

- It is difficult to read text that is all in capital letters. It is easier to read words and sentences that use mixed uppercase and lowercase letters. This is because the shape of a word conveys a lot of information. Suppose you are reading the sentence, "Washington D.C. is the..." and out of the corner of your eye you see that the next word has the shape as shown in Figure 2. Your brain calculates that it is a seven-letter word with the letter p or g and two letters, such as t and l. You may even be able to guess that the word is *capital* without reading it. Information about letter shape is lost when you use capital letters.
- Moving text is more difficult to read than static text. Try to fit one page of text onto a single screen, because it is difficult to read text when the page has to be scrolled.
- People read double-spaced text faster than single-spaced text.
- Do not vary the type size by more than three points.

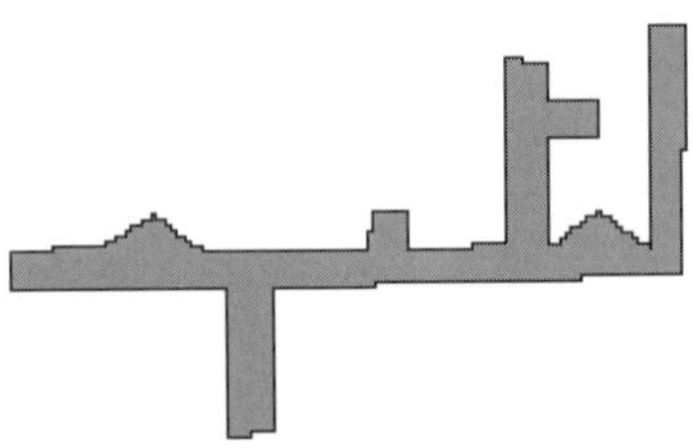

FIGURE 2
The shape of the word.

Table 2 Font Sizes for Comparison

Layout	Font size
Telephone directory	6 point
Newspaper	8 point
Novels	10 point

- Lines of text should not be more than 40–60 characters. At the end of a line, the eyes have to jump to the beginning of the next line; try not to make this a very long jump.
- Choose a simple typeface. Decorative fonts look nice but are difficult to read. Go with a legible font. Although we are used to Serif typefaces on paper, they are less legible on the computer screen. So, choose a Sans Serif font.
- Use the same typeface throughout a project. You can vary the style to make text bold, italic, or underlined if you want to emphasize information.
- Be consistent. Use the same font for information of the same type. When the font size changes, the reader assumes that a different kind of information is signaled and will pay attention. Use one font for all titles, another for all subheadings, and another for all buttons.
- The font size should be readable. Children do not like reading small print and neither do adults who wear reading glasses. A font size between 9 and 12 points is the best (Table 2). Below a font size of 9, your reader has to peer at the screen. Above 12 points, the text becomes too large to read comfortably. Save the larger fonts for titles where you want the user to pay attention.
- A neat finish—When pages are typeset by hand, the letters are adjusted so that the page looks neat. The same can be done to text on-screen. A lot of space is left around letters—between lines of text, between letters, and in the margins. These blank spaces can interfere both with reading and with the look of your text. For a neat finish, you have to adjust letters to get the best fit. Spaces between lines of text, between letters, and in the margins can be adjusted to give a neat finish.

  - Spaces between lines of text—The space between lines of text is called leading. You can manipulate this by adjusting the spacing. Remember that single-spaced text is difficult to read.
  - Spaces between letters—Some letter combinations look awkward because there is too much space between the letters. You can adjust the spaces between letters by using Kerning so that the combinations look more even. Look at combinations of letters below:

    - WA, MW, TA, and VA. are not kerned
    - WA, MW, TA, and VA. are kerned

  - Margins—We all know that the left margin should be aligned. The right margin is usually uneven because we rarely get the exact number of letters on the line (Figure 3). How do we make the right margin look neat? There are several options.
  - Justify the text—The text is spaced so that it aligns on both the left and right margins (Figure 4). Justified text looks better but is more difficult to read because of uneven spaces between the words.
  - Hyphenate the text—Hyphenation breaks words at appropriate places (Figure 5).

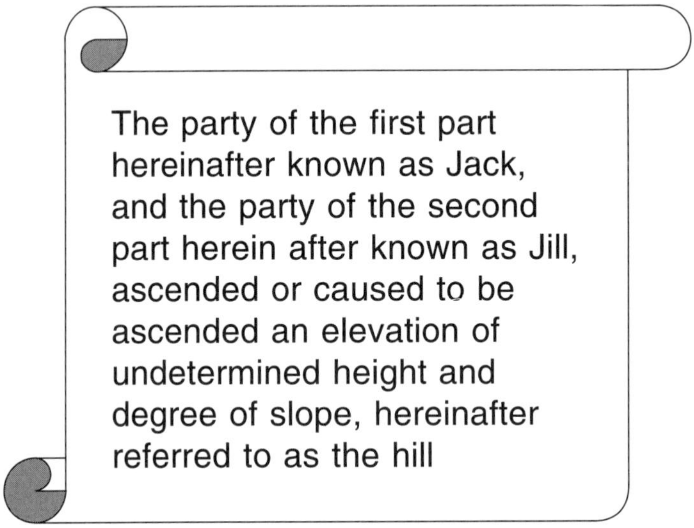

FIGURE 3
Normal text.

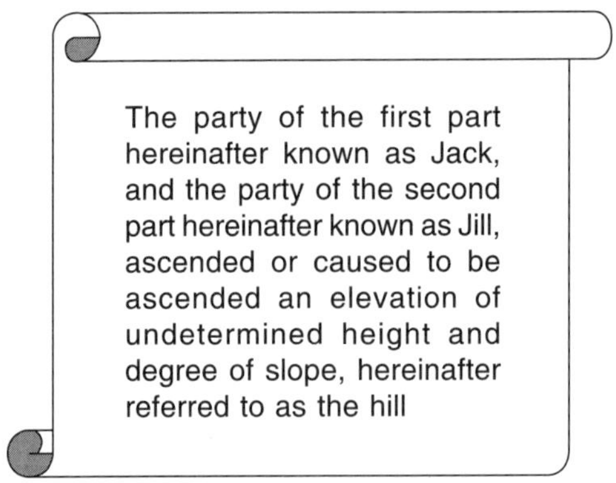

FIGURE 4
Justified text.

- Edit the words—Add and remove words so that they are spread correctly over the page. Can you imagine doing that to a whole page of text?
- When all else fails, left align the text and leave the right margin ragged.
- In longer texts, there may be awkward breaks. You may find that a paragraph is broken awkwardly—the paragraph may start at the bottom of one page and after a single line it goes to the next page. Alternatively, the opposite may happen—the final sentence of the paragraph may appear on the next page. This is not tragic but it looks untidy. It can be fixed through widow and orphan control which ensures that related text is not broken at awkward points.

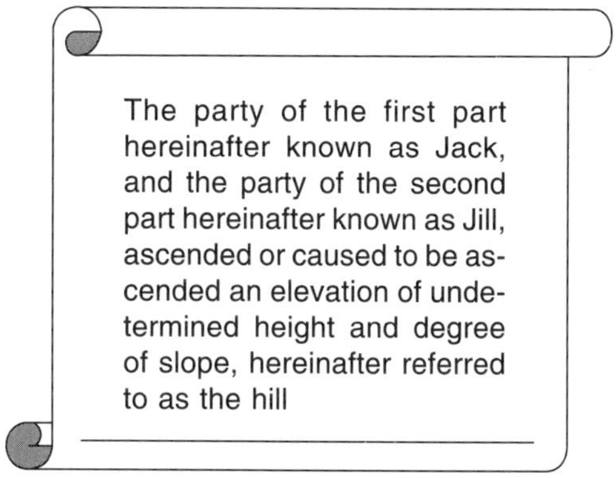

FIGURE 5
Hyphenated text.

FOCUS

Important information must stand out.

- Use different font or text effects, such as text animation.
- Movement in our peripheral vision attracts attention.
- Use font size to indicate the relative importance of the content. Use large sizes for important information and smaller sizes for less important information.

SPECIAL EFFECTS ON FONTS

Two- and three-dimensional effects make your text stand out by adding depth and visual impact.

TEXT ANIMATION

When you want the user to focus on text, and specifically on certain words in it, you can use text animation which makes the text move, flash, or change. This way you can capture the reader's attention.

- Most packages allow you to animate text through the *Font* option. A simple version is available in MS-Word. PowerPoint allows effects that are more complicated; for example, words can fly onto a screen or a title can appear one letter at a time.
- More sophisticated text animation effects are possible by using graphics effects on text. For example, letters can be made to move. You can also use morphing to animate small amounts of text, such as letters or words.

Avoid too many effects, as this can become distracting or even boring after a while.

WordArt

MS-Word allows you to create text effects through WordArt. In WordArt, text is treated as a drawing object; this means that text can be manipulated like an object. You can add color and depth, and rotate it in different ways.

WordArt provides a gallery of predefined styles for text. The gallery includes text that is vertical, tilted in different directions, or gives the impression of depth. In addition, there are a number of tools on the Drawing toolbar that allow you to customize the effects.

Here are a few examples of what you can do with WordArt:

- Shadowed text
- Skewed text
- Rotated text
- Stretched text

Text does not have to be boring but neither should it be too busy. One way to use text forcefully in multimedia is to combine its form and content.

WordArt EFFECTS

Common WordArt effects are

- DEPTH—You can create an illusion of depth through either the Shadow tool or the 3-D settings. Through these tools, the dimension of depth is added to text. You can adjust the degree of depth, the direction of lighting, the surface texture, and the color of the shadow
- DIRECTION—In English, written words run from left to right. In WordArt, you can manipulate the direction of text. It can be placed so that it is read vertically or tilted.
- SHAPE—Text can be fitted to a predefined shape. WordArt provides a small set of shapes that are available through the WordArt toolbar. Text can be fitted into these shapes.
- COLOR AND TEXTURE—Sophisticated color and texture effects can be added to text through the drawing toolbar. These allow you to manipulate textures and add multiple colors to text.
- INCORPORATING PICTURES IN TEXT—With some manipulation, you can insert a picture in the middle of text.

PUTTING TEXT ON SCREENS

Location—Look at the screen from a children's multimedia title (Figure 6). It is part of an animated sequence that shows an apple coming to meet the main character.

Look at the layout and answer the following questions:

1. What caught your eye first?
2. Where did you look next?
3. Which was the last spot that you looked at?

FIGURE 6
A screen layout.

Keep in mind the following essential points about the location of objects on a screen when designing a layout.

- The center of the screen receives the most attention while the corners receive the least. If text conveys important information such as content, place it in the center of the screen. When text is required for navigation, place it in the peripheral areas. The bottom right of the screen gets the least attention from readers; they look at it last, just before they move to the next screen or activity. Design your page according to these principles and readers will appreciate your efforts.
- Use precise and powerful language. Compare *Terrific*! to *That Answer Was Correct.*
- The amount of text has to be carefully chosen. If there is too little text on one screen, the user has to keep clicking to get to the next screen of text. If there is too much text, reading it on the screen can become tiring.
- Titles should be short. Use lots of white space around titles.
- Pack information so that the reader does not have to scroll sideways. To calculate this, use only 40–60 characters, including spaces. Sometimes, text will not fit on a single page and the reader has to scroll down. Minimize this because the reader will have to remember information from the top of the page.

4. Some of the problems are: text has to be scrolled, location of the buttons, too much text so that the page has to be scrolled, too many textboxes carrying different content. Remember that these are only guidelines; at some level, these decisions are a matter of your own taste.

TEXT ON THE INTERNET—HYPERLINKING

Paper-and-pen technology presents text in a linear way. Suppose you are reading a movie review in the newspaper and would like to know the other movies in which the hero has acted. You can read ahead and hope that the review includes this information or you can look at a few film magazines to get the information. This takes time and you have to search. Hypertext is designed as a way around this problem. In a hypertext system, these documents would be connected; even within a document, ideas that are connected are linked. These links between hypertexts are called hyperlinks. A hyperlink is a link between some point in one hypertext document to a point in either another document or another place in the same document.

By using hyperlinks, users can rapidly access and browse through large amounts of text. Hyperlinks allow users to navigate in a nonlinear manner. The pieces of text are called nodes and the relations between the nodes are called links.

Hyperlinked information is often organized in a hierarchy. In a printed encyclopedia or dictionary, you can find the contents only through a static, linear, alphabetic index. Hypertext links are useful in two cases:

- When the amount of information is very large but can be broken down into several smaller, related pieces.
- When the user needs only a small part of the information at any one time.

ADVANTAGES OF HYPERTEXT

The advantages of hypertext are:

- You can place bookmarks. A history mechanism allows you to return to a page you visited earlier.
- You can search for related documents.
- Audio, video, and animation fragments can be added to hyperdocuments.
- Documents worldwide can be linked.

DISADVANTAGES OF HYPERTEXT

The disadvantages of hypertext are:

- You need a computer to access the documents. Reading text on a computer is more difficult than on paper because of the low resolution on-screen.
- If navigation aids are not provided, a heavy cognitive load is placed on the reader; the reader can also become disoriented.

NAVIGATION IN HYPERTEXT

In a book, the information is arranged in a linear sequence. So, each page assumes that you have read and remembered what the previous pages contained. This is not true of hypertext, where the information is presented as independent chunks.

However, a major issue in hypertext is navigation. In a book, even if you flip through it in random order, you know where you are in the document because the pages are numbered and you can hold the entire document in your hand. This is not possible with hypertext and there is a real danger of the user becoming disoriented.

Most hypertext documents resemble a maze in which it is easy to get lost. Even in small documents, users get lost in hyperspace. For this reason, navigation is a major issue in the design of hypertext and several aids have been developed to help users find their way through the mass of material.

NAVIGATION AIDS

Here are some aids that have been developed to help users find the information they want without getting lost in hyperspace.

- BACKTRACK—It allows you to go back repeatedly until you reach the first node you visited. If a hypertext system does not offer backtracking, the user may get stuck at a node that has no outgoing links. Most hypertext systems offer a back button that lets you return to the last visited node.
- SNEAK PREVIEW—Some systems provide additional information before you actually follow the link. For instance, when the cursor is moved over the anchor, a short description of the destination node or the full URL is displayed.
- HIGHLIGHTING LINKS—Some systems depict links that point to "old" nodes in a different way than links to "new" nodes. They use a different color or different underlining.
- BREAD CRUMBS—To avoid getting lost in hyperspace, you can leave a trail. When you leave "bread crumbs" behind, you will recognize a node that was visited before. The bread crumbs facility assumes the user has a poor memory.
- HISTORY—History lists allow users to directly jump to previously visited nodes. There are two possible ways to implement a history list:
  - A complete history list shows all nodes that have been visited. If a node has been visited twice, it will appear twice in such a list.
  - An abbreviated history list only keeps those nodes that were not "backed out of" by following links backward.
- BOOKMARKS—You can mark a page by including the name of the node in a list of bookmarks.
- OVERVIEW MAPS—These help users get an overview of the structure of the entire document. Such overviews are usually in the form of pictures.
  - *Bird's eye view*—The document is shown as a tree or forest, with the links as exceptions. One can view details by zooming in or by using a scrolling window.
  - *Fish-eye view*—This shows the structure around the current node in detail.
- GUIDED TOURS—Guided tours take the user through an information base along a predetermined path. This would be useful in an educational context.

NAVIGATION STRATEGIES

Users follow different browsing strategies:

- *Breadth-first* navigation means visiting all nodes that are only one link away from the "starting" node. So, the user follows the link to one node, reads it, and returns to the starting node.

- *Depth-first* navigation is following links to nodes farther and farther away from the "starting" node. When a node with no outgoing links is reached, the user backtracks until a new forward link is found.
- *Random* navigation refers to visiting nodes in random order.

USING TEXT OVER THE INTERNET

Writing hypertext documents is more difficult than writing text because the author must make sure the reader is able to absorb the information in text and also the structure of the hyperdocument.

There are nine considerations for writing hypertext:

- CHUNKING—Organize the information into small chunks. Each chunk should deal with only one topic, theme, or idea.
- INTERRELATIONSHIPS—Each document should contain links to other documents.
- SIMPLICITY IN NAVIGATION—Navigation should be simple, intuitive, and consistent.
- SCREEN DESIGN—Visual layout is very important; screens should be designed so that the information can be easily understood.
- LOW COGNITIVE LOAD—Minimize the burden on the user's short-term memory. Do not expect the user to remember things from one screen to the next.
- MAINTAIN MULTIPLE PERSPECTIVES—It is easy to be sidetracked by technical requirements. Keep the user and the organization of the document in mind during the design phase.
- CONSISTENCY OF DOCUMENT NAMES—Maintain a list of names of nodes when you create them. This will help you identify links when they are created.
- MASTER REFERENCE LIST—Create a master reference list to prevent redundant or missing citations.
- EARLY REVIEWS—Review the technical, legal, and management aspects of the document as early as possible. It is difficult to make changes when the hyperdocument becomes larger.

EXERCISES

1. Which are Serif fonts and which are Sans Serif?
   a. Arial
   b. Comic
   c. Courier
   d. Garamond
   e. Gothic
   f. Technical
   g. Times New Roman
   h. Univers
2. Which of the given typefaces are easy to read on paper and why?
3. Type the above words on a computer in the given font and view the effect on the screen. Which typefaces are easy to read on the screen and why?

Projects

1. Create a 3-D text effect using WordArt.
2. Make a personal Web page. Decide on the contents of the Web page and use graphics to make it aesthetically pleasing. You may consider putting one or more of the following:

   - Information about you and your family.
   - Your resume.
   - Links to samples and demos or projects you have done.
   - Your favorite people and things.
   - Your favorite subjects.

Later on, if you have Internet access, you can make your own Web page and upload it to a free site. Remember, design it so that your message comes through!

Solutions

1. Serif fonts: Courier, Garamond, Gothic, Technical, Times New Roman,
   Sans Serif fonts: Arial, Comic, and Univers
2. The Serif fonts because the ends of the letters have flags that direct the eye.
3. Sans Serif fonts are easier to read on the screen because the flags, which can be distracting, are not present.

An Interlude: Meaning in Binary Strings

> **About Meaning and Distortion**
>
> While we understand a lot about sound and light, we know very little about how they carry meaning. Why does a piece of sound make you happy, or sad? Why do we say a picture is "scary" or "beautiful"?
>
> In computers, all information is stored as strings of zero and one bits. Whether it is a picture, some text, sound, or light, it is all represented as strings. Where and how do strings carry their "meaning"? If we change some of the zeros and ones will the meaning change?
>
> We don't know the answers to these questions, but we have some guesses. Enclosed is a purely experimental piece of work. If you find the contents interesting, read through it. Maybe you will be able to think of some answers that others have missed!

MEANING IN BINARY STRINGS

Abstract

This chapter deals with the existence of meaning in binary strings. A set of experiments to determine where and how meaning resides in such strings is described. It is found that a string with meaning is indistinguishable from a randomly generated one. The paper examines the postulate that the presence or absence of a byte has little bearing on the meaning of a binary string. Further experimentation seems to show that consciousness is a prerequisite for the creation and perception of meaning in binary strings. The paper proposes a timeless matrix where the interactions of strings produce finite and conscious perception of meaning.

The Meaning of "Meaning"

In this chapter we report our findings on a set of experiments performed on binary strings. In the process, we find that we are plunged into a discussion on meaning and consciousness.

If indeed Cognitive Science has reached a stage where it can say something about these subjects, we hope this chapter will be of use in the formulation of an eventual physics of consciousness.

Introduction

Computers process information using binary strings. All information in current digital computers is stored and manipulated in the form of strings of zero and one. All data consists of such strings, as do all programs that manipulate data. The operating systems of digital computers consist of binary strings, as do their memories. There is no evidence that current computers have any awareness of the meaning of the data they process. On the other hand, the human beings that use the results of data processed by computers deal essentially with the meaning that these strings of zero and one contain. We have attempted to determine where and in what form meaning exists in binary strings.

Definition of "Meaning"

We will define meaning as an evocation (Simon, 1995) of links in memory. For instance, when a reader views words in a text, certain symbol structures stored in the reader's memory are activated. Moreover meaning is associated with recognition (Feigenbaum and Simon, 1984), that is, the evoked structures are recognized and in the process understood or associated with the input text.

In this chapter, we will see how the meanings of binary strings are dependent on expression. That is, a string will have meaning only when expressed through an appropriate method.

BINARY STRINGS

Definition

We will define a binary string as a linear sequence of bipolar states. Zero and One (or One and Minus One) are the most common form in which binary strings exist in computers. However, the term itself need not be defined only with respect to computers. Presence or absence of anything could constitute a bipolar state and, as such, strings are widespread throughout real and imaginary spaces.

Computers and Binary Strings

Digital computers are essentially collections of switches and are, therefore, totally dependent on bipolar states for their functioning. Data of any kind, (numbers, text, sound, graphics etc.,) consist of binary strings. Such data is manipulated through sequences of instructions (programs) that are expressed as binary strings. All input and output is through binary strings under the control of an Operating System, which itself is a program and, therefore, a binary string.

All binary strings in a computer are labeled using "headers" that describe the nature, structure, and function of these strings. Headers are also binary strings.

Bit Patterns in Binary Strings

Binary strings in computers are usually combined into bytes (groups of eight bits, each bit being a zero or a one). There are 256 bytes that constitute the "alphabet" of the digital computer. The assignment of a character or a symbol to a particular group of eight bits is arbitrary and decided by the American Standard Code for Information Interchange (ASCII). However, the complete ASCII set, if represented as one string, would contain the same number of zeros and ones.

Experiment 1—Bit Patterns in Sounds Pictures, and Programs

In this experiment, we counted the number of zeros and ones in strings that represented sounds, graphics, and programs. In order to do so, we used a small program to skip the target files header, read the data bytes, convert these to bits, and total the zero bits and one bits. A part of the results are shown in Table 1.

Observations

As may be expected, the distribution of 0 and 1 bits appears close to 50:50 in most files. It may be noticed that for certain types of files, e.g., "WAV" (sound) and "BMP" (picture files), this distribution is sometime violated. This is not considered significant as the effect can be generally explained as an artifact. For example, the most common byte in a sound file is the silence byte (1111 1111). Hence, any sound file will show a larger proportion of 1 bits. However, since the choice of the ASCII character 255 as the silence byte is arbitrary, its effect on the distribution is merely an artifact. In fact, if the silence byte is removed, the distribution shifts more toward the 50:50 proportion.

On the basis of the data and the above observations, we assume that the proportion of 0 and 1 bits are the same in meaningful and meaningless strings. We state that: A string with meaning is indistinguishable from a randomly generated one.

In this context, it is interesting to note that it is impossible to determine the nature of a string (i.e., sound, picture, or program) from a segment of it, even if the segment is large. In some instances one may be able to guess from artifacts such as the proliferation of the silence bit, but only if one knew from where to begin counting the bytes. If the string segment does not start from the beginning of a byte, there would be no way to tell what the segment might mean.

Table 1 Distribution of Zero and One Bits in Files

File name	Description	Size (bits)	Percent 0	Percent 1
excel.exe	Program	44,796,032	55.69	44.31
winword.exe	Program	42,543,232	56.59	43.41
alarm.exe	Program	89,472	73.88	26.12
Bitbybit.c	C Program	15,120	53.45	46.55
Showfile.c	C Program	35,040	54.10	45.90
arcade.bmp	Bitmap	5,040	52.34	47.66
castle.bmp	Bitmap	6,224	50.13	49.87
setup.bmp	Bitmap	307,696	39.49	60.51
rec45.wav	Wave	1,005,520	48.60	51.40
beep.wav	Wave	46,112	48.88	51.12

Byte Patterns in Binary Strings

With the above observations in mind, we decided to investigate the distribution of the 256 ASCII characters in meaningful strings. We used another program to determine the distribution of bytes in the same files whose bits had been counted earlier.

Experiment 2—Byte Patterns in Sounds, Pictures, and Programs

In this experiment, we took the target files, removed the headers and counted the bytes. For each file, a plot of the frequency of occurrence of bytes against the ASCII numbers of the bytes was produced. Typical plots for sound, graphic, and program files are shown in Figures 1, 2, and 3.

Observations

Sound files have a distinct signature as far as the frequency of occurrence of bytes is concerned. The dominant byte is the one representing silence. This is due to the nature of audio information as it is perceived by the human ear. Without a liberal punctuation with silence, the meaning of a sound is not obvious. This would be so in text as well, if one were to count the blank character as a part of the text. However, if one treats the silence byte and the blank character as artifacts, the distribution of the other bytes follows no discernible pattern. Nor is there any great variation from one audio file to another.

In the case of graphic files and computer program files, no pattern can be seen. We state that: The presence or absence of a byte has little bearing on the meaning of a binary string.

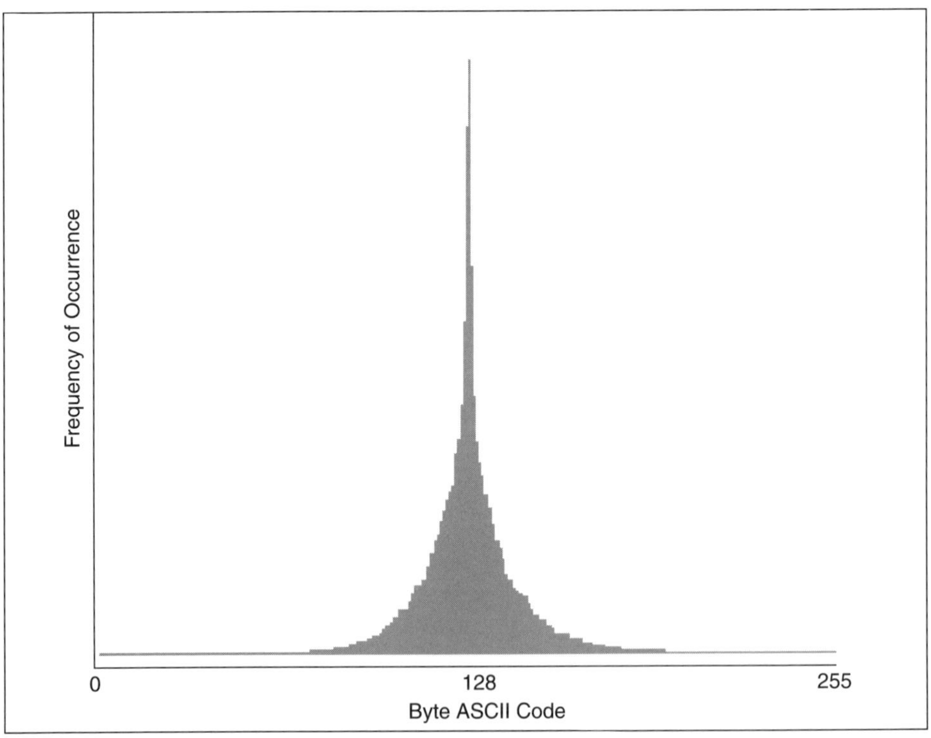

FIGURE 1
Frequency distribution of ASCII bytes in a sound file of 66 Kbytes (11 kHz, 8 bit, mono).

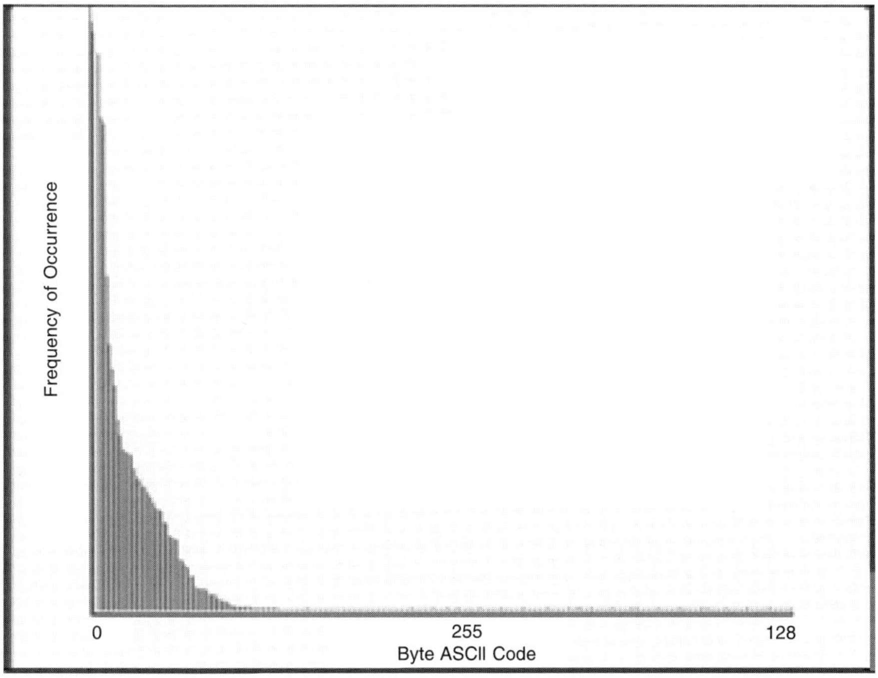

FIGURE 2
Frequency distribution of ASCII bytes in a bitmap file with a size of 301 KB.

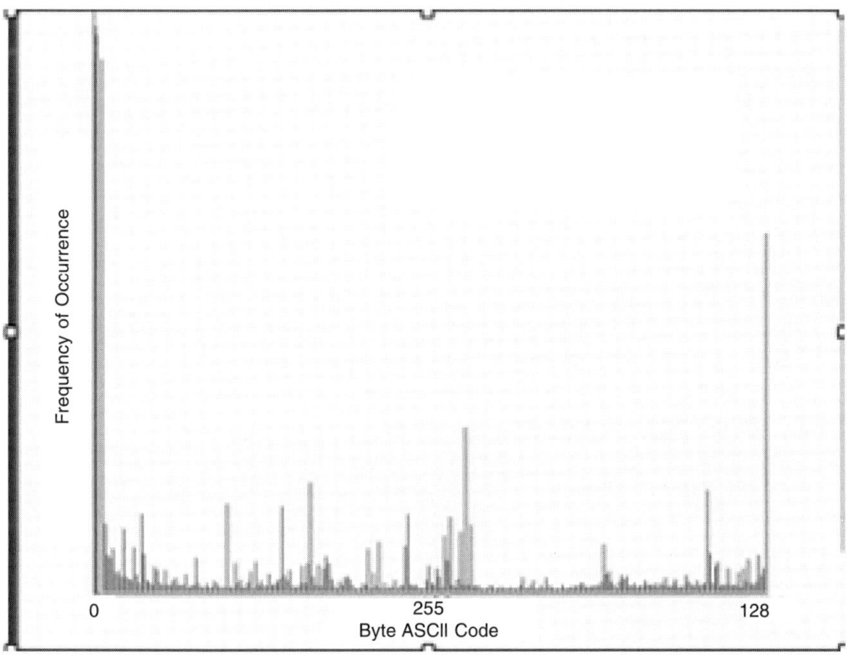

FIGURE 3
Frequency distribution of ASCII bytes in an EXE file with a size of 5.07 MB.

In this connection, we need to note that the byte is an artificial construct with an arbitrary (conscious) allocation of meaning to each group of eight bits. It is, therefore, further stated that: Consciousness is a prerequisite for the creation and perception of meaning in binary strings.

Bit Shift Distortion in Binary Strings

Since the proportion of zero and one bits in a meaningful string is no different from that of random strings, we decided to study the effect on meaning by changing the position of bits in strings.

Experiment 3—Meaning Degradation in Sound and Text Files

In this experiment, we shifted the position of a single bit from the beginning to the end of a data file and studied the effect of such a shift on the meaning of the file. Each target file was progressively changed by shifting the starting bit to the end, shifting the next bit to the end, and so on. To do this we removed the header from the target string, converted the bytes of the string to binary, shifted the relevant bit, changed the bit structure back to bytes, and replaced the header. The tests were performed on audio and text files and the results were checked for meaning by listening and reading for audio and text files, respectively.

Observations

It is intuitively obvious that a shifted bit will seriously degrade the meaning of a file. This is because once the first bit is shifted, every byte in the file will have a changed value. It may indeed be assumed that the entire content of the file will no longer be meaningful. We were surprised to find that this is not so.

In the case of audio files, we observed a steady degradation in the audio quality as bits were shifted. The degradation increases gradually and the file degrades into noise by the seventh bit shift. After this, when the eighth bit shift takes place, the entire original meaning returns since now, effectively, an entire byte has been shifted to the back of the file and the remaining byte sequence restored to its original condition.

We do not, as yet, have an explanation for this graceful degradation. Perhaps it is due to the fact that the silence byte (1111 1111), in the one-bit shifted condition will result either in 1111 1110 or 1111 1111, both of which are silent bytes. Since silence, ironically, is the principal component of audio files, a single bit shift does not render the file meaningless.

Table 2 shows the most prevalent byte in a sound file after 1 through 8 bit shifts. A clear pattern is evident from the table. This may indeed provide the explanation for why audio files retain meaning even when bytes are changed.

In the case of text files, a single bit shift completely destroys the meaning of the file.

In view of the foregoving, we may hypothesize that the meaning of a string is more sensitively connected to its structure than to its contents or constituents.

Surprisingly, such results have been observed in chemical physics as well (Mathur and Mitra, 1979).

Headers—Strings to Look at Strings

Headers are strings that carry information about other strings. For example, the header of an audio string will carry information about its format, the sampling rate, whether it is

Table 2 The Effect of Bit Shifts on the Most Frequently Occurring Byte in an Audio File (11 kHz, 8 Bit, Mono)

No. of bits shifted	Most frequent byte	Hex value[a]	Binary value
1	254	FE	1111 1110
2	253	FD	1111 1101
3	251	FB	1111 1011
4	239	EF	1110 1111
6	223	DF	1011 1111
7	191	BF	1011 1111
8	127	7F	0111 1111

[a]The Hex value equals the base 16 value. In the base 16 representation of any number, the digits from 0 to 9 are represented by 0 to 9. The digits 10 to 15 are represented by A, B, ..., F in order. For example, the decimal number $127 = 7 \times 16 + 15$. So 127 = 7F in Hex notation.

mono or stereo, etc. Typically, headers are extremely small compared to the data strings they describe. However, they are extremely important to the meaning of strings as, without them, there would be no way to determine in what way the data needs to be processed to express meaning.

Experiment 4—Bit Pattern and Degradation in Sound Headers

In this experiment, we caused bit shift degradation in audio headers using the same methodology as for experiment 3.

Observations

All meaning is destroyed in a single bit shift. In fact, the data is no longer recognizable as sound at all. The data can no longer be expressed and, therefore, remains a string without meaning for as long as we like. However, with the original header, it can be played and, therefore, has a beginning and an end. It is tempting, though perhaps unwarranted, to compare the situation to an ancient verse that states: "That which is expressed (or has form) is temporal, that which is unexpressed (or has no form) is eternal." (*The Gita*, Hindu religious text of unknown authorship and chronology.)

Human Memory as Binary Strings

In our definition of meaning, we have postulated that memory is essential for the perception of meaning. In this context and in the context of the above experiments, it is important to examine the structure of human memory.

The Brain and Neural Networks

The human brain consists, for the most part, of a large network of neurons. Each neuron is essentially a biochemical electrical switch. Neurophysiology has not yet discovered by what biological mechanisms human memory is accomplished. Nor do we know, physiologically, how neurons store memories. We do know, thanks to computers, that memories can be stored in physical devices and that such processes as evoking, activating, and associating can be carried out with them (Simon, 1995, Braitenberg, 1984). Memories in neural networks are stored in a repetitive and multiplexed fashion. As a result they show graceful degradation when bits are randomly changed in the network (Mitra, 1994).

If an artificial neural network can be constructed on a digital computer that has sufficient complexity to match the size of the human brain, it is possible that thought would result. While this is a controversial matter, for the purposes of this chapter, such a possible simulation seems to indicate the possibility that a brain can be represented as a binary string, much as an artificial neural network can.

Memory in Neural Networks

Artificial neural networks store data in several well-understood ways. The most common method is through the interconnection and weights of interconnections between neurons. Once again, the detail of the storage method is not important in our context. It is clear that memories can be stored as binary strings in other binary strings that represent neural networks.

DISCUSSION AND SPECULATION

Structure, Function, and Content

From the above experiments and analyses, it would appear that binary strings could be constructed out of anything and could represent any meaning if preceded by an appropriate header that can enable the string to be processed by an "expression engine" that expresses its meaning. The meaning is encrypted in the string through a conscious schema that can create an arbitrary meaning list for an arbitrary group of bits (8 in our case).

The meaning of strings would be dependent more on the structure and sequence of these groups of bits than on their specific content. The header string would entirely determine whether the string could be expressed or not. When expressed, a string would have a finite meaning.

Several questions remain unanswered in this work. Can a string have multiple meanings? Can strings be transmuted—audio to video, memory to meaning? In our future work we will attempt to answer some of these questions.

Strings, Meaning, and Consciousness

There would appear to be three functions that a string is capable of performing in the context of meaning. A string could represent a conscious memory that derives meaning from other strings that it interprets using appropriate header strings. Since all three functions are performed using strings that are indistinguishable from random strings, it is tempting to speculate that any string can have a meaning to a memory string through an appropriate header string.

Given this scenario, consider an n-dimensional matrix containing an infinite number of bipolar elements distributed randomly. Such a space would contain all possible forms of conscious memory, all possible forms of headers, and all possible meanings. In effect, the interplay of finite string lengths within this matrix would create all possible conscious realities. Whenever a string is expressed as a meaning, it would have a beginning and an end in an otherwise timeless situation.

ACKNOWLEDGMENTS

One of the authors (Sugata Mitra) is grateful to the other two (Harita Gupta and Arun Narula) for assistance with the programming and performing of the actual experiments. We are grateful to Sanjay Gupta for constructing the frequency distribution program for bytes. A short but encouraging discussion with Margaret Boden is gratefully acknowledged.

REFERENCES

Braitenberg, V., *Vehicles: Experiments in Synthetic Psychology,* Cambridge: MIT Press, 1984.

Feigenbaum, E. A., and Simon H. A., EPAM-like models of recognition and learning, *Cognitive Science*, 8:305–336, 1984.

Mathur, S.C. and Mitra, S., Crystal structure sensitivity of the band structure of organic semiconductors. *J. Phys. C Solid State*, 12, (2), 1979.

Mitra, S., The effect of synaptic disconnection on bi-directional associative recall. Proc. IEEE/SMC Conf., Vol. 1, 989, 1994.

Simon, H. A., Literary criticism: a cognitive approach, *SEHR*, Vol. 4, Issue 1, 1995.

CHAPTER 16

Art and Design

INTRODUCTION

We have learned a lot about various elements of multimedia. Now we have to combine them and make a multimedia system. But first we have to design the system. In this chapter, we will learn about some important design issues faced in designing multimedia systems.

When computers were first introduced in the 1950s, using them was a multistep process. The systems analyst specified how the computer would be used to solve a problem. This specification was given to the programmer, who would make the control and flowchart to implement the program. A coder would then translate the flowchart into a computer code and debug the system. Finally, a keypunch operator would encode the program for the machine and then run it.

By 1960, the development of assemblers and compilers combined the jobs of programmer and coder into one. With further development of the keyboard, one person was able to design, program, and run programs on the computer. Slowly, as hardware prices crashed (in the 1970s), this trend of "every person a computer user, every person a programmer" became even more widespread. However, the skills required to use the computer were still quite high, and consequently the computer was used only for very technical and difficult jobs. Word processing and the use of spreadsheets changed all that. With the development of a good monitor, a personal computer or a workstation could be used by many users with very little training. For example, a user could directly enter, correct, edit, and format documents that looked better than what could be obtained on a typewriter.

The success of these programs, and the tremendous rise in the number of personal computers led to an explosion of applications of the personal computer. Computers started being used in all aspects of our life. With multimedia systems, and now Web-based products, millions of people have become computer users. For this reason it has become very important to design systems in such a manner that users have no difficulty in using them. It has almost become an axiom in the computer industry that users will not buy computers or computer programs unless we make them easier to work with. Thus, it has become important for the programmer to design the user interface of the system with care.

Another consequence of the rise of the Internet and of multimedia systems is that the programmer has to design multimedia systems too. With programs like MS-PowerPoint, it is easy for anyone to make a multimedia presentation. On the Internet, the situation is similar. Using HTML is very easy, and a large percentage of Web pages have been designed by individuals rather than by corporations. In addition, Web pages are increasing the use of multimedia elements, even though it takes a long time for multimedia Web pages to load. Thus it is becoming important to understand what is involved in choosing appropriate media elements in your multimedia systems, and in putting them together to make your multimedia system.

In this chapter we will learn a little about the issues involved in both these aspects of design—the design of user interfaces and the design of multimedia systems.

MAKING THE RIGHT DESIGN CHOICES

There are many things involved in coming up with a good design of your multimedia system. The most important consideration is to understand the audience of the presentation (or the user of the system). The audience requirements will drive the use of appropriate media elements, the choice of colors used, the quality of the language used, the amount of interactivity included in the system. In a multimedia software product, the emphasis should be on the ease with which a new user can use the system. In a multimedia presentation, the main objective is to pass a message to the viewer. Each multimedia element used should go toward giving that message to the audience.

Keeping the message and the audience in mind, the script is developed. Essentially, a script is a plan of how the message will be delivered. The script shows how the message will be given. The information given in each screen has to be planned. The script also contains a plan of the interactivity of the system, with the different paths a user can take by clicking on various buttons on a screen. Further, one important aspect of interactivity is to give feedback to the user once the user performs an action. For example, when the cursor is placed over a button, there is a small change in the button, which reminds the user that the button can be clicked to perform an action. Often, a help text also comes up and tels the user what happens in case that button is pressed.

After the script, the designer constructs the storyboard. During the storyboarding phase, appropriate media elements are selected. This is a detailed design, and information is provided by the designer on what the media elements will be like. For example, will there be a narration by a person when a particular screen is shown? If the storyboard gives this information, the producer can plan to pass the job on to the audio specialist. If there are particular graphics which require an expert graphic artist, then the storyboard will have to contain a detailed visualization of the graphics to be made. The graphic artist can look at the visualization and construct the appropriate graphic elements.

What can you do to make the right choices while designing your system? There are no easy prescriptions to follow. But if you make it a habit to observe various media around you, and note the reasons why these fail or succeed, you will be able to apply your learning to the design of your multimedia systems. Remember that it is observation that makes a good designer great.

USER INTERFACE DESIGN—EVENT-DRIVEN PROGRAMMING

In the traditional programming paradigm, the user begins the program and then the program takes control and prompts the user for inputs as needed. Slowly, as graphical interfaces evolve, "event driven" programs replaced this paradigm. Events are messages that the user gives to the program, for example, moving the mouse, clicking, double-clicking the mouse at a button on the screen, or typing a letter on the keyboard. In the word processor MS-Word, if the user types a key in a document, the program prints the letter in the document and waits for the next event. Now if the user selects the save option in the file menu, the program saves the document and again awaits the next event.

At the heart of event-driven programs is a simple loop that waits for an event to happen. Earlier, programmers had to explicitly program the event loops. Nowadays, Visual Basic, for example, allows you to just build objects (such as windows and menus) and to specify how they are to respond to messages. For example, the event loop of MS-Word would notice a keystroke event, display the character on the screen, and wait for another event. If this package notices a mouse-click event it would take the cursor to wherever it has observed the event.

For example, when the cursor is placed over a button in MS-Word, the button is highlighted. Another example is of a double click event: When we double click on a shortcut, it finds the target of the shortcut.

USER INTERFACE

The term *user interface* in the context of the computer is usually understood to include such things as the windows, menus, buttons, the keyboard, the mouse, the sounds that a computer makes, and, in general, all the information channels that allow the user and the computer to communicate. Most successful multimedia systems are used by people who do not have any knowledge of programming. A graphical user interface should be designed with this in mind and should allow ordinary people to use computers easily.

A good graphical user interface uses pictures rather than text to give users an understanding of how to work on a system. A common understanding of symbols allows us to make systems that can be used with little instruction. For example, in MS-Word, if you click on the floppy disk icon, the file is saved. By using an icon with a graphic of a floppy disk, the designer has tried to communicate the function of the icon to the user.

There are other screen objects that are used for graphical user interfaces. Screen objects are also known as Windowing system components. Some examples of common screen objects are:

- Windows
- Menus
- Controls
- Dialog boxes
- Control panels
- Query boxes
- Message boxes

The design of these screen objects has become standard within the Windows programming environment. Using the same kinds of dialog boxes across various programs allows the user to transfer the knowledge gained from using one program to another. Usually, most programs for windows follow the design used by Microsoft Windows. However, path-breaking companies that develop a particular type of product for the first time often have to define their standards for themselves. For example, there are many icons in Paint Shop Pro which are not used in Office programs. But if PhotoShop (another bitmap editor) uses the same icons and organization of menus for common concepts like layers and filters, it will make it easy for Paint Shop Pro users to use these tools in PhotoShop. That is the main reason why various vendors try to standardize their menus and icons as much as possible.

APPROPRIATE USER INTERFACE

The best way to understand how to design a good user interface for your programs is to observe the user interfaces of the popular programs that you use. However, it may be necessary, especially in the case of Web pages, to design your own user interface, which looks very different from the standard Windows interface. In that case, it is important to remember the following simple guidelines.

The screen should not be too cluttered. Do not put too much on the screen. There is only so much that a user can grasp at a glance. If there are too many new and unfamiliar navigation controls on the screen, the user will not be able to figure out how to navigate the system.

There should be some logical chunking of similar functions in the menus and groupings of buttons. In stand-alone multimedia programs this is done by putting similar functions in the same toolbars or under the same menu. In a big Web page, such as that for a news site, this is a very important issue since the number of users is potentially very large. If the information is difficult to find, users are not likely to return to the Web site.

The icons should be as intuitive as possible. This is easier said than done, but by asking a large number of people to guess what a particular icon stands for, a designer can tell whether the icon they designed works or not. For example, look at all the icons used in Paint Shop Pro. Can you understand what the icons are communicating to you?

There should be uniformity in the multimedia system or Web page. It is a good idea to use similar screens for similar functions. As the users become familiar with the system, they will find it easier to use. As another example of uniformity, well-designed programs often use the same buttons when they perform the same functions in every screen. For example, the help buttons should be the same wherever they appear in various screens of the multimedia system.

Frequently used controls should be obvious. Hide less-used controls, which the user can find as they become more experienced in the use of your system. In a small multimedia system this is not an issue, but in a large system such as MS-Word, it is important to do this carefully, or new users will never be able to begin using the system.

Give feedback. Often the best designs fail because the user does not get appropriate feedback after performing an action. Every action of the user should be accompanied by a response from the system that it has taken notice of the action of the user and that something is going to happen. For example, when the cursor moves over the printer icon, it gets highlighted. Remember, every action of the user should give rise to a reaction from the system!

Again, remember that the best way to make the right choices is to always observe the good practices of others, to evaluate them constantly, and to transfer your learning to your own designs.

THE USE OF MEDIA IN THE STORYBOARD

Since the audience has been identified at the research stage, the storyboard describes media elements appropriate for the target audience of the presentation. The storyboard contains detailed information about all the media used in the multimedia system. The storyboarding stage contains visualizations of all the media elements used in the system and forms the detailed design of the system.

While making the storyboard, we have to give information on which media elements to use for each screen of the multimedia presentation. We have to take care in selecting the specific media elements, so that they have the maximum impact on the users of the system. For example, to show the comfort of traveling in a luxury car, it is better to show a comfortable passenger in a picture than describing it through text or voice.

While choosing the specific media elements, we have to keep in mind that some information may be appreciated only by certain cultures, and some by all. Some examples of culture-specific information are the dresses that people in a scene wear, the language used, and the backdrops. Cross-cultural communication is something that appeals to or has meaning for masses at large. For example, ice in a picture may represent cold, and champagne may represent celebration across many cultures. Or, we can use national colors or sentiments in our presentation, if the target audience has a strong sense of national identity.

The theme of this section is to understand the appropriate use of the multimedia—audio, graphics, and video. The appropriate use of text, the most important element in Web pages, was considered in Chapter 15.

APPROPRIATE USE OF AUDIO

Audio can be used to attract the attention of the user of the multimedia system and also to add realism to the environment.

There are three ways audio is used in a multimedia system:

- Music—Music sets the tone and creates a mood for the multimedia presentation or system.
- Sound Effects—Sound effects give a certain message to the user. A sound effect could be short clip that is played to warn the user when the system does something wrong or to attract the attention of the user when giving a message box.
- Voice-Overs—It is helpful if a voice explains the object in question when explaining something about a particular picture or a complicated diagram.

APPROPRIATE USE OF GRAPHICS

They say that a picture is worth a thousand words. In most multimedia systems, graphics are the primary means of communication. It is very important to choose the right graphic elements. An accomplished artist will be able to communicate complex emotions and thoughts using pictures. However, it is not easy for everyone to be able to communicate easily using graphics. For us, it is more important to be aware of the graphics around us, and to consciously discuss the messages a drawing or a painting is trying to communicate. By doing so we can judge whether what we create is pleasant or not.

In general, when selecting or making graphics for a storyboard, choose graphics that convey the message you wish to convey. Some animation can be used to grab the attention of the user in a static screen. Animations can be used to describe events or processes that cannot be videotaped, such as biochemical processes, prehistoric ecological systems, or fantasy tales. Even text can be animated in interesting ways.

However, care should be taken not to use very long animations and also too much animation at the same time.

Color also serves as a means of communication: On roads, red lights tell us to stop, green lights tell us to go. On a map, blue colors indicate water (rivers, seas, and oceans), greens indicate forests and parks. We use the names of colors to describe our moods—a sad person feels blue, a person can be green with envy, and so on.

We have seen the classification of colors in different ways, as in the RGB system, or according to Hue, Saturation, and Brightness. In this section, our purpose is to classify colors more according to color harmony. That is to say, we wish to write down some rules for putting colors side by side so they have a pleasing effect on the eyes. Again, to really get a sense of color harmony, it is very important to keep observing various objects around us and to see whether their colors go well together.

It is also useful to talk to friends, discuss these issues, and try to vocalize these observations. Many designers use the color wheel (for paints now, rather than lights) to select colors. The three primary colors, yellow, red, and blue form an equilateral triangle in this wheel (see Figure 1). There are four such triangles in Figure 1. Can you find them?

A mixture of primary colors is called a *secondary* color. For example, orange is formed by adding yellow with red. A general rule of thumb is that colors that lie on a triangle go well together. So too do *complementary* colors. Colors that lie opposite each other are called *complementary* colors in paint, for example, red and green, orange and blue, and yellow and violet. A color may harmonize well with colors that are *nearly complementary*, that is to say, colors that lie next to the complement. For example, red goes well with blue-green or yellow-green. Colors that lie next to each other on the color circle, such as blue-green, blue, and blue-violet, may also go well together.

Another way of getting pleasing color effects is to take various *shades* and *tints* of the

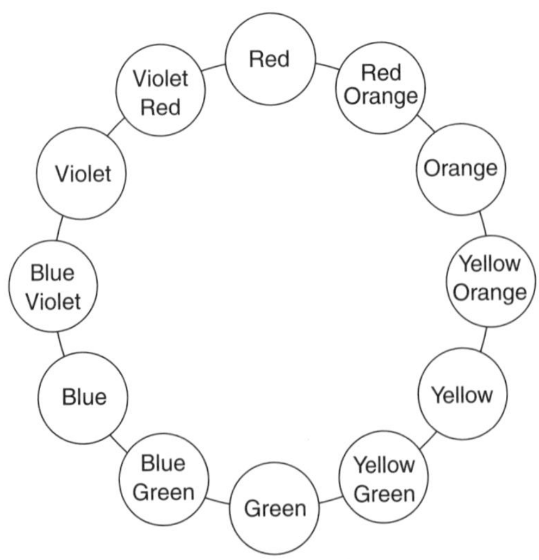

FIGURE 1
Color wheel.

same color. Shades and tints of a single color are formed by adding white or black to the colors. For example, pink is a tint of red formed by adding white to red color.

We should mention that these are just rough guidelines for choosing colors. The harmony of colors is a very subjective thing, and often you see color schemes that break all the rules and yet become fashionable for years. Good designers are always observing colors around them. In choosing the color combinations for a Web page, for example, it is a good idea to browse the Internet and see what colors are fashionable. It is a good idea to keep track of sites that have won design awards and note what color combinations they use. Finally, it should be kept in mind that what works in one media may not work so well in others, and often there may be cultural reasons why some color schemes work while others do not.

APPROPRIATE USE OF VIDEO

Video is the newest medium available for use on PCs, and is, very quickly, becoming popular. This is true even on the Web, where many sites are putting live video of important events. Since people are familiar with video through movies and television, the use of video in multimedia is very popular. Video has an innate ability to engross people and to persuade them. Video can be especially good for capturing personal information in interviews, for teaching by example, and for demonstrating processes difficult to describe using text. Video can also be used to communicate to a wider audience crossing all cultural and linguistic boundaries.

TESTING A MULTIMEDIA SYSTEM

Testing the system is perhaps the most important of all the stages of multimedia production. Testing is studied in great detail. Many companies have defined their own process for testing software. Here we will list some issues that have to be considered.

The main question that needs to be answered is whether the various parts of the system work as they should. For example:

- Do buttons work when clicked?
- Does the video really play on the system that you have made it for?
- Does the system satisfy all the specifications given by the client?
- Does the system cause errors on the machine it is supposed to run on?

As far as the design of the system and its various elements is concerned, we have to determine whether the system really accomplishes the communication objectives it was designed to accomplish. For example, some of the questions that need to be answered are:

- Do real users always get the right message?
- Does it attract attention?
- Is the interface easy to use?
- Does it hold the attention of the intended audience?

Most of these can be tested by observing the work of real users on the system. You should plan to test prototypes of the system with as many users as possible.

Most big companies provide a checklist to enable their developers to test the systems they create.

Somc of the things you can do as an individual are:

- Test the functionality of the product on the machine.
- Test the functionality on somebody else's machine with the same configuration.
- Check if all components adhere to the specifications laid down by the client.
- Test design without users. Imagine yourself to be the user as you develop the system. Put yourself in the user's shoes, and think about what you are doing. Programmers may find many defects in the design of the system by imagining themselves to be the users.
- Choose users similar to the intended audience to test the design. Give them specific parts of the system or prototype to test. Tell them to think aloud as they navigate the system, record their comments, and analyze it later. Do not ask questions such as: Why did you press this button,? Did you notice this feature.? Users tend to reply affirmatively to such questions, even if they do not mean it. What should be requested from the user is: Tell me what you are thinking; keep talking.
- Record any data you wish to measure. (For example, how much time does somebody take to navigate the tasks that the user was unable to do without looking at the help file.)
- Analyze the data appropriately.

Programmers usually do many of the items in this list as they develop the system. The problems they find at this stage can be fixed quickly. The design problems are harder to fix, but some can be managed on the fly.

Testing systems made by other programmers is a much more difficult proposition and is not covered in this book. Companies that develop complicated products often have entire divisions of program
ers who are responsible for testing the system and delivering it to the client. But all the developers should do the kind of testing described here.

EXERCISES

State whether the following statements are True or False.

1. The audience and the message to be imparted are the most important issues in Multimedia Design.
2. Choosing appropriate media elements is done during the scripting phase.
3. The script contains the plan of how the user will navigate the system.
4. The storyboard is the detailed design of the system.
5. In MS-Word, if the cursor moves over a button, an event takes place.
6. The user interface includes the keyboard.
7. A control panel is a windowing system component.
8. The reason for making similar screens for similar functions is to make the navigation intuitive.
9. For a program it is a good idea to put in all the controls on the main screen.
10. We should give feedback after the user does something.
11. Cross-cultural information is something that appeals to a particular culture.
12. The storyboard consists of a description of all the media elements to be used in a system.

13. To get a darker shade of the same color of paint, we add black paint to it.
14. Colors that lie opposite each other in the color circle (for paints) are called complementary.
15. Video should be used in showing fantasy tales.
16. Animation can be used when video is not possible, such as in describing the structure of the atom.
17. Testing is done at the end of the project.
18. The design of various media elements cannot be tested.
19. While testing the system with a user, we should make sure to ask the user whether they noticed a particularly important feature of the system.

Project

1. Look at the design of your home page (made in a previous project). Go through various do's and don't's in this chapter and redesign your Web page appropriately. Who are the users of your Web site? Your design should communicate what you wish to communicate, be easy to navigate for your intended audience, and look good!

Solutions

1. True
2. False
3. True
4. True
5. True
6. True
7. True
8. False
9. False
10. True
11. False
12. True
13. True
14. True
15. False
16. True
17. False
18. False
19. False

CHAPTER 17

Cognitive User Interfaces

WHAT DOES "COGNITIVE" MEAN?

Humans think and learn. These are cognitive (or mental) activities. The following are among our cognitive skills:

- We can speak and understand languages.
- We can reason and use logic to solve problems or discuss matters.
- We can see things, recognize objects, and understand the meaning of what we see.
- We can form mental images in our head.
- We can invent, create, design, and program computers.

Cognitive Science is the scientific study of our cognitive skills. To study cognitive skills scientifically, psychologists study people to see how their minds work—how quickly they can solve problems, how changes in the body and brain are related to mental changes, how people differ in their responses, and how they are similar.

Another recent trend is to use computers to imitate or simulate human cognitive skills and to test theories about how the human mind works. Medical scientists learn about human brains, about the different functions performed by different parts of the brain, and about changes in behavior that are caused by damage to the brain. Educationist study how cognitive abilities are used in working with computers and other machines. Thus, we see that Cognitive Science is a multidimensional subject being studied by many scientists.

How can this knowledge be applied in real life? Cognitive Science is applied:

- In the development of computer systems with human capabilities, such as speech, speech recognition, or even vision; and in the development of machine hardware.
- In the design of software which is easy to understand and allows people to work efficiently. In short, it is used in the design of user-friendly software.
- In writing software, particularly communications, multimedia, virtual reality, and other

applications requiring computer intelligence with an understanding of human cognitive abilities.

The first item in the foregoving list deals with hardware and complicated programming issues; the other two are very much design issues. All three are very important. In Cognitive Design, we try to come up with features that make our systems appear to be intelligent. Going even further, we might say that we would like our products to be as human-like as possible.

In this chapter, we will look at strategies for coming up with ideas to make our software appear endowed with cognitive abilities, or simply put, to appear intelligent. We will also discuss an important new model for understanding our ideas, called the APE model of Cognitive Systems. Finally, we will see how Web pages are driving the need for Cognitive Design.

Some Definitions

Cognitive Systems: Those (biological or artificial) systems that show adaptive, proactive, emotive, and other behavioral characteristics of living things.

Cognitive Engineering: The design and development of an artificial cognitive system that has properties similar to, identical to, or indistinguishable from biological cognitive systems.

Cognitive User Interface: An interface that changes or rearranges itself (adapts/customizes), acts proactively, and/or shows emotions in response to the information and/or experience it has gathered about the user and the environment.

THE APE MODEL OF COGNITIVE SYSTEMS

The purpose of this section is to understand how to bring a "human" element into your design. To think about "intelligent" or "human-like" features of a program, we begin by comparing a human being doing a job with how the current program does the same job. An example of this "thought experiment" follows.

Consider the job of Notepad, which is a text editor. Its job is to store and print documents. If a secretary were to do this same job, in what ways would it be better? The secretary would:

- Point out mistakes in spelling and grammar (and suggest alternatives).
- Format letters like you formatted the ones a day before.
- Correct minor spelling mistakes, without confirmation.

Actually, all these features, which are not present in Notepad, are available in MS-Word (part of Office 97).

Let us now formulate a model for a cognitive system. This helps us get more ideas on how to make our programs smarter and to recognize cognitive features of other programs.

The following three are properties of the human being that can be included in varying degrees in a program to make it more human-like.

- *A*daptive—A human being adapts to other humanbeings and objects. In other words, we learn and change our behavior over a period of time.
- *P*roactive—A human being is often proactive in dealing with other humans, or even with objects. We act without being prompted to do something.

- *E*motive—A human being uses emotion to communicate effectively.

This is the APE model of Cognitive Systems.

To continue our example, let us try to classify the features of the intelligent word processor that came up earlier as Adaptive, Proactive, or Emotive. Note that there could be some overlap.

- Suggest alternative spellings when the user makes a spelling mistake. (P)
- Format letters like you formatted the ones yesterday. (A)
- Correct minor spelling errors, without asking for confirmation. (A)
- Fill in the name of a person, given partial information about the person. (A/P)

Note that we have not looked at any emotive aspects yet. For example, our smart word processor could have the following features:

- Remind you about birthdays, special dates, and show you how to make cards for the occasion.
- It should give you encouragement when you figure out something difficult.
- It should laugh at the jokes in the document that you are writing. Over a period of time, the system should understand the types of jokes you like, and tell you such jokes occasionally.
- It should remind you if some document has to be finished soon and offer encouragement to get to work.

Making the program "emote" is very delicate and has to be done with care.

Note that many of these ideas, like taking dictation at one time seemed to appear futuristic. But in fact, many seemingly impossible ideas give directions to technology. For example, there is a lot of research on "Voice Recognition Systems." There are essentially two types of voice recognition systems. User-Independent voice recognition software recognizes words spoken by any user. However, the systems now available in the market can only recognize a few words with some accuracy. There are other problems with such software. The program often gets confused by different accents, and is accurate only about seven times out of ten. Some better results are achieved by User-Dependent software. This variety of voice recognition software is adaptive and learns words over a period of time from the user. This type is probably going to be useful for personal software such as our intelligent word processor. The recognition rate is higher in a user-dependent voice recognition software, and it only gets better with time. The only drawback — which makes it unsuitable for many situations—is that it has to be trained by a particular user.

The example of MS-Word that we have used is not by accident. It seems likely that sooner or later user-dependent voice recognition software will appear in MS-Word to take dictation. (In fact beta versions are already being tested.) Microsoft products are the first examples where cognitive ideas are being implemented. Over time, some of the "smart" features they have implemented will only get smarter.

The APE model of Cognitive Systems was developed by the R&D Center of NIIT. This model encompasses both programming and design issues. As we have seen (in the case of Voice Recognition Software), the programming required to implement even simple design ideas may be very difficult. Nevertheless, as we design and program our products, we should first get as many ideas as we can, and then think which among them can be implemented easily.

EXAMPLES OF COGNITIVE PRODUCTS

We know the "trick" to come up with ideas to make our product cognitive, and we know how to classify the ideas into the APE model. Now let us see how these ideas apply to two common products.

First, let us consider a Computer-Based Training package (CBT). Let us say that we have decided the content of what we have to teach and that the mode of delivery of the content is via computer-based training. We now think about the human elements in a normal teaching-learning process.

The main human element in a teaching-learning situation is the instructor. So we consider what this human being does that your CBT doesn't, to improve the effectiveness of your CBT. For example, a human teacher checks to see whether the students are understanding enough or not, answers questions in different ways, often tell jokes to relieve the tension in the class, keeps track of how each student is doing, encourages students in different ways, gives positive (or negative) feedback, or even helps the student when needed.

There is another, perhaps more interesting, human element in this situation.

Friends and classmates—who can laugh, tell jokes, interrupt occasionally, make fun of the teacher/subject—help make a class interesting. In order to "humanize" the CBT, many CBT designs include a cartoon character to guide the student through the CBT. Often this guide is a good candidate for becoming a friend for the user.

Usually CBTs have a fixed script, and often show very little recognition of the user. Ideally, a cognitive CBT would come to know the user's likes and dislikes, the speed at which the user understands a concept, and adjust accordingly. The challenge for the designer here is to come up with ideas completely in tune with the instructional objectives of the CBT, and that are relatively easy to apply.

Note that while choosing the features to implement, it is very important to keep in mind that the primary purpose of the CBT is to be an effective educator. So any features that reduce the efficacy of instruction should be discarded.

As another example of cognitive design, consider what an intelligent newspaper should be like. Suppose we were given the option of getting a newspaper made especially for us. What are the features we would like the newspaper to have? It should:

- Present only the news that interests us.
- Not repeat the same news, unless asked to do so.
- Give editorials based on our likes and dislikes.
- Give only our favorite cartoons.
- Include news items about our families and friends.
- Include messages from our families and friends.
- Advertise products that might benefit us.

The key to all these ideas is that the newspaper should get to know the person whom it is servicing and react accordingly. For example, the newspaper should figure out what news interests us and customize itself accordingly over a period of time.

The early newspaper, which was produced for the masses in a city, is now being replaced by newspapers that are for the entire world. Since the readers in different parts of the world require different news, some customization is necessary. (For example, readers in Australia may prefer cricket news to baseball news, and the situation in the United States is reversed. However, an Australian student studying in the United States may follow both sports!) Even this broad level of customization is not very satisfactory. What is really needed is a newspaper designed for a particular individual that gets to know the individual over a period of time and becomes a single product addressing all the information needs of a person.

One essential idea is that we are moving away from designing for the masses toward designing for an individual. This would require some automatic personalization from our programs. This would require cognitive abilities from the programs we write.

COGNITIVE WEB PAGES

The Internet is the chief driving force for the design and development of cognitive products. Here, all at once, the Web page you create is available to all types of people across the world. On many Web pages, you cannot really focus on a particular target segment. For example, people of all nationalities, all ages, and coming from all kinds of backgrounds will access the newspaper you create on the Web. The advertisements you design for your products will be viewed by everybody in the world. The Web page you design for the little corner shop delivering flowers will get orders from all over the world. So how will you design something effective if you cannot pin down your audience?

Among the many different industries and individuals populating the Internet, the advertising industry was the first to need the help of cognitive design. Advertising on the Web usually takes the form of banners which usually come at the top of various pages. For example, there are banners at the top of common search engine pages that advertise various products (see Figure 1).

Earlier, the advertising agencies that created these kind of banners had a problem in charging their clients. Clients wanted proof that their advertisements were being looked at by their targeted customers. One of the first methods to track the usage for clients was to check how many times the Web page has been loaded by a browser in a user's machine (the number of "hits"). However, this method is not very satisfactory. For one thing, the number of hits increases each time you refresh the page. Further, it is not clear whether the right people saw the advertisement. Advertising companies then began tracking data to figure out when people actually clicked on the banner. They also began figuring out the location and characteristics of the people who actually were coming to that page. This is done by means of some data that is captured by the server that hosts the Web page. After a couple of years, advertising agencies began using this data to show only those banners that are likely to be interesting to the user. This movement is continuing and Web designers are becoming more and more sophisticated in their approach to the development of Web pages.

To return to the newspaper of the future that we have designed, you will find that many of the features we listed are actually implemented on newspapers on the Web. Some more simple examples of cognitive features in many sites follow.

Our first example is of amazon.com, a bookstore on the web (see Figure 2).

Note that the buttons on top of the bookstore's Web site represent some of the broad headings under which the bookstore is advertised. There is also a shopping cart which you can use to select items before paying for them. You can search for specific books and can browse under various topics. There are also special sections for kids and a music section.

If you are a regular customer, you will find many cognitive features on amazon.com. If you select a book on a particular subject, books on similar topics (or by the same authors) are recommended to you. Similarly, if you have bought a few books before, the bookstore offers to "make recommendations" based on your previous purchases (see Figure 3). These features are meant to reproduce many of the typically human things an alert salesperson

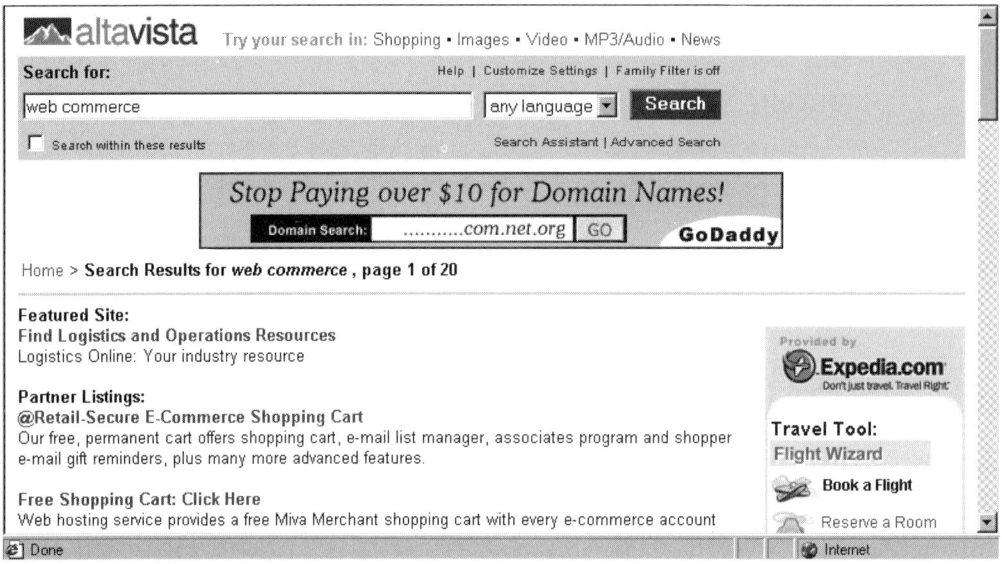

FIGURE 1
A popular search engine—Altavista.

would do. Let us say that you are interested in science fiction and always buy your books from a local bookstore. Suppose all the salespeople know you well and remember that you enjoy science fiction. The next time you visit the store, the salespersons will surely bring your attention to the new science fiction books that have arrived. This is exactly what amazon.com would want in their bookstore. As another example of a cognitive Web page consider my.yahoo.com. This site gives you an opportunity to customize it according to the kind of information you wish to see every day. Each user is given a unique login ID and password, and information on the users likes and dislikes is maintained. This information may be used to customize the site for the user over a period of time. This site comes close to being your personalized newspaper, with an e-mail account, news you wish to see, and the latest stock quotes. You can even get information on the weather, and follow the exploits of your favorite movie and sports stars (see Figure 4).

CREATING COGNITIVE SYSTEMS

We have now been exposed to many cognitive ideas. One of our central themes has been that a product we have been designing has to be aware of its human masters to be able to adapt to them. For example, the intelligent word processor is aware when we have made a spelling or grammatical error and reacts accordingly. Our smart newspaper gets to know when a particular individual is logged on and adjusts accordingly. Our CBT classmate knows what kind of interruptions we prefer. Finally, we saw that the bookstore amazon.com remembers which books we bought the last time we came to the store. In fact, in designing a cognitive Web page or a presentation, it is necessary to think about what data to capture. This is especially true of adaptive features of a program.

FIGURE 2
amazon.com, a bookstore on the Internet.

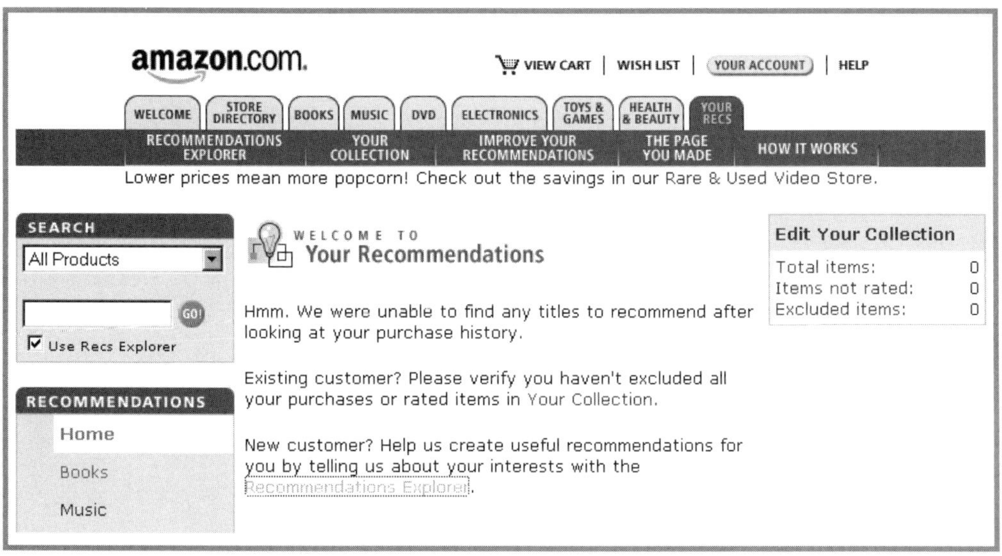

FIGURE 3
amazon.com makes recommendations.

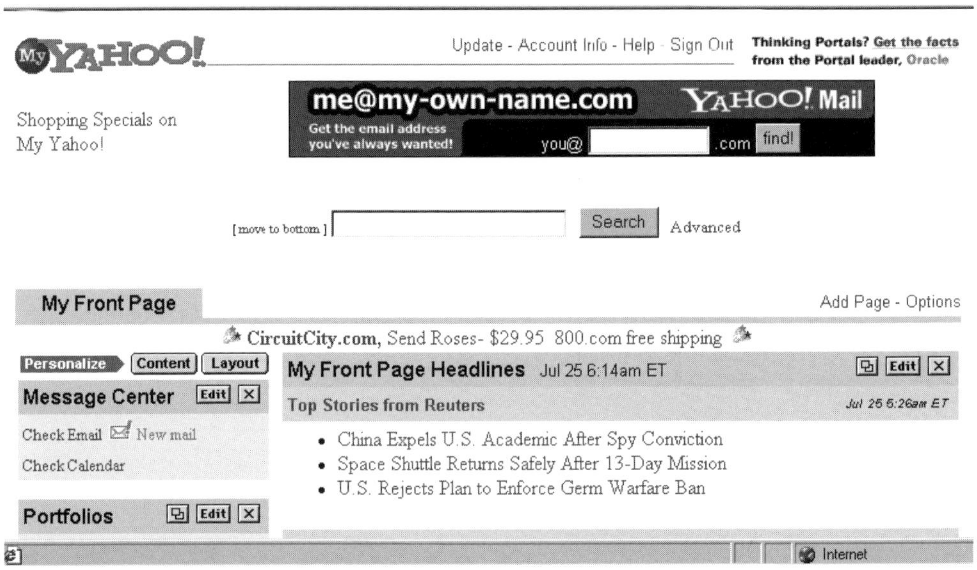

FIGURE 4
my.yahoo.com—a personalized newspaper.

In most cases, this is the bottleneck in creating cognitive products. This is because capturing the data is not the easiest thing for designers to do. In the case of Web pages, the server often captures some data but it is not easy to use that data for adding cognitive elements. For example, the server can tell us the browser used by the customer, so we can adjust our page to make it appear best in the user's browser.

To summarize the entire process of Cognitive Design, you should keep the following in mind as you design your presentations or Web pages.

- Begin by understanding and thinking about the user.
- List the jobs of the product you are designing.
- Think of how humans do these jobs.
- Think about ways of replacing specific jobs that humans do.
- Classify your ideas according to the APE model of Cognitive Design.
- See if you can capture the data to make Adaptive ideas work.
- Finalize the features that can be implemented.

Projects

1. Write a paragraph with at least five sentences that make some kind of sense (to your team), where each sentence should have one three-word phrase made by selecting one word from each column in the table below (in order, from left to right.) For example, a sentence can be: The Cognitive Engineering Forum (CEF) is a small group in NIIT, searching for ways to make intelligent anthropomorphic interfaces.

Intelligent	Cognitive	Multimedia
Emerging	Anthropomorphic	Ability
New	Human	Interface
Strategic	Social	Methodology
Corporate	Randomized	Agent
Chaotic	Definitive	Resources
Infant	Transformational	Management
Advanced	NetCentric	Architecture
	Learning	Software
		Perception
		Paradigm
		Systems
		Engineering
		Design

2. Make a list of features that a "cognitive" newspaper should have. Try to give as many specific features as possible. The word "cognition" means understanding.

> **Tip**
> Sometimes it helps to consider what jobs a newspaper does currently (inform readers, report on important events,...) and think about how a human being would have done the same jobs. Would the human being have done the jobs differently?

3. a. Classify the features that you came up with in the previous exercise into three heads (features that make your system Adaptive, Proactive, or Emotive). Note that some features may have to be split in two to fit separately under these heads. Some features may appear under two heads.
   b. Do you think some more headings (aside from A, P, and E) should be made?
   c. What technologies are needed to implement these ideas?

An Interlude: Development of Cognitive Systems

About Cognitive Systems

When a person is particularly cold and heartless, we often describe that person as a machine. A machine is meant to have no emotions, and does not care about others. The computer too is a machine and does not care about others. But the world is witnessing the development of computer vision, computer-generated art, even computer systems that do mathematics. We may shortly see the rise of computers which show emotion.

The paper *The Development of Cognitive Systems* argues that it is desirable for computers to become more *cognitive*, and shows a way we can think about such computers. The paper talks about how we can make effective computers by giving them the habits of effective humans. Read about these ideas of the future today. Maybe, you will be able to bring in the future tomorrow!

THE DEVELOPMENT OF COGNITIVE SYSTEMS

The Current Computing Environment

Modern computing environments have undergone considerable changes in the last 5 years. The computer is no longer considered a special-purpose device whose "serious" usage is by organizations and specialists. The computer today is a part of media and the home in many ways similar to the television set. Its usage by organizations has also increased dramatically, but the really large numbers are present in the nonspecialist segments, whether at home or at the office.

The term "computer" is generally considered synonymous with the term PC (personal computer). PCs have been around for over 17 years, most of this time as stand-alone machines with an operating system and specific applications such as word processors, spreadsheets, etc.

The PC today is generally a node in a local area network of any organization. At home, too, it is generally a part of the Internet and, therefore, it is in a network. Local and wide area networking are so prevalent and the technology so important that the line "the network is the computer" is often used to describe the computing environment.

Client-Server Technology

This is the most "traditional" of the technologies that define the current environment. Arguably, the most popular platform for networking today consists of the Windows NT operating system. Transfer Control Protocol (TCP) and the Internet Protocol (IP) represent the most prevalent manner in which data is transferred over networks.

The nature of data over networks has changed from alphanumeric to multimedia and requires considerably larger rates of data flow. This can be achieved either through modern compression technology or through larger bandwidths and other transfer mechanisms such as Asynchronous Transfer Method (ATM).

The Internet

Over 20 million servers connected over a global-wide area network now provide connectivity to over 300 million people. The Internet is not only the largest network ever created, it is also considered an anthropological phenomenon unparalleled in human history.

The Internet today is a system of continuously changing links between millions of computers. It is almost organic in nature. It does not belong to anyone, nor can it be controlled by anyone. It is growing at an exponential rate and is likely to continue to do so for many years to come.

Almost any kind of data or information is available on the Internet. It also permits most kinds of interaction, starting with e-mail (the most prevalent application at present) to Internet telephony, video conferencing, and many other collaborative computing methods.

Another fascinating aspect of the Internet is the absence of space and time as we understand it in the physical world. Since connections between computers on the Internet are nearly instantaneous irrespective of the location of the machines, space loses much of its meaning as do time zones. The possibility of creating "worlds" on the Internet that follow alternate physics is resulting in the development of a host of new applications from cyber shopping to virtual universities.

While it is impossible to determine what the future of the Internet will be, it is quite evident that it will impact every sphere of human activity and change forever the way in which we live, learn, and work.

The User

As the PC gets internalized in societies, the nature of the user becomes more and more heterogeneous. A PC user today can range from a research scientist to an illiterate child. Hence, people from almost any location in the world and from any social, economic, and linguistic strata could simultaneously access material resources on the Internet. Such a heterogeneous mass of users expect a lot more from the PC than the current technology is designed to provide as will be evident from what follows.

The Need for Cognition in Systems

Computers have no knowledge of the environment or the user. In fact it does not "know" of the existence of either. Critical comments from lay users usually refer to this ignorance.

Human beings tend to have an anthropomorphic view of machines. Hence terms such as "stupid," "dumb," or "insensitive" are often applied to machines. A normal PC is capable of acquiring and using environmental data with little or no modification. It is proposed that such data would increase the effectiveness of computers.

Product Differentiation and Technology

Rapid standardization is occurring in the technologies of client-server computing and multimedia. Due to the proliferation and ease of use of PCs, there is very little that technology can do to differentiate one product from another. "Company X has better multimedia than company Y because they have better technology" is not a credible sentence anymore. It is conception and design that are the key differentiators between products. Since both conception and design are cognitive processes, the future of products would seem to depend on a kind of "Cognitive Engineering" that would take into account the anthropomorphic features the general user is likely to expect in products. The products of such engineering could be called "Cognitive Systems."

PROACTIVE SYSTEMS

Proactive and Reactive Software

Proactive and reactive management are important topics for social scientists. Reactive means you wait for something to happen before you react while proactive means that you make things happen. Proactive is generally believed to be better than reactive. It is interesting to think of this in the context of programming, both digital and cognitive.

We have a lot of programs in our heads. A large number of these are reactive. The way you close your eyes a split second before an insect hits you. The way you swerve on the road a split second before an accident. The sneeze, the cough, the smile, and the tears are all reactive programs. Vital programs that keep us alive used to be called by many names such as involuntary reactions, instinctive reactions, or even impulse. In today's terms, I think we ought to call them Event-Driven Programs. Such programs cannot be controlled by free will. Interestingly, most new generation visual, object-oriented computing schemes are also event driven.

The trouble is, all programming, in effect, is event driven. Hence the famous insult of the uninitiated, "A computer will only do what it is told (programmed) to do." A good program, therefore, gives us an idea of what it would be like if we were only reactive. Total obedience, complete predictability, uniform quality, and complete compliance.

However, most science says that between stimulus and response in living things, there is always some processing that goes on somewhere in the system. So, there is nothing that is purely reactive. It's a question of how much processing to do before responding. The words Reactive and Proactive are simplistic. The word Processing is important. On the assembly line, there is not much processing to do between stimulus and response. With your back against the wall in the board room, you need to do a lot of processing.

That gives us a clue as to why computers get to some places so easily and not to others. One could generalize and say that current computing paradigms will work well in those situations where reactive behavior is desirable. Earlier, we used the words "repetitive behavior." I think "reactive" is a better word and captures the spirit of current "intelligent" computing.

Proactive Programming

Let us examine some of the issues with proactive versus reactive computing. These terms are not generally used to describe computer programs; they describe human behavior. Suppose you are sitting harmlessly in your office and a visitor storms in hurling abuses. You could get up and shout at him and your secretary rushes to call the security guards. That would be reactive behavior. On the other hand, if you consciously control your rising adrenaline level, take a few deep breaths, wait until the visitor's tirade is over, and then ask him what the matter is—that is proactive behavior. It is generally considered more effective to behave proactively.

Almost all computer programs behave reactively. In particular, all Graphical User Interfaces (GUI) are purely reactive. They wait passively for someone to do something to them before they do anything. Whatever they do is purely a reaction to the user input. The most modern programming languages are described as Event Driven; that is, they are blatantly reactive. They will operate only when an "event" occurs. When you click on a button in such an application, the program responds as programmed. It does not pause to analyze the input or to "think" about how it should react.

Like in the case of human behavior, if programs could behave proactively they would be more effective. The next generation of algorithms should be based on the concepts of such proactive programming.

How could a program be made proactive? I think the first step is to analyze the inputs before reacting to them. For example, if you always type the word "and" as "dan," then a word processor that remembers this and automatically corrects the error would be a proactive program. In fact, such word processors do exist and form the first examples of commercially available proactive systems.

To be truly proactive, a computer needs to be aware of its environment and its user. This does not mean that we have to wait until PCs acquire eyes and ears and the necessary software to analyze what they see and hear. After all, nature took several hundred million years to figure out how to do this in biological systems. But there are organisms much simpler than us that can behave proactively using simple signals from the environment.

To begin programming proactively, we should look for signals that are already available to the PC that we are ignoring today. What can a PC figure out about its user? Quite a lot, I think. For instance, it can figure out how quickly you can type. A person who types quickly on a PC keyboard is probably used to computers and knows a lot about them. Such a person does not need to be told something like "Click on the NEXT button to see the next screen." So a proactive program could remove that redundant instruction when it detects a computer-aware user.

Other such involuntary signals from a user that can tell a PC something about him or her could be reading speed and hand eye coordination. Reading speed is easily measurable every time there is text on the screen that you have to read and acknowledge by pressing a button such as OK. Once a PC has measured your reading speed, it can tell when you are skipping things and when you are reading slowly and sluggishly. It could even tell from your reading speed whether you use English as a first language or not.

The way a person uses a mouse contains hidden information about hand-eye coordination, acuity of vision, and familiarity with GUI environments. You might even be able to figure out whether the user is a child or an adult! Armed with such information, the program could decide proactively about what typeface and size to use, how long to keep text on the screen, where to place buttons of what size, and many things like that. The result would be a program that adjusts to a user's convenience automatically. In a world where most people ignore other's convenience completely, this may be a nice relief, in the cyberworld at least.

Another important factor that contributes to proactive behavior is experience. Computer programs usually do not gather experience, even when they can. For example, I always keep what I write in a directory called "docs." Every time I want to save, I have to click through a maze of directories and subdirectories before reaching the "docs" directory. I have been doing this for years but my computer is not programmed to remember this. If it was, it would have proactively saved my word processed files in the "docs" directory without asking me.

Such proactive interfaces are beginning to emerge and several large software companies are working on them. I think the first major impact of proactive programs will be on Computer-Based Education. One of the reasons why a human teacher continues to be far better than any automated system of learning is because teaching is a proactive process. The teacher observes the student and works out instructional strategies based on such observations and personal experience. Teaching programs of the future should be designed to do similar things. Such programs will detect a student's learning style, psychosocial characteristics, physiological limitations, and other parameters important to learning. It will then use its experiential data about other students it has "taught" to decide on a teaching strategy. Finally, it will reach into its bank of educational materials to find appropriate content for the teaching task at hand.

One of the interesting features of such proactive teaching programs will be that two identical programs may become totally different in their educational approach over a period of time depending on the student populations that have used them! They might even be programmed to solicit advice from each other!

The Properties of Highly Effective Systems

To work out the anthropomorphic properties that effective systems should have, we can take Steven Covey's book *The Seven Habits of Highly Effective People* (New York, 1989) as a starting point. The systems approach itself has been mapped onto these seven habits earlier (Haimes and Schneiter, 1996). However, in this chapter we will use the seven habits as guidelines for software designers. In effect, we are proposing that the same habits, appropriately practiced by computer programs, would make more effective systems. Table 1 shows some of the ways in which systems design may be affected by the seven habits.

Definition of Cognitive Systems

Cognitive Systems can be defined as "Systems whose behavior changes in an adaptive and proactive manner in response to and in anticipation of changes in the environment and user characteristics."

Recognizing and Reacting to the External Environment

There may be future hardware and software innovations that will enable the development of cognitive systems, but it is our contention that several cognitive components can already be incorporated into software with minor or with no modifications to the present PC architecture. Some possibilities are described in the following pages.

Table 1 The Seven Habits

Habit	Description	Implications to systems design
1	Be proactive	System behavior should be affected by concern and anticipation.
2	Begin with the end in mind	System behavior should be determined by long-term goals and also the immediate task.
3	Put first things first	System priorities should vary according to environment.
4	Think win-win	System behavior should give equal priority to the user's welfare as it does to its own.
5	Understand, then be understood	System design must include continuous monitoring of user's self and environment.
6	Synergize	The system and user must operate as a team.
7	Sharpen the saw	Systems must continuously adapt to changes in the environment, user characteristics, and goals.

Sound

Most PCs today are equipped with hardware that enables sound recording and reproduction. Most PC users utilize the sound playback facility for audio cues, music, and software that uses speech and music. The recording facility of the PC is seldom, if ever, used by the average user. A microphone connected to the PC and turned on and off periodically can form an effective "ear" for the PC. In an experiment conducted by the author it was found that such an arrangement can enable the PC to monitor the audio environment sufficiently to perform several tasks. These include:

- Changing the volume of playback to suit the ambient noise level
- Detect telephone rings and interrupt audio playback or take other action
- Detect voice and take appropriate action
- Detect usual noises such as door opening, cups and glasses, applause, etc.
- Detect unusual noises such as coughs, cries, animal noises, sirens, etc.

In general, it is important to notice that even though speech recognition continues to make slow progress, systems designers can integrate recognition on standard sounds into programs.

Light

Ambient light level (amplitude and frequency) can be sensed through light-detecting resistors connected to the parallel or serial port of the PC. This would enable a PC to:

- Distinguish between day and night
- Adjust monitor brightness
- Detect shadows
- Detect if the CPU (and sensor) is being moved

Temperature

Thermal sensors connected to any part on a PC would detect temperature. There is valuable information in such measurements, particularly in tropical regions. A PC that can measure temperature could do the following:

- Observe diurnal variations and correlate this with user behavior patterns
- Detect seasons
- Detect air conditioning problems
- Detect self-overheating
- Detect human body temperature

Movement

Movement detectors are commonly available for home security purposes. These can be easily interfaced with PCs through A-to-D convertors. A PC capable of movement detection can do the following:

- Detect human or animal presence
- Detect vehicle movement

Other Possibilities

In addition to such simple detectors, it is also possible to envisage more complex measurements on the environment that an average PC could be capable of. However, for purposes of this paper we will restrict ourselves to only the foregoing possibilities, since other forms of "senses" involve more complex and expensive hardware that may not be easily available to systems designers. The following is a list of other environmental data that can be captured by PCs if they are required to do so:

- Electromagnetic radiation
- Radio and TV broadcasts
- Infrared radiation
- Bio-electric signals as discussed later

Recognizing and Reacting to User Characteristics

Current PCs recognize their users through a name and password as entered by any person. Other than this, the PC is able to detect the presence of a human being only when there is activity on the keyboard or mouse. At the moment these inputs are generally treated by programs in a binary mode, that is, only a presence or absence is noticed. A number of user characteristics can be detected through simple analysis of available data as is described here.

Name

Names generally consist of vowels and consonants and carry information about the owner's race, religion, language, and sex. This information is used frequently by human beings for communication and other purposes. For example, a "Dr. Smith" would be visualized differently from a "Janet," "Joshua," "Chandrashekar," or "Li." Such information can be used to make initial assumptions about users (as is done by humans) and later modified, based on more data. Also, programs should be able to guess that "Mxyzptlk" is not a name.

Reading Speed

Almost all computer programs are page turners in the sense that they change from one screen to another in reaction to keyboard or mouse events. Most programs have sections that are meant to be read by users. This is particularly true of educational material. Whenever text has to be read before some further action can take place, a computer is capable of estimating the speed with which the reader has read the text by measuring the time between the appearance of the text and the users input to continue. This information, when averaged over time, can allow a computer to estimate whether a user has:

- Read the text normally
- Read the text fast (already knows the content)
- Not read the text
- Read the text slowly (has difficulty in understanding or has been disturbed)

Reading speed is a simple measurement that can be interpreted in many ways.

Keyboarding Speed and Signatures

Almost all computer programs require a user to type in information at some time. As in the case of reading, computers are capable of measuring and analyzing the keyboarding patterns of a user. This information could be used as follows:

- High keyboarding speed could indicate familiarity with computers
- "Pecking" at keys can be easily detected and associated with occasional users
- Patterns of keyboarding, for example, the speed with which individual keys are pressed, often have characteristics unique to a user. In an experiment performed by the author, it was found that different persons type the same password differently. Thus, while there is not enough information to detect who is typing, it is often possible to detect who the user is not.

Mouse Movements

Easily measurable parameters of mouse movement include the direction of motion, velocity, and acceleration. When moving from one point to another, users tend to converge on the target in different ways. It is suspected from a set of experiments being conducted by the author that experienced users tend to move at high starting velocity and decelerate as they approach the target, while users unfamiliar with the mouse tend to do the reverse.

Mouse movements can also be used to estimate hand-eye coordination, unusual muscular conditions (shakes, tremors, etc.), and other physiologic parameters.

Activity Log

An analysis of the switching on and switching off times for a PC and the applications run on it can provide a large amount of information about a user. The author has identified the following possibilities:

- The most frequently used application indicates the users profession or function
- Regular patterns of logging on or off can indicate office hours, home usage, leave patterns, coffee breaks, etc.
- Frequency of usage of certain disk areas or files can indicate the relative importance of data and hence the possibilities of automatic backup, defragmentation, etc.

- PC behavior can be programmed to adapt by analyzing logs and determining what actions would minimize user effort for frequent or favorite activities.

Voice

Voice recognition is an active area for research and development, but continues to be the Promised Land for user interfaces. The attraction of voice communication with a PC is clearly anthropomorphic since this is the way humans communicate. Several attempts to make practical voice recognition systems have been made. However, at this time none is in widespread use. The algorithms for understanding accented speech and for ignoring extraneous noises are still not efficient enough to solve the "cocktail party" problem. A human being can focus on a single, heavily accented conversation in the middle of a noisy cocktail party and still understand most of what is being said. No system can do this.

Voice synthesis is a more well-understood subject and several systems that can produce good quality synthesized speech are available. However, developers continue to use recorded human voices rather than synthesized speech. This is becouse of the fact that synthesized voices lack a "human" quality that is hard to define. More understanding of the role of emotion in voice modulation is required before artificial voices can become indistinguishable from real ones.

Other Possibilities

The area of Cognitive Systems is a nascent one. It is difficult to predict all the possible outcomes and fallout technologies from it. Some of the possibilities are listed below:

- Personality Storage and Retrieval—This is an attempt to create a multimedia, dynamic database containing personality-related material from a single person. Using a combination of Relational Database Management System (RDBMS) and psychological models, the goal is to create a digital copy of a person that would respond and converse in ways identical to the real person it is modeled after. Initial attempts have shown some success.
- Direct Links between Human Beings and Machines—It is possible to link physiological factors such as EEG and EMG signals. Such interfaces provide new ways of bidirectional communication between human beings and machines. In experiments conducted recently, we found that interfacing EEG signals from human brains to PCs is feasible and inexpensive. The PC is then able to detect, for instance, the state of alertness from the relative intensities of the emitted alpha and beta waves. Moreover, the user can control these emissions to a certain extent, with considerable practice, and this can be used to control or signal to the PC.

Emergent Behavior

Emergent behavior is usually considered a property of complex systems. In programming behavior into systems, one would generally associate one kind of behavior with a particular state of the system. Moreover, each behavior would generally modify the state of the system, thus giving rise to another behavior. One can then state that each behavior is an indirect function of every other behavior. If a system has a sufficiently large number of behaviors, then, over a period of time, the system behavior would tend to be chaotic, but not necessarily meaningless. Groups of behavior that result in system activity not envisaged by the system designers can follow. Such behavior would generally be called emergent behavior.

The approaches to cognitive computing described above, if related to each other, can result easily in complex and emergent behavior.

CONCLUSIONS

It is concluded that current PCs can be programmed to behave in a cognitive fashion as defined above. Cognitive Engineering of systems is dependent more on the programmer's attitude to systems than on the technology. While certain cognitive features will have to wait for the development of new algorithms and hardware, a large amount can be achieved now through sensitive planning of system behavior. Such behavior can enhance the performance of systems in much the same way as "good habits" enhance the performance of human beings.

Interrelated system behaviors can lead to emergent behavior. The nature or utility of such emergent behavior is unknown at this time.

ACKNOWLEDGMENTS

The author is grateful to his colleagues at the NIIT R&D Centre and the Cognitive Engineering Forum at NIIT for many stimulating discussions on this topic.

REFERENCES

Haimes, Y. Y., and Schneiter, C., Covey's Seven Habits and the Systems Approach: A Comparative Analysis, IEEE Transactions on Systems, *Man and Cybernetics,* 26(4), 1996.

Covey, Steven, *The Seven Habits of Highly Effective People*, Fireside, 1990.

Towards Immortality, Technology Section, The Telegraph, Calcutta, India, May 29, 1995.

Mitra, S., Multimedia Design for the Internet, presented at the Parallel Convention, 13th Commonwealth Conference of Education Ministers, Gaborone, Botswana (1997).

CHAPTER 18

Authoring Multimedia in Visual Basic

TEXT

Introduction

Textual communication is the most common form of communication, next to the spoken word. It is very rare that you will find any multimedia that does not use text as one of the media for communicating any idea. Text remains an intrinsic part of multimedia though good multimedia will seldom use text in plain and unimaginative ways. In Visual Basic, there are means to use text creatively as part of multimedia.

Label Control

As you have already learned, Visual Basic provides only one intrinsic control whose primary purpose is to display text, which is the label control. The label control displays text that cannot be directly modified. Like all the controls that display text, a label has properties like Font, Forecolor, and other such properties. We will discuss only those properties that make the label a useful control for multimedia applications. These are:

- Caption Property
- Alignment Property
- Autosize Property
- Wordwrap Property
- BackStyle Property

The text content of a label is set using the Ca*ption property* of the label, which can be done at run time and also at the design time. The maximum length of Caption property cannot be more than 1 KB or 1024 bytes.

Within the label control, text can be aligned using the *Alignment property*. Text can be left aligned, right aligned, or centered.

If the length of text in the label exceeds its width, the control expands horizontally to accommodate text if the *Autosize property* is set to True. The default value for Autosize property is False.

If the *Wordwrap* property is set to True and the content of the Caption property exceeds the width of the label control, text wraps to the next line, that is, the control expands vertically to accommodate text.

You can use the *BackStyle* property to create transparent label control when you want text to be displayed over the background color on a Form object or picturebox control or when you want to place a label over a graphic. On the other hand, use an opaque control when you want text to stand out. The BackColor property of the control is ignored if BackStyle = 0 (transparent). This is an important property as most of the good multimedia applications display text on transparent controls using a graphic as the background. But using a transparent label is not the only way to display text over a graphic. This brings us to the use of a graphic method that can do the job just as well, the Print method.

Print Method

The Print method is used to display text on a form or picturebox at run time. The font characteristics and the color of text are inherited from the form or picturebox control. The FontTransparent property of the object controls whether text is shown transparently or not.

The Print method is often used in conjunction with the TextHeight and TextWidth method. The TextHeight method returns the height of a text string, as it would be printed in the current font of a form or picturebox. The TextWidth method, on the other hand, returns the width of the string. The values returned by these methods are expressed in terms of the ScaleMode setting of object. The TextHeight method returns a value that includes normal leading space above and below text. It also takes into account any carriage returns, so you can use the height to calculate and position multiple lines of text within the object. On the other hand, the TextWidth method is used to determine the amount of horizontal space required to display text. If the string contains embedded carriage returns, TextWidth returns the width of the longest line.

The text displayed using the Print method is positioned using the CurrentX and CurrentY property of the object on which text is displayed. The CurrentX property indicates the horizontal coordinates for the next graphic method, whereas the CurrentY property indicates the vertical coordinates. Again, the values returned or set by these properties depend on the ScaleMode setting of the object.

GRAPHICS

Pictures in Visual Basic

Pictures can be displayed in three objects in Visual Basic applications:

- On a form
- In a picturebox
- In an image control

Graphics formats recognized by Visual Basic include .bmp files (bitmaps), .ico files (Icons),

.rle files (run-length encoded files), .wmf files (Windows Metafiles), .emf files (Enhanced Metafiles), .gif files, and .jpg files (JPEG's).

You use different techniques to add a picture to a form, a picturebox, or an image control depending on whether you add the picture at design time or at run time.

Adding a Picture at Design Time

There are two ways of adding a picture at design time:

- Load a picture onto a form, a picturebox, or an image control from a picture file by using the Picture property in the Properties Window.
- Paste a picture onto a form, into a picturebox, or an image control by copying a picture from another application (such as Microsoft Paint) onto the Clipboard and pasting it using the Edit menu in Visual Basic into the control.

Once you have set the Picture property for a form, picturebox, or image control, the word displayed in the Settings box is "(Bitmap)," "(Icon)," or "(Metafile)." To change the setting, load or paste another picture. To set the Picture property to "(None)" again, select the word and press the DEL key.

Adding a Picture at Run Time

There are four ways of adding a picture at run time:

- Use the LoadPicture function to specify a file name and assign the picture to the Picture property.
  The following statement loads the file Flowers.bmp into a picturebox named picView:
  picView.Picture = LoadPicture("C:\MyPicture\Flowers.bmp")
- Use the LoadResPicture function to assign a picture from the project's resource (.res) file into the Picture property.
  The following statement loads the bitmap resource ID, 10, from the resource file into a picturebox named picRes:

  ```
  Set picRes.Picture = LoadResPicture(10, vbResBitmap)
  ```

- Copy a picture from one object to another.
  Once a picture is loaded or pasted onto a form, a picturebox, or an image control, you can assign it to other forms, pictureboxes, or image controls at run time. For example, this statement copies a picture from a picturebox named picSource to an image control named imgView:

  ```
  Set imgView.Picture = picSource.Picture
  ```

> **Note**
> If you load pictures from files at design time, the pictures are saved and loaded with the form, and the application copies pictures from one object to another. Then, when you create an executable file, you do not need to give your users copies of the picture files; the .exe file itself contains the images. Also, consider supplying a resource file and using LoadResPicture. The .res file gets built into the .exe, and the bitmaps are saved in a standard format that any resource editor can read. If you load pictures at run time with the LoadPicture function, you must supply the picture files to your users along with your application.

Removing a Picture at Run Time

You can also use the LoadPicture function to remove a picture at run time without replacing it with another picture. The following statement removes a picture from an image control named imgView:

```
imgView.Picture = LoadPicture()
```

AutoSize Property

If you want a picturebox to resize automatically to the size of a new picture, set the AutoSize property for the picturebox to True. When a picture is loaded or copied into the picturebox at run time, Visual Basic automatically expands the control down and to the right, enough to display the entire picture.

> **Note**
> Image controls do not have an AutoSize property, but automatically size themselves to fit the picture loaded into them. Instead, image control has the Stretch property. If you want a picture in an image control to automatically expand to fit the size of the control, set the Stretch property to True. Forms do not have an AutoSize property, and they do not automatically enlarge to display all of a picture.

Additional Controls

There are two other graphic controls that can be used in any application to represent geometric shapes. These are the Line control and the Shape control. These controls do not support any events and are only for decorative purposes.

The shape control supports certain properties to control the appearance of the shape. By setting the Shape property, it can be displayed as a rectangle, a square, an oval, a circle, a rounded rectangle, or a rounded square. The BackStyle property determines whether the shape is displayed transparently over the form or not. The line control is similar to the shape control but can only be used to draw straight lines.

Using Graphics Methods

Graphics methods are summarized in Table 1. In addition to the graphical controls, Visual Basic provides several methods for creating graphics. Table 1 applies to forms and pictureboxes.

Table 1 Graphics Methods

Method	Description	Used with
Cls	Clears all graphics and Print output.	Form, Picturebox
PSet	Sets the color of an individual pixel.	Form, Picturebox
Point	Returns the RGB color value of a specified point.	Form, Picturebox
Line	Draws a line, rectangle, or filled-in box.	Form
Circle	Draws a circle, ellipse, or arc.	Form, Picturebox
PaintPicture	Paints graphics in selected area.	Form, Picturebox

> **Note**
> The Print method can also be considered a graphics method because its output is written to the object and is saved in the memory image (if AutoRedraw is True) just like the PSet, Line, and Circle methods.

Advantages of Graphics Methods

Graphics methods work well in situations where using graphical controls require too much work. For example, creating gridlines on a graph would need an array of line controls but only a small amount of code using the Line method.

Graphics methods offer some visual effects that are not available in the graphical controls. For example, you can only create arcs or paint individual pixels using the graphics methods.

Graphics you create with these methods appear on the form in a layer of their own. This layer is below all other controls on a form, so using the graphics methods can work well when you want to create graphics that appear behind everything else in your application.

Graphics created using graphics methods can also be saved as bitmaps using the SavePicture statement provided the AutoRedraw property of the control or the form is set to True. This provides a way to create bitmaps through the Visual Basic code.

Limitations of Graphics Methods

Creating graphics with the graphics methods can only be seen at run time; that is, you have to run the application to see the effect of a graphics method. Graphics methods, therefore, do not work as well as graphical controls for creating simple design elements of an interface. Changing the appearance of graphical controls at design time is easier than modifying and testing the code for a graphics method. For example, it makes more sense to use Shape control if you want to display a static circle on the form rather than writing code to do so.

Most of the graphics methods work only on forms and in pictureboxes and not on any other control.

Microsoft PictureClip control

An ActiveX control that can be handy in any multimedia application for creating small animations is the Microsoft PictureClip control. PictureClip control stores multiple images that can be used by other Visual Basic controls. It is not meant to be used alone but as a central repository to conveniently supply other controls with images.

In the PictureClip control, all images are contained in a single bitmap. Selected regions can then be "clipped" from the bitmap and used with a picturebox control to create animations.

The PictureClip control can be used with any control that assigns a Picture object to a Picture property, such as the picturebox, Image, and CommandButton controls. Storing multiple images in a single PictureClip control conserves Windows resources and speeds up the retrieval of images.

Assigning Images

In creating a set of images, cut and paste all the separate images into a single bitmap. Ensure that all the images are of the same dimensions so that when individual images are retrieved into any control, there are no inconsistencies. In Figure 1, a set of images depicting a flying butterfly is shown.

FIGURE 1
A single bitmap created from a set of images.

After creating an image resource bitmap, load it into the PictureClip control. The PictureClip control has a Property Pages dialog box which allows the bitmap to be loaded into the control and the grid set by specifying the number of columns and rows. The bitmap in Figure 1 consists of 1 Row and 2 Cols.

The resource image bitmap can also be loaded into the PictureClip control at run time using the Picture property, as in the following example:

```
Picture Clip1. Picture = Load Picture ("C:\VB\SAMPLES\COMPTOOL\_
                         PICCLIP\BUTTERFLY.BMP")
```

Retrieving Images from a PictureClip Control

Once you have created and loaded an image resource bitmap into the PictureClip control, you can determine how you want to retrieve each image.

You can select any portion of the image resource bitmap as the clipping region using the ClipX and ClipY properties to determine the upper-left corner of the clipping region and the ClipHeight and ClipWidth properties to define the area of the clipping region. The Clip property then contains the clipped region.

You can divide the image resource bitmap into a specified number of rows and columns. The rows and columns create cells that can then be accessed using an index number. The cells are indexed beginning at 0 and increase from left to right and top to bottom using the GraphicCell property. Using the Property Pages dialog box, you can set the number of rows and columns at design time.

You use the GraphicCell property to specify which cell in the image resource bitmap of the PictureClip control you want to load into a picturebox control. The following example loads a single image (one cell) into a picturebox control in the Form-Load event procedure:

```
Private Sub Form_Load()
PictureClip1.Picture = LoadPicture("C:\VB\SAMPLES\COMPTOOL\_
PICCLIP\BUTTERFLY.BMP")
  PictureClip1.Cols = 2
  PictureClip1.Rows = 1
  Picture1.ScaleMode = vbPixels
  Picture1.Picture = PictureClip1.GraphicCell(1)
End Sub
```

If you have previously defined the numbers of rows and columns using the PictureClip Property Pages, you can simply load the image into the picturebox control with the GraphicCell property. If not, you must specify the number of rows and columns by using the Cols and

Rows properties. To use the GraphicCell property you must define at least one column and one row.

For creating animations, the PictureClip control must be used in conjunction with the Timer control. If the images from the PictureClip control are assigned to any VB control in a sequence in the Timer_Event of the Timer control, this gives the illusion of continuous movement.

AUDIO AND VIDEO

Multimedia Controls in Visual Basic

Visual Basic does not provide any intrinsic controls/methods for integrating audio and video into your multimedia applications. The application has to depend on ActiveX controls for managing audio and video. Fortunately, Visual Basic is shipped with scores of ActiveX controls and among them is the Microsoft Multimedia control. The Multimedia control allows you to manage Media Control Interface (MCI) devices. These MCI devices include: sound boards, MIDI sequencers, CD-ROM drives, audio players, videodisc players, and videotape recorders and players. In Figure 2, the buttons are defined, from left to right, as Prev, Next, Play, Pause, Back, Step, Stop, Record, and Eject.

Multimedia Requirements and Supported Device Types

The functions provided to you by the Multimedia control depend on the hardware and software configurations of a particular machine. For instance, if your application uses specific multimedia devices and drivers, they must be installed on the user's machine.

Driver support for many multimedia devices (audio and video files, for instance) is provided for in the Windows 95 and Windows NT operating systems. Other devices, such

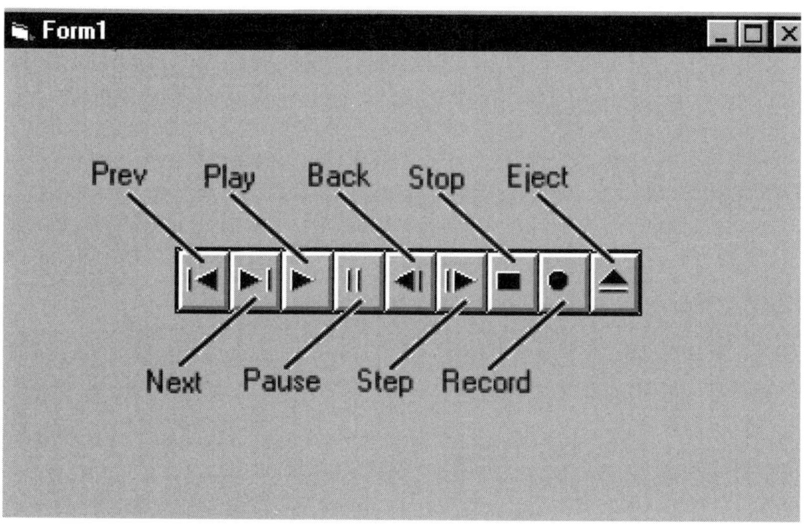

FIGURE 2
Microsoft multimedia control.

Table 2 Devices Supported by the Multimedia Control

Device type	File Type	Description
Animation	–	Animation device
CDaudio	–	Audio CD player
Dat	–	Digital audiotape player
Sequencer	.mid	MIDI sequencer
Vcr	–	Videotape recorder or player
Video	.avi	Video file
Videodisc	–	Videodisc player
Waveaudio	.wav	Audio device that plays digitized waveform files, for example, PC sound card.

as digital audiotape players or image scanners require separate drivers, which are usually provided by the manufacturer.

Table 2 lists some of the devices supported by the Multimedia control. Those listing an accompanying file type are compound devices.

MCI Commands

The Multimedia control uses a set of high-level, device-independent commands, known as Media Control Interface commands, that control various multimedia devices. Many of these commands correspond directly to a button on the Multimedia control. For instance, the Play command corresponds to the Play button.

The Multimedia control is essentially a Visual Basic interface to this command set. Commands like Play or Close have equivalents in the MCI command structure of the Win32 API. For instance, Play corresponds to MCI-PLAY. Table 3 lists the commands used by the Multimedia control along with their Win32 equivalents: In Visual Basic, these commands are initiated using the Command property of the Multimedia control. For example:

```
MMControl1.Command = "Open"
```

While the implementation of the MCI command set in Multimedia control is sufficient for most uses, directly utilizing the Win32 API can provide advanced programming functions and techniques.

Programming the Multimedia Control

The Multimedia Control can be either visible or invisible at run time by setting the Enabled and Visible properties. By default, the Enabled and Visible properties are set to True and the control is visible at run time. If you do not want the user to interact directly with the buttons on the Multimedia control but want to use the control for its multimedia functionality, set the Visible property to False. An application can control MCI devices with or without user interaction. To enable or make individual buttons visible or invisible, you set the visible

Table 3 Commands Used By the Multimedia Control, along with Their Win32 Equivalents

Command	MCI command	Description
Open	MCI_OPEN	Opens MCI device.
Close	MCI_CLOSE	Closes MCI device.
Play	MCI_PLAY	Plays MCI device.
Pause	MCI_PLAY or MCI_RESUME	Pauses playing or recording.
Stop	MCI_STOP	Stops MCI device.
Back	MCI_STEP	Steps backward through available tracks.
Step	MCI_STEP	Steps forward through available tracks.
Prev	MCI_SEEK	Goes to the beginning of the current track using the Seek command. If executed within three seconds of the previous Prev command, goes to the beginning of the previous track or to the beginning of the first track if at the first track.
Next	MCI_SEEK	Goes to the beginning of the next track (if at last track, goes to the beginning of the last track) using the Seek command.
Seek	MCI_SEEK	Seeks track forward or backward.
Record	MCI_RECORD	Records MCI device input.
Eject	MCI_SET	Ejects Audio CD from CD drive.
Save	MCI_SAVE	Saves an open file.

and enabled properties of each button. For example, the Back button contains the properties BackEnabled and BackVisible. Each of the nine push buttons has corresponding properties.

In most cases, the default functionality of the individual buttons is sufficient to manage MCI devices. However, the Multimedia control contains run-time properties that allow you to augment or redefine the button commands.

The Notify, NotifyMessage, and NotifyValue properties provide valuable feedback on the failure or completion of a command.

Opening the MCI Device

After you place the Multimedia control on a form, whether it is set to be visible or not, the first step is accessing the MCI device. To do this, you set a number of run-time properties. For example:

```
'Set initial property values of the media device
With MMControl1
.Notify = False
.Wait = True
.Shareable = False
.DeviceType = "CDAudio"
End With
```

The Notify property, if set to True, generates a Done event when the next command is completed. The Done event provides useful feedback indicating the success or failure of the command. The Done event is also used to synchronize the occurrence of other events based on the completion of the audio/video file. The Wait property determines whether or not the Multimedia control waits for the next command to complete before returning control to the application. The Shareable property either restricts or allows use of the media device by other applications or processes. The DeviceType property is used to specify the type of MCI device.

Finally, the Open command is used to open the MCI device:

```
'Open the media device
MMControl1.Command = "Open"
```

When the control is visible, setting the properties discussed earlier and issuing the Open command enables the push buttons of the Multimedia control that are inherently supported by the MCI device. For instance, opening the CDaudio device enables the Prev, Next, Play, and Eject buttons. When Play button is pressed, the Stop and Pause buttons are enabled.

Multiple instances of the Multimedia control can be added to a form to provide concurrent control of several MCI devices. You use one control per device. But you cannot use more than one control for any given device concurrently.

For the devices that require a file to play audio, the Filename property is used. A typical Visual Basic code for playing audio looks like:

```
With MMControl1
.Notify = False
.Wait = TRUE
.Shareable = FALSE
.DeviceType = "WaveAudio"
.FileName = "C:\WINDOWS\MEDIA\TADA.WAV"
.Command = "Open"
.Command = "Play"
End With
```

On the other hand, video is played slightly different using the Multimedia control. The output of a video is visual and, therefore, has to be displayed in a window. You can use the `hWndDisplay` property to specify the handle to such a window. If no handle is specified in the `hWndDisplay` property, as is the default setting, the Multimedia control plays the video in its own window known as the Stage Window. If you need to embed the video in your application's window, then you can use the form or a control like picturebox to do so. In the example below, a picturebox named picVideo is being used to display the video whose handle is assigned to the `hWndDisplay` property.

```
With MMControl1
.Command = "Close"
.Notify = False
.Wait = TRUE
.Shareable = FALSE
.DeviceType = "AVIVideo"
.Filename = "C:\WINDOWS\HELP\EXPLORER.AVI"
'Provide a handle for video output
```

```
  .hWndDisplay = picVideo.hWnd
  .Command = "Open"
  .Command = "Play"
  End With
```

You should always close those MCI devices that are open before exiting your application. For example, you can place the following statement in the Form-Unload procedure to close an open MCI device when the form containing the Multimedia control is unloaded.

```
Private Sub Form_Unload (Cancel as Integer)
  Form1.MMControl1.Command = "Close"
End Sub
```

Error Handling

You can handle errors encountered by the Multimedia control using the Error and ErrorMessage properties. You can write error handlers that can check the Error and ErrorMessage properties. If there is an error in the Open command, you can test for the existence of a CD drive. If the CD drive is not available, an error message is returned. For example, the following is the code for an error handler called ErrHandler:

```
ErrHandler:
If Form1.MMControl1.Error Then
  MsgBox Form1.MMControl1.ErrorMessage, vbCritical, "CD Player_
  not installed or not working properly"
End If
```

ACCESSING EXTERNAL PROCEDURES AND WINDOWS API

Using DLLs

Visual Basic is a powerful Windows development environment. Its strength comes from the fact that a programmer is able to develop powerful software applications in no time. In that sense, Visual Basic is a RAD (Rapid Application Development) tool. This speed of development does come at a price. Visual Basic is not able to provide all the functionality of the Microsoft Windows operating system that the operating system possesses. When you need capabilities that go beyond the core language and controls provided with Visual Basic, you can make calls to procedures contained in dynamic-link libraries (DLLs).

DLLs are libraries of procedures that applications can link to and use at run time rather than link to statically at compile time. This means that the libraries can be updated independently of the application, and many applications can share a single DLL. Microsoft Windows consists of a large number of DLLs, and other applications call the procedures within most of these libraries to display windows and graphics, manage memory, or perform other tasks. These procedures are sometimes referred to as the Windows API, or application programming interface.

This ability to make direct calls to DLLs makes Visual Basic even more powerful; the applications gain in speed and flexibility, even more so, in case of multimedia applications. Multimedia applications, by their very nature, are resource intensive, that is, they require more memory and CPU processing than, say, an ordinary database front-end application.

Access to the Windows API not only means more speed for the software but also the ability to accomplish tasks that otherwise would not be possible through the core language.

Declaring a DLL Procedure

To use a DLL procedure, you append a Declare statement to the Declarations section of the code window. Depending on whether the procedure returns a value or not, use either of the syntax given below:

```
Declare Function publicname Lib "libname" [Alias "alias"]
[([[ByVal] variable [As type] [,[ByVal] variable [As
type]]...])] As Type
Declare Sub publicname Lib "libname" [Alias "alias"]
[([[ByVal] variable [As type] [,[ByVal] variable [As
type]]...])]
```

The procedure name replaces the *publicname* and the *libname* is substituted by the name of DLL. By default, the DLL procedures are declared as public in the modules but these can be declared privately by using the Private keyword to restrict their scope. For example, the GetWindowsDirectory procedure in the kernel32.dll is used to get the path for the Windows directory on the system.

```
Declare Function GetWindowsDirectory Lib "kernel32" Alias
"GetWindowsDirectoryA" (ByVal lpBuffer As String, ByVal nSize
As Long) As Long
```

Calling the DLL Procedure

It is a simple job to call a DLL procedure once it has been declared; you call it as you would call any other procedure in Visual Basic.

```
Dim strPath as String*255
Dim intReturn as Integer
Dim strReturnPath as String

intReturn = GetWindowsDirectory (strPath, Len(strPath))
strReturnPath = Left (strPath, intReturn)
MsgBox strReturnPath & "is the Windows directory!"
```

Let us see how the function GetWindowsDirectory works. GetWindowsDirectory takes a fixed-length string buffer as the first argument and the length of that buffer as the second argument, and returns the number of characters written into the first argument. This is because the function writes data into the first argument and, in case the length of the data is longer than the size of the string received by it, then the function will write beyond the string and corrupt other data with catastrophic effect on your program. To avoid such a scenario, a long fixed-length string is sent as the argument that is long enough to take any length of data; for Windows API, 255 characters are generally long enough. In any case, the second argument does inform GetWindowsDirectory the length of the sent buffer. This is also a good example of the care you need to take while calling DLL procedures.

API Text Viewer

The Windows API contains thousands of functions, subs, types, and constants that you can declare and use in your projects. These procedures are, however, written in the C language, so they must be declared before you can use them with Visual Basic. Since the most commonly used set of external DLL procedures in any program are those that make up Microsoft Windows itself, these Windows API declarations are available along with Visual Basic in the form of a file Win32api.txt. API Text Viewer—a program to view and use these declarations in your programs is also available (Figure 3).

> Though accessing the calls in DLLs is a potent feature of Visual Basic, caution must be exercised while using it. When you make a call to any procedure that resides outside Visual Basic, then that part of the program is no longer in control of the Visual Basic's Integrated Development Environment (IDE). For example, when any run time errors occur, hardly any intelligible error messages are reported back as Visual Basic's IDE has no way of knowing the probable cause of the error. This means that the risk of system failure increases as debugging and testing the code becomes trickier. So, does this mean that the power of calling DLLs is something good in theory but tough to implement in practically? The answer is No. But there are certain caveats to be kept in mind while calling DLLs. You should be fairly safe of your observe the following steps:
>
> 1. Be sure that you know the right procedure to call to achieve your objective, and also the side effects that the call might have.
> 2. Pay special attention to the declaration of DLL procedures.
> 3. Take care that you pass the arguments to the calls in the right order and of the right data type.
> 4. Save your work often.

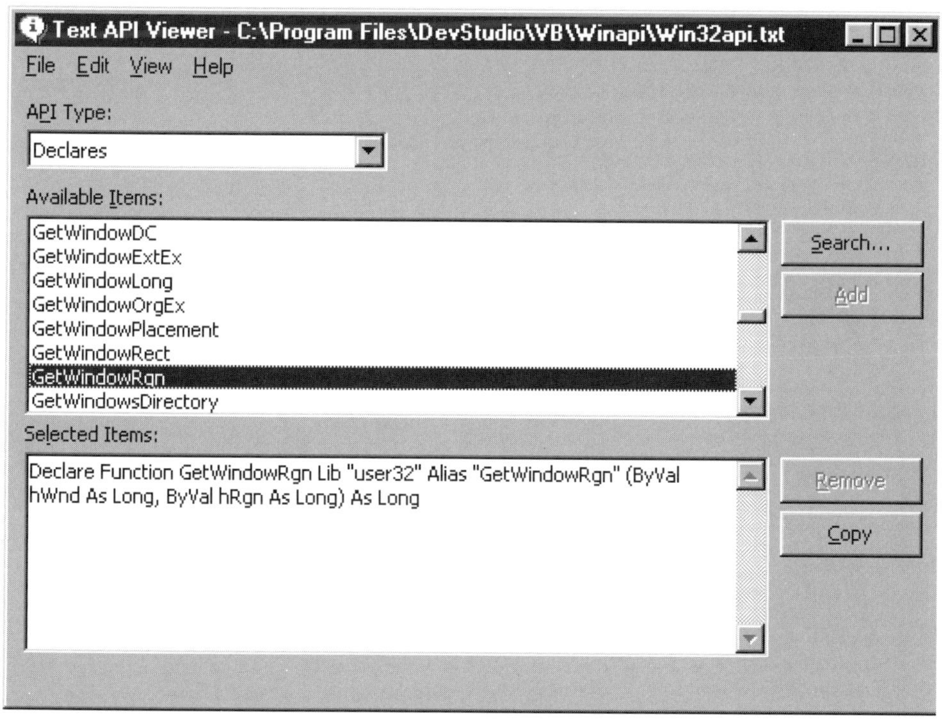

FIGURE 3
API text viewer.

EXERCISES

1. For displaying scrolling text, which set of properties of a Label control is most applicable:
   a. Caption, BackStyle, Alignment, Autosize
   b. Left, Top, Wordwrap, Caption
   c. Caption, BackStyle, Left, Top
   d. Alignment, Top, BackStyle, Wordwrap
2. The CurrentY property of an object returns:
   a. The vertical coordinates in the current ScaleMode
   b. The horizontal coordinates in pixels
   c. The vertical coordinates in twips
   d. The horizontal coordinates in the current ScaleMode
3. State whether the following statements are True or False:
   a. The LoadPicture method of the PictureClip control is used to assign and display an image.
   b. The AutoRedraw property affects the way a picturebox or a form is repainted.
   c. The Paint event is invoked when the Refresh method of the Shape control is called.
   d. The default setting of the hWndDisplay property of the MMControl allows embedding a video in an application.
   e. MCI_SET is the Win32 equivalent command for the Seek command of the multimedia control.

Projects

1. Make a multimedia presentation using Visual Basic as the language to integrate various multimedia elements. Choose a theme that you feel strongly about and locate appropriate media elements, modify them if necessary, and make an interactive multimedia presentation on this theme.

Solutions

1. c
2. a
3. a. False
   b. True
   c. False
   d. False
   e. False

Index